THE COMPLETE BOOK OF
KITCHEN DESIGN

THE COMPLETE BOOK OF

KITCHEN DESIGN

Ellen Rand, Florence Perchuk,
and the Editors of
Consumer Reports Books

CONSUMER REPORTS BOOKS
A Division of Consumers Union
Yonkers, New York

With the exception of Consumer Reports Ratings found in Appendix C, products discussed in this book were not tested in CU's laboratories. Products mentioned elsewhere have not been tested by CU and represent the collective, expert judgments of the authors. The design ideas and floor plans reproduced in this book have not been tested in actual use by CU. Their inclusion does not represent an endorsement of the plans or the professionals who created them.

Library of Congress Cataloging-in-Publication Data
Rand, Ellen.
The complete book of kitchen design / Ellen Rand and Florence
Perchuk, and the editors of Consumer Reports Books.
p.   cm.
Includes index.
ISBN 0-89043-474-3
1. Kitchens—Remodeling—Amateurs' manuals.   2. Consumer
education.   I. Perchuk, Florence.   II. Consumer Reports Books.
III. Title.
TH4816.3.K58R36 1991
643'.3—dc20   91-8551

Design by GDS / Jeffrey L. Ward
Drawings on pages 54–55, 69–70, 75, and 91 by Mona Mark
First printing, September 1991
Manufactured in the United States of America

The Complete Book of Kitchen Design is a Consumer Reports Book published by Consumers Union, the nonprofit organization that publishes *Consumer Reports,* the monthly magazine of test reports, product Ratings, and buying guidance. Established in 1936, Consumers Union is chartered under the Not-for-Profit Corporation Law of the State of New York.

The purposes of Consumers Union, as stated in its charter, are to provide consumers with information and counsel on consumer goods and services, to give information on all matters relating to the expenditure of the family income, and to initiate and to cooperate with individual and group efforts seeking to create and maintain decent living standards.

Consumers Union derives its income solely from the sale of *Consumer Reports* and other publications. In addition, expenses of occasional public service efforts may be met, in part, by nonrestrictive, noncommercial contributions, grants, and fees. Consumers Union accepts no advertising or product samples and is not beholden in any way to any commercial interest. Its Ratings and reports are solely for the use of the readers of its publications. Neither the Ratings nor the reports nor any Consumers Union publications, including this book, may be used in advertising or for any commercial purpose. Consumers Union will take all steps open to it to prevent such uses of its materials, its name, or the name of *Consumer Reports.*

Contents

CONTENTS

CONTENTS

Introduction

It may be a small event that triggers the beginnings of visions of a new kitchen: a burn mark on an old countertop, or an old appliance breaking down one time too many. Or perhaps you've recently bought an older home or apartment and want to redo it before you move in. You may have just signed a contract to buy a newly constructed home or apartment and dislike the builder's kitchen plans so intensely that you decide to do your own. Your children may have grown and left the nest, and you think it's time for a new look.

Whatever the trigger, suddenly your kitchen seems drab, dark, cramped, and dysfunctional. You envision a room that looks better, works better, and adds value to your home. You imagine an open, warm, and well-lighted space that allows you to enjoy a cup of coffee in peaceful solitude or to comfortably orchestrate an informal buffet dinner for 30.

Fortunately, there has never been a better time to contemplate a kitchen remodeling project. Over the past few years, significant changes have been made in products and materials. Technological advances—most notably, the use of the computer—have made appliances "smarter," more versatile, and easier to use.

Great strides also have been made in synthetic surface materials for countertops and flooring—not only in the variety and vibrancy of designs, colors, and patterns but also in the more practical arena of maintenance and durability. Natural materials, such as stone, tile, and wood, are increasingly being used in the kitchen; when employed appropriately, they add immeasurably to a room's beauty and function.

In kitchen cabinets, special storage features such as roll-out drawers, cutlery trays, bins, and pantry shelving that once were produced only in more expensive, custom lines are now routinely available in all price categories.

European-influenced product design has brought a cleaner, sleeker appearance to today's kitchens. The white-on-white look, including built-in appliances and frameless cabinetry with no visible hardware, is the most striking example of that influence.

At the same time, the romance of a country-style kitchen, with elaborately carved cabinetry and hand-painted tile, continues unabated. There has been such a profusion of new products and materials in the past several years that virtually everyone's stylistic tastes can be readily accommodated.

This profusion of choice also has its drawbacks, of course. How can you find your way through this ever-changing maze of products and materials and still stay within the time and budget you've allowed? When you are offered a choice of spending from $5,000 to $35,000 on cabinetry, for example, what information do you need to make the proper decisions?

This book will help you make the choices that are right for you and your household. With its focus on careful and detailed planning as the foundation for the project, it will dispel your apprehension about the pitfalls of tackling a major home improvement project. Since kitchen remodeling involves all the utilities in a home, the book will also help you understand how the "body" of your home functions: its respiratory system (ventilation), circulatory system (plumbing), and nervous system (electricity). In this way, you'll be prepared to translate your taste and your household's requirements into a remodeling project that's both realistic and attractive.

Kitchen design itself is an ever-evolving art. It need not be wedded to a traditional concept of how the room should function. Rather, the key lies in creating a plan that suits your individual needs—and the home's or apartment's structural conditions—with imagination and style.

Is there more than one cook in your family, for example? A multipurpose island—or even two separate islands, if space permits—can create separate "stations" to allow each cook to work with ease. Is your kitchen the hub of all family activity? A planning desk incorporating a home-entertainment center, an informal dining area, a children's area, and a built-in bar can provide a comfortable backdrop. You'll find an abundance of design ideas and guidelines for such noncooking needs in the pages to come.

HOW THIS BOOK IS ARRANGED

A kitchen remodeling project should be approached methodically, and for that reason the book is divided into two main sections. Part I addresses conceptual issues, such as how to begin the process, how to define your needs and preferences, understanding planning and design principles, how to find qualified design and construction professionals, and how construction proceeds. Part II addresses specific product categories, including cabinetry, appliances, flooring, plumbing fixtures, and countertops.

A unique feature of this book is chapter 11, devoted to "Floor Plans That Work—and Why." The 11 plans presented there are all *real* solutions to *real* kitchen remodeling challenges posed by homes of greatly varying sizes, shapes, ages, and family situations. You'll see precisely why each plan satisfies each particular household's requirements.

Appendix A lists a number of sources you can consult for additional information, including industry associations that certify design and construction professionals and professional organizations responsible for building-code standards and product testing and certification. Appendix B gives sources of additional information about kitchen design for people with special needs.

You'll find *Consumer Reports* product Ratings and guides to product features in Appendix C. They give Consumers Union's evaluations of some refrigerators (top-mount and built-in), ranges, microwave ovens, microwave/convection ovens, and dishwashers. The Ratings of individual brands are based on CU's laboratory tests, controlled-use tests, and/or expert judgments.

Included, too, is a glossary of the terms you'll need to know when gathering information, discussing your project with designers and contractors, and reviewing and evaluating their plans as well as the progress of construction.

PART ONE

Planning and Design

1
Getting Started

Chances are, you've already begun to envision the kind of kitchen you want. But getting past the fantasy stage can be a daunting process, even to the most sophisticated homeowner. Where do you begin? How do you gather reliable and relevant information? How do you find the right people to plan and install the kitchen? How much will the project cost, and how long will it take?

There is no question that the remodeling process involves a major investment of money *and* time, disruptions in your daily routine, dealing with unfamiliar craftspeople, paperwork, and a potentially dizzying array of choices in products and materials. The good news is that you *can* turn a dream into reality, and the result will be a kitchen that you love, that will serve you and your household well for many years to come.

Even if you don't have an ideal kitchen in mind, or can't define in detail your stylistic likes and dislikes, there are simple, methodical ways to do so. You can start by collecting information and design ideas from books and magazines. Although home magazines usually show some kitchens every month, there are specialty magazines devoted solely to kitchen (and

bath) remodeling. Keep a file of clippings of kitchens you like, and make some notes to yourself about the specifics that appeal to you.

Don't be put off if the kitchens you like seem to be beyond your budget. Remember that, in some ways, kitchen design is like fashion. Couture designs, for example, may be created initially for the very wealthy, but their shapes, colors, and patterns are usually reinterpreted and made affordable for a wider market soon after their introduction. If you see a $100,000 kitchen, don't hesitate to make note of the elements and details you like. A creative designer or contractor may be able to adapt them to suit your budget.

A word of caution: Some of the dramatic kitchen photos you'll see in consumer magazines may have serious design drawbacks that are masked by the excellence of the photography. These kitchens should be approached with an educated, critical eye. As you read this book, you'll learn how to evaluate a plan and you'll understand why a particular plan may not work for you.

Your armchair tour of the latest in kitchen plans and materials can continue if you write to various associations and manufacturers for more specific information. Summaries of manufacturers' literature currently available are generally found toward the back of consumer magazines; the literature usually is supplied free or for a nominal sum.

A word of caution here, too: Much of what you will read is likely to seem self-serving in terms of brand names and specific companies. But some manufacturers and most professional associations make a real effort to provide useful design and planning tips as well as general product information. An additional benefit is that you can begin to focus on your own style preferences, according to your reactions to the kitchen settings displayed in the brochures' photographs.

Consumer-oriented home improvement and kitchen and bath shows, which are frequent events in some areas, present an opportunity to learn more about kitchen products and design. Most exhibitors—often from your local area—are only too happy to talk to you about your project, even in preliminary or hypothetical terms, and may offer helpful free advice as a way of establishing their credibility or helping you to remember them when your project is closer to becoming a reality.

Shows are also a good place to pick up product literature. Once you skim past the hyperbole, you'll find useful information about product specifications and sizing.

The producers who organize these shows often arrange for remodeling experts to present seminars on a variety of home improvement–related topics. It may be helpful to attend those that address kitchen design, planning, trends, and product choices.

One of the best ways to obtain information on the tremendous variety of products and materials currently on the market is to visit showrooms and see them for yourself. Showroom visits can also help you get a sense of pricing and of "good-better-best" differentiations. Be ready to ask critical questions about why one product costs so much more than another, whether it doesn't have drawbacks of its own, and whether it can be adapted to your specific situation.

Pay particular attention to how designers or sales reps answer your questions. Do they seem more interested in making a sale than in providing you with product and design information? Do they seem to understand your concerns? Do they help you clarify what you're looking for? Do they seem rushed, distracted, or impatient with your questions?

If you establish a rapport, these designers or sales reps are good contacts to pursue when you are ready to have plans drawn.

COMMON PROBLEMS, CREATIVE SOLUTIONS

The first step toward planning your new kitchen is to understand what is wrong with your present one and what are the current needs of your household. That will help you determine whether your kitchen needs a simple "cosmetic" facelift; the replacement of appliances, cabinetry, countertop, and flooring based on your existing floor plan; or a total remodeling that includes structural changes, such as an extension of the home.

No matter how problematic or limited your present space may be, a creative solution can be found. Much depends on examining your space from a new perspective and avoiding the limitations that surface when you're fixated on its present configuration.

If the kitchen is poorly located in relation to the rest of the house, for example, perhaps it can be "swapped" with an adjacent space that would function better. Or the kitchen can be extended by means of an addition, or by expanding into an existing adjacent space that may be large and underused, such as the dining room.

As specific as your own particular needs might be, there are a number of common problems and dissatisfactions that prompt homeowners to tackle a kitchen remodeling project. In older homes, for example, the kitchen is likely to suffer from an overabundance of entries and exits, which not only creates chaotic traffic patterns but also interrupts wall and counter space that might be used for additional storage and working areas.

Creative solutions might involve blocking off one or two entries and relying on one main access. This allows for longer cabinet runs, which add to storage and counter space and a more coherent traffic pattern that lets the cook(s) work undisturbed. More radical solutions might involve closing off all old entries and creating a new one, or switching the adjacent breakfast room into a kitchen, and vice versa.

Older homes typically feature relatively small, compartmented spaces that do not fit with contemporary preferences for large, open spaces in which families and friends can gather, children can play, and informal dining can take place. These older, compartmented spaces are precisely the opposite of the contemporary open-plan dilemma: that is, how to define the kitchen space so that you know where the kitchen ends and living/dining/entertainment spaces begin.

Creative solutions to the "rabbit warren" layout usually involve breaking down partition walls to literally open up the space. This allows for a more logical placement of appliances and work spaces, for more comfortable dining, and sometimes for a home office/planning/computer center.

If storage is your problem, look at the space adjacent to the kitchen. Can you use some of that space, creating a pass-through or barrier wall between the two spaces? If so, you can create more base cabinet storage space as well as an additional countertop to increase your working surface. You can use sliding or louvered doors to close off the view to the kitchen if you are entertaining. In an apartment kitchen, consider removing the partition between the breakfast area and the kitchen and placing tall storage cabinets along one wall extending into that area.

Or, if ceiling height permits it, you can have a double tier of wall cabinets installed to increase storage. You can double your present storage space by using 24-inch-deep cabinets for the top level and cut back to a depth of 12 or 13 inches for the lower wall cabinets.

Insufficient lighting in the kitchen can be oppressively bleak. A kitchen that's dark and dreary is not very inviting for cooking or leisure time activities. Solutions may involve dropping the ceiling, installing recessed lighting or under-cabinet lighting, or adding skylights. A more radical solution might entail adding a sunroom extension to the kitchen, or installing greenhouse or expansive Palladian-style windows.

DEFINING YOUR NEEDS

When you're ready to determine your household's specific needs, you need to take a thorough and detailed inventory of all your kitchen equipment, your cooking and shopping style(s), how you and your family live and entertain during the week and on weekends, and what activities are usually centered in your kitchen, as well as your general style and color preferences.

Remember that a kitchen remodeling project should serve you into the twenty-first century, so the plan must be flexible enough to suit your household as it evolves over time. Be mindful, too, that you should plan for more storage space for trash handling than you presently have, for recycling purposes.

The following guidelines can help you define your needs.

• *List your overriding objections to your present kitchen.* Is the kitchen too small, dark, cramped, and inconveniently compartmented? Does it lack room for informal dining? Is the work space inefficient? Is it impossible for two cooks to work simultaneously? Is the room's appearance uncomfortably outmoded? Are the colors unappealing? Are cabinets or appliances outmoded or worn? Are countertops scratched or burned? Is the lighting insufficient? Are there too few outlets? Is the ventilation poor?

• *Consider how you and the members of your household use the kitchen space.* Are there family members with special needs and considerations—infants, toddlers, the elderly, a physically handicapped person? When and how do you prepare and eat meals? How many members of your household cook? Are there specialties that need to be accommodated, such as baking? How often do you entertain? Formal and/or informal? What nonfood-related activities take place in your kitchen? Are a television and a computer to be incorporated?

• *List the types, sizes, and quantities of equipment you have.* How many pots, pans, and lids? Tureens and stock pots? Poachers, steamers, woks? Small appliances? Baking equipment (including pans, muffin tins, molds, measuring cups, spoons, cookie cutters, cake decorating equipment, baking sheets, soufflé bowls)? Mixing bowls, colanders, strainers, long-handled equipment? Cutting board, casserole dishes, containers for leftovers? Spices? Tableware (including everyday dishes, glasses, and utensils, chinaware, silverware, crystal, cups, saucers, serving pieces, tablecloths, napkins, placemats)? Nonperishables (canned, boxed, and bagged foods, pet foods and supplies, paper goods, storage bags, wraps, foil)? Cleaning and recycling items?

• *Determine your style preference.* Are you more comfortable in a formal or informal setting? Do you prefer a pristine "laboratory" look, with everything put away, and nothing on display? Or do you like a cluttered kitchen, with your pots, books, canisters, and collectibles displayed? Do you want traditional decor, "Country" (American, French, or English), American Shaker, Contemporary, "high-tech," Art Nouveau/Deco, a strong regional influence, or an eclectic mix? How about your color preferences? Do you prefer countertop dining? A banquette? A separate table? A combination of countertop *and* separate table? How important are the views from the dining area? From the working areas?

BUDGET CONSIDERATIONS

Because the kitchen is the most costly room to remodel in your home, it is doubly important to prepare a plan wisely that will work well and be a constant pleasure. Even if you invest a significant sum in top-of-the-line equipment and materials, the plan can still be dysfunctional, cramped, or otherwise inefficient and can prove to have limited financial and emotional value.

To understand how and where you can save money to stay within your budget, you need to know where the greatest costs are. Labor costs will consume the biggest portion of your budget: as much as 40 percent or more of the total project cost. Plumbers and electricians are not concerned whether you are spending a few hundred or a few thousand dollars on an appliance; their rates are the same, no matter what.

The second highest cost in the kitchen is the cabinetry; it can amount to as much as half of the total cost of all materials. Built-ins—swing-out and roll-out shelves and drawers, tilt-out drawers, spice racks, fitted flatware storage, pull-out wastebaskets, and pull-out cutting boards—all add to the total cabinetry cost.

Appliances, countertop and backsplash materials, and flooring account for the next largest sums, followed by fittings and accessories. Prices vary dramatically in every category. A faucet, for example, can cost less than $100 or more than $400, depending on quality and material. A built-in refrigerator can cost several thousand dollars, as can a top-of-the-line imported cooktop/grill. Solid-surface synthetics,

marble, and granite can cost two-and-a-half to three-and-a-half times as much as comparable-size laminate countertop materials, and ceramic tile is approximately twice as expensive as laminate.

Although you can cut costs by doing some of the work—such as painting, wallpapering, and tiling—yourself, these tend to be lesser items. However, if you are a handy person, it is certainly worth taking these on. The Remodelors Council of the National Association of Home Builders, a trade group, surveyed its members and found that homeowners perform some of the work in 80 percent of their jobs.

Gutting your kitchen yourself and arranging for debris to be hauled away before construction begins is another way to save money. Whether it is worth it to you, in terms of the time and effort you will have to expend, is a decision only you can make.

The important thing is to make these decisions before contracts and prices are set—and stick to them. The best way to avoid "extras" is to keep changes to a minimum once construction begins. If a plan is well-thought-out, there should be little need to ask for changes at a later date. Changes cause time delays and possibly scheduling conflicts with various subcontractors. Delays are costly. Of course, working in an older home often uncovers structural "surprises" that need to be taken into consideration as they arise, but that's another matter.

Most of our dream kitchens include some "wish list" design elements that far exceed our more realistic "must haves" and budget requirements. One of the difficult tasks you have to tackle before construction begins, then, involves making trade-offs and compromises in design, products, and materials without sacrificing the look and conveniences you are seeking.

THE DECISION-MAKING PROCESS

Most people are amazed by the number of decisions that must be made before remodeling a kitchen. Ask yourself the following questions to determine your needs:

- Will a simple, cosmetic facelift provide a functional, aesthetically pleasing room?
- Can the main work centers (sink, cooktop, refrigerator) remain where they are, or will

they function more efficiently in a different configuration?

- Are structural changes—such as a room extension, relocating doors and windows, or relocating the kitchen itself—necessary?
- Can you reuse existing appliances to help conserve costs, or are they so outmoded that they must be replaced?
- Will you do any of the work yourself—for example, painting, wallpapering, or installing tile or flooring?

The next important decision concerns financing. How will you pay for this project? If you are not going to use discretionary income, what type of loan might be appropriate and possible?

Probably just as important as financing the project is selecting the professional(s) to design and install your kitchen (see chapters 3 and 4). There are no guidelines or formulas to follow in determining your budget, and there are no standard ways to approach a kitchen remodeling project as far as staffing is concerned. The "lead" individual you hire might be an architect, interior designer, kitchen designer, kitchen dealer, or a remodeling contractor.

The design professionals can draw plans and turn the project over to you to have the kitchen installed by a contractor or they can supervise the construction. You can give your designer or contractor the responsibility for specifying products and materials based on an understanding of your tastes, make these selections in consultation with him or her, or do it yourself.

If you already have some expertise in the home construction field—and the time and patience—you can act as your own contractor, hiring the tradespeople you need (carpenter, plumber, electrician, tile setter, etc.) and coordinating their work schedules.

Since you will literally be living with the contractor and his or her crew for several months, and you will be living with the results of their work for perhaps 10 to 15 years or more, you must choose a "lead" professional whom you feel you can trust, with whom you share a rapport and common goals for the project. The danger of choosing "Mr. or Ms. Wrong" for your project cannot be understated. A sketchy review of designers' or contractors' qualifications and track records only opens the door for serious, costly problems as the project progresses. (See chapters 3 and 4 for our suggestions in this regard.)

COST/VALUE CONSIDERATIONS

Unfortunately, there is no easy answer to the question of how much a remodeling project should cost. No specific formulas or guidelines can help you determine what makes the most sense for you, particularly since every single kitchen remodeling is unique.

Every year, trade associations and consumer and trade magazines publish figures showing "average" prices for kitchen remodeling projects, on a national or regional basis. Although these figures are helpful, they can be misleading because the studies on which they're based include even the smallest, most superficial home improvements, such as a simple appliance or countertop replacement.

To complicate matters even further, prices for materials and labor can vary dramatically not only from one region to the next, but even from one county to the next. Prices in urban locales can easily be double to triple what they might be in a suburban or rural setting.

A more accurate gauge of how much you should spend is your local housing market. How much is your home worth, based on homes in your own area? It is realistic to plan to invest between 10 and 20 percent of the home's current value on kitchen remodeling. You want to avoid overimproving your property so you do not price it out of the market should you decide to sell it in the future.

For example, in a million-dollar home it is not unreasonable to expect to find the homeowner spending $100,000 to renovate the kitchen. That figure is easy to reach with custom cabinetry, specialty designs (for example, handpainted tiling), and imported materials and equipment. But for a home valued at $165,00 to $200,000, such a budget would be unreasonable. An attractive, functional kitchen can be achieved in that home for $25,000 to $30,000 or less.

Cost recovery is difficult to calculate. Here, too, trade associations and consumer and trade magazines annually publish figures that estimate the amount a homeowner might reasonably expect to recover for various types of remodeling projects. These surveys have consistently estimated that a kitchen remodeling should recapture from 70 to 125 percent of its cost when the home is sold.

This figure cannot be taken at face value, of course. Much will depend on

- the overall neighborhood and the value of surrounding homes
- the age of the home
- the size of the home
- how recently the remodeling project was completed

If you sell your home five years after the kitchen has been remodeled, it is unrealistic to expect to recover all your costs. Remodeling the kitchen is a capital improvement, though, and adds to the cost basis for the house, lowering your capital gain when you sell. In computing that gain, you add the cost of the capital improvement to the purchase price of the home when you bought it.

On the other hand, remodeling a kitchen will undoubtedly add value in an intangible—but very important—way. Builders and brokers alike point out that in home sales, the two most important rooms are the kitchen and the bath. Particularly in a very competitive market, when buyers have a wide array of housing choices in any given price range, a modernized kitchen will help the home "show" well and will give that home a competitive edge over a comparable home with an older kitchen.

FINANCING A KITCHEN REMODELING

A consumer survey commissioned by the Remodelors Council found that more than 80 percent of homeowners questioned use personal savings as the major source of financing for remodeling jobs, followed by bank credit cards, home-equity loans, and other financial institution loans. Here, too, you must exercise as much care in choosing a financing source as you would in selecting a contractor. Lending laws vary from state to state, and loans and credit lines vary widely from one institution to the next. Be sure to shop around to see who offers the most attractive rates and terms.

You can seek a personal loan or use your home as collateral for a second mortgage. You can also refinance your home. Be aware that if you use your home as collateral and are unable to pay back your loan, you could lose your home. Before making any final decisions, consult your accountant or tax adviser regarding possible tax advantages for different types of financing. Interest on mortgages and home-equity credit is tax deductible. Many other types of interest are not.

Before choosing a finance source, ask yourself the following questions:

- What is the interest rate on the loan, and is it fixed or adjustable?
- If the rate is variable, what is the "cap" (or maximum) amount to which it can rise? Can it be converted to a fixed rate? What is the initial annual percentage rate? What is the index based on? How often can the rate change and in what increments?
- What is the length of the loan? Are there penalties for prepayment? For late payment? Can the loan amount be refinanced at the end? Can the loan term be extended?
- Are there fees involved? Closing costs? Property-appraisal costs? Attorneys' fees? Title search? Points? Continuing costs throughout the life of the loan?
- Are payments for interest only, or do they combine principal and interest? Is there a balloon payment required at the end of the loan term?
- Can terms be changed without the borrower's consent?
- What are the default provisions?

You should also expect a lender to ask to see the project's finished plans, specifications, and cost estimates for materials.

Some contractors offer home improvement loans from finance companies. The lure of these loans is that you will be approved regardless of your current income or employment situation or job history, as long as there is sufficient equity in your home. In such an arrangement, the finance company typically routes the payment for a job directly to the contractor. That gives you considerably less leverage in dealing with your contractor, should disagreements arise concerning the progress, timing, and/or quality of the work being done. Once the power to withhold payment is outside your control, you have relinquished your major negotiating strength. Worse— your home can be seized for nonpayment of the loan. Financing obtained through a contractor often has less attractive terms than that offered by local lending institutions, so it pays to shop around.

For those who are remodeling a kitchen to accommodate the needs of a handicapped person, the Veterans Administration is a source for below-market financing. In some states "reverse-mortgage" loans are available for senior citizens who wish to make home improvements, financed by borrowing against the equity in their homes. In many cases, the loans don't have to be repaid until the homeowner moves, dies, or sells the home.

SCHEDULING

If you want your new kitchen to be ready in time for Thanksgiving dinner, don't start the remodeling process during your summer vacation.

Builders and remodeling contractors usually caution clients that major projects take longer and cost more than anyone might anticipate. Since each project is unique, there is no hard-and-fast rule regarding how long a kitchen remodeling should take. The construction process can take less than a month for a simple facelift or last four months or more for an extensive renovation. But here are a few general guidelines:

- Drawing plans can take one to three weeks; if revisions are required based on your review, the process certainly can take a month.
- Cabinetry should be ordered 8–12 weeks in advance if it is stock; European or custom cabinetry should be ordered 12–16 weeks or more in advance.
- Construction will start about 4–6 weeks before cabinets are delivered.
- Flooring, countertops, and backsplash materials can be ordered while a room extension is being built.

The more detailed and well planned your project, the fewer surprises and delays you'll encounter once construction begins. Because you cannot predict the vagaries of manufacturers' and suppliers' businesses, however, it makes sense to have second choices to rely on. That way, if there is a problem with delivery of the appliances, flooring, countertops, or cabinetry you have selected, either because of a factory or shipping delay, or if a line has been discontinued, your project need not come to a halt; you can simply switch to your second choice.

2

Planning Your Kitchen

We live in exciting design times. There has been not only an explosion in the shapes, colors, sizes, and varieties of materials available but also a recognition that much of the conventional wisdom about kitchen design should be rethought and reworked.

Outstanding kitchen design is usually the result of a happy marriage of layout, style, texture, materials, light, and color, all blending in a way that best responds to an individual household's needs.

CHANGES IN KITCHEN DESIGN PRINCIPLES

Kitchen design was once based on the assumption that a stay-at-home mom prepared meals for a family. Because the kitchen was used only for cooking, it could thus be separate from the rest of the house, with its facilities confined only to a single function.

The advent of the working woman has had a profound impact on kitchen design over the past 25 years. During the week, when everyone's schedule is full and people are busy, meals are as likely to be "zapped" in the microwave as created from scratch. In addition, men and children are now active participants in meal preparation.

Our current time constraints, which allow for less time to devote to cleaning chores, have also meant more emphasis on ease of maintenance as a major criterion in selecting materials for the kitchen.

As social and family roles have changed and evolved, the kitchen has changed also, becoming the heart of the home for some families. The kitchen's isolation ended as it opened up and connected to other areas of the home, becoming the central gathering space for family and friends.

Other major social and economic changes have had an impact on kitchen design. Kitchens have grown in size during real estate "boom" cycles, focusing the design challenge on how best to plan sizable, rather than very limited, compartmented spaces. Concern with health changed the types of foods we buy, store, and serve: more fresh foods and fewer canned and packaged goods. Garbage handling has become an important issue, increasing the space needs for recycling household trash.

TRADITIONAL DESIGN

Current kitchen design still owes much to traditional planning principles; however, there is no one perfect solution to your design needs. Multiple solutions are available, depending on the restraints of architectural, structural, budgetary, and building/zoning code requirements. Ultimately, it is more important for your kitchen to function well and to provide an appealing aesthetic environment than it is to follow design guidelines precisely.

The Work Triangle

Classic kitchen design has always relied on the concept of the *work triangle*. This term refers to the path of the tasks you perform in the kitchen: removing food from the refrigerator, moving to the sink to wash and prepare food, and moving again between the sink and the cooktop for cooking and cleanup. The points of the work triangle are generally referred to as *work centers*.

Classic design principles include the following:

- The perimeter of the work triangle, between the stove, sink, and refrigerator, should be between 12 and 22 feet, with each leg ranging from 3½ to 7 feet.
- The optimum work triangle has equal-size legs.
- Traffic patterns should not interfere with the triangle.

Classic Kitchen Shapes

Classic kitchen design has grouped these various "centers" into work triangles within different-shaped kitchens. The most popular shapes have been:

The "Galley," or "Corridor," Kitchen. In this kitchen the main work centers (range, refrigerator, and sink) are located along two opposite walls. The efficiency of this plan is that it allows the cook to pivot between work centers with relative ease. The drawbacks are that counter and storage space are often limited, and traffic can go through the cook's path. This shape is often found in apartments and townhouses.

The L-shaped Kitchen. In this kitchen the range, refrigerator, and sink are located along two

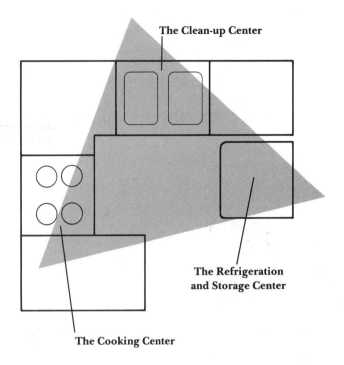

The Clean-up Center

The Refrigeration and Storage Center

The Cooking Center

Figure 2.1   The Work Triangle

walls that are perpendicular to each other. The benefit of this plan is that it allows for a natural triangle and workable counter space.

The U-shaped Kitchen. In this kitchen, the range, refrigerator, and sink are located along three walls that form a U. Designers like the U shape because it enables the cook to save steps; the cook is surrounded on three sides by countertop and storage.

If they are spacious enough, L- and U-shaped kitchens may also lend themselves to variations with the introduction of an island or peninsula. Islands or peninsulas are particularly useful when there is more than one cook present; they help establish separate work areas. They also improve traffic flow by directing it away from the cook's path.

The G-shaped Kitchen. In this kitchen, the U is extended, with an extra wall for cabinets and appliances. The extra wall might take the form of a peninsula instead of a solid wall. The advantage of this shape is that it allows for the separation of functions, encourages practical traffic patterns, and provides for some privacy. The potential drawback is that the space may seem too enclosed.

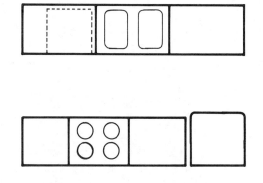

Figure 2.2   The Corridor Kitchen

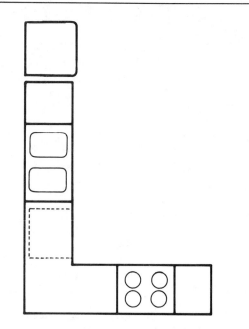

Figure 2.3   The L-shaped Kitchen

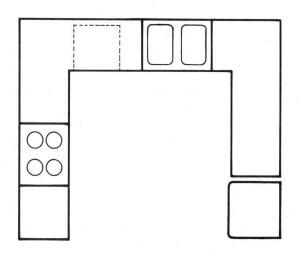

Figure 2.4   The U-shaped Kitchen

HOW THE KITCHEN FUNCTIONS

A kitchen layout must enable you to perform a great many specific tasks efficiently and comfortably. Among these are

• *Bringing in groceries and other household goods from outside.* This is one of the reasons that the location of the kitchen, in relation to the rest of the house, is important. The location has to pass what we'd like to call a *torn-bag-of-groceries test.* If you're hauling in a torn, heavy grocery bag from the nearest entry, you need a convenient surface on which to set it down before the bag breaks.

• *Storing groceries and other household goods.* Your cooking and shopping habits will dictate how much and what kind of storage you need. For example, do you buy mostly fresh fruits, vegetables, meats, and fish, or do you rely primarily on packaged goods? Do you shop in bulk or on an as-needed basis?

• *Preparing food.* The relationship between the sink and the cooktop is still the most important one in kitchen planning. Think of it in terms of how it passes the *hot pasta test.* That is, you need to be able to remove a boiling pot of pasta from the cooktop to a colander in the sink *quickly and efficiently.* If you have to walk around an island or other appurtenance to do it, or if your path is usually crossed by kids at play, your kitchen plan fails the test.

The relationship between the sink and the refrigerator is also critical. It must pass the *dripping Romaine lettuce test.* That is, you need a quick, direct path so that you can retrieve fresh foods from the refrigerator and take them to the food preparation center without danger of dropping them or otherwise creating a mess in the kitchen.

Vital to efficient meal preparation is enough continuous counter space for chopping, cutting, slicing, or otherwise processing and arranging food before it's cooked.

If two cooks prepare meals together, there should be a mini-work pattern, for example, between the refrigerator, microwave, and a secondary sink, and sufficient aisle space to allow one person to work without interrupting or bumping into the other.

Food preparation is also made simpler when the utensils, cookware, and spices are easily available to the cook close to the most-used appliances.

Before the advent of the microwave oven, the cooktop was the most-used cooking appliance, and ovens were the least. The microwave has changed cooking methods, however, so its placement has become important.

Serving and Preparing

Counter and aisle space recommendations: 36 to 48 inches of continuous counter space in the food preparation center of a large kitchen; 24 to 30 inches of counter space in a small kitchen; 24 to 36 inches of continuous counter space in the cooking area; 39 inches of aisle space between island and wall cabinets. Exceeding these amounts leads to inefficient use of space.

• *Serving meals.* You need adequate room to set down pots, casseroles, and dishes. Such "landing space" should be provided next to key appliances: cooktop, ovens (microwave and conventional), and refrigerator. If you have a sizable kitchen, an island can be used not only as a food preparation area but also as a "landing" and serving area. Landing space next to a cooktop or oven should be heatproof. Note that laminate counters, by themselves, are not heatproof, so a trivet or other heatproof material should be kept handy.

If the path between serving and dining is circuitous, it should be reworked. Similarly, it should be easy for you to go to the refrigerator from the dining area in the kitchen, to get the extra soda or ketchup you may have forgotten, without crossing the sink/cooktop path.

• *Cleaning up.* Everyone's least favorite task—cleaning up after meals—is much simpler if the sink, dishwasher, and storage areas for dishes, utensils, and glassware are grouped in close proximity. Beware plans that show dishwashers angled next to the sink, however; unless there's enough clearance space, you won't be able to load or unload the dishwasher without feeling completely hemmed in.

If you have sufficient space, consider using one sink for cleanup purposes, clustered with the dishwasher, storage for everyday dishes and glassware, and the recycling center. A secondary sink can be devoted to meal preparation tasks.

Cleanup counter space recommendations: 36 to 39 inches (including dishwasher), with 24 inches on one side of the sink for draining.

• *Providing for a home office.* Whether or not you work in your home, you and/or your family may well pay bills, do homework, keep the books, plan meals, make phone calls, and manage the schedule in the kitchen. This "center" is the ideal place to keep cookbooks, family records, files, and even the computer.

The ideal location is separate from the cooking area. The office can be adjacent to the cleanup area or serve as a bridge between the dining or pantry area.

• *Specialties.* Sewing, indoor gardening, and specialty baking such as pastry making are examples of the kinds of additional activities for which many people use their kitchen.

Baking may require a different type of countertop material, such as marble, and a countertop height that is lower than the standard 36 inches for easier dough making, rolling, and filling. Ovens and storage should be sufficient for a variety of pans, utensils, and other equipment.

Counter placement and height recommendations: Standard counter height is 36 inches. For baking, a 32-inch-high counter section can be placed between the food preparation area and the cooktop, or put in a section of a center island, and lowered from standard height to 32 inches.

• *Dining in the kitchen.* Although this cannot be considered a "task," it can certainly be an unpleasant experience if you are cramped, crowded, and inconvenienced at mealtimes. Conversely, a well-planned table and a seating arrangement near a bank of windows, flooded with light and air with perhaps a volume ceiling (whose height exceeds the standard 8 feet) and a skylight, will invite family and friends to linger.

If your kitchen is spacious enough, seating may include both a table and chairs or built-in banquette against a wall plus island countertop dining or peninsula countertop extensions. A banquette offers the additional benefit of increasing storage space for bulky items.

The height of a snack counter can vary, from the standard table height of 30 inches to standard countertop height of 36 inches or to the raised bar height of 42 inches. If the snack area is part of an island or peninsula that also houses a cooktop or sink, consider setting those functional elements at a different height from the dining section. Not only will it be more appealing visually, but it will also help shield diners from spatters and splashes from cooking and cleanup.

Be aware that older people and young children often have difficulty getting on and off of tall stools, and that the danger of tipping over and falling is ever-present. An alternative to freestanding stools might be seats that are attached to the base of the counter but can swing out for easier maneuvering.

One of the biggest mistakes made in kitchen design is the failure to provide walking space around the dining table and chairs, a particular concern in kitchens where the separate seating area abuts a snack counter.

Plan on a minimum of 42 inches between counter and wall or furniture.

The size of the table will depend on household size and structural constraints. Assuming that each person needs 21 to 24 inches of table space, four people can be comfortable at a round table that is 42 inches in diameter, although in a small kitchen, a 36-inch table will suffice. If you have young children, a snack counter is often very useful. When you buy stools, however, be aware that the average person needs 14 inches of knee space below the counter. For maximum comfort, a footrest 18 inches from the seat should be provided.

If you want to incorporate a dining area into a small kitchen, it may involve redesigning the space to incorporate all appliances along one wall, installing tall storage cabinets along another, and using the available open space for seating. A range/oven that houses the oven, a cooktop, and perhaps an overhead microwave will save space in such an instance.

Another solution may involve building in a small pull-out table in a drawer space, which can be stored away when you don't need it. Similarly, a small fold-down table against a wall or under a window, in a square, rectangular, or half-round shape, can create a cozy dining nook in a limited space.

APPLIANCE PLACEMENT: DOS AND DON'TS

Many plans place appliances according to a "sprinkler" system: that is, appliances are sprinkled throughout the room with little logical connection to the progression of tasks that takes place in a kitchen. In fact, appliance placement logically follows the progression of tasks that takes place in the kitchen.

Sink/Dishwasher

- Provide sufficient "loading space" at the sink and the dishwasher to make loading and unloading easier. The average person needs approximately 20 to 24 inches to stand and perform these tasks comfortably.
- Place the sink cleanup area near the middle of the work pattern, if possible, since it is so heavily used.
- Provide sufficient counter space for a dish drain on one side and food preparation, cleanup, and leftover storage on the other, particularly if the plan does not call for a second sink.
- Take a fresh look at the sink location. It need not go directly under the window; it can function just as well in an island or peninsula setting. If you do choose the more traditional window location, though, remember to center the sink under it.
- The dishwasher door should not obstruct the aisle when it is open.

Microwave Oven

- Place the microwave at or, preferably, below eye level. Otherwise, it is awkward and dangerous to remove hot dishes. Other good alternatives are placing it at countertop level (if you have the luxury of significant available counter space), hanging it below a wall cabinet, or setting it several inches up from the countertop, housed on a shelf.
- Plan on using a pull-out board for "landing space" if the microwave is housed with a conventional wall oven outside the primary work pattern.
- Place the microwave so that it relates easily to the refrigerator/freezer.
- Allow for landing space near the microwave unless you expect to use it only occasionally.
- Do not place the microwave below countertop level in an island unless you provide a pull-out board for landing space. This type of arrangement may be suitable for a wheelchair-bound cook (see below). It could be hazardous if there are young children in the family, however, particularly if they use the appliance unsupervised.

Refrigerator

- Place the refrigerator so that it is easily accessible not only to the cook but also from a snack counter or dining table.
- Provide enough landing space adjacent to the refrigerator, preferably on the side of the handle, so that such space won't be blocked by the open refrigerator door.
- Provide sufficient clearance (2 to 3 inches) at one side if the refrigerator is up against a wall.
- Avoid placing the refrigerator next to ovens, unless there is an aesthetic imperative to do so and sufficient landing space is provided along adjacent countertops or a nearby island or peninsula.
- Place the refrigerator at the end of a run of cabinets.

Conventional Ovens

- Plan double wall ovens so that the upper oven, when open, is about 3 inches below the cook's elbow. The break between the ovens should be at 36 inches off the floor.
- Avoid placing ovens within the primary work pattern unless the cook relies heavily on them for day-to-day cooking.
- Avoid placing the dishwasher opposite a lower oven; it creates a traffic crunch if both doors need to be open at the same time.

Cooktop

- Provide a short, direct path between the cooktop and sink so that other household traffic will not intrude.
- Provide sufficient counter space adjacent to the cooktop so that food can be "staged" for serving.
- Provide sufficient clearance in front of a drop-in or freestanding range/oven combination so that you can comfortably bend down, open the door, and use the oven.
- Don't place a cooktop near a combustible wall.
- Don't place a gas cooktop close to a window, where an open flame can ignite curtains.
- Don't place a cooktop at the end of a cabinet run, adjacent to a traffic aisle, because of the danger of knocking over a pot whose handle may protrude into the aisle space.

STORAGE IDEAS

As the years go by, most people acquire a lot of kitchen items, ranging from the small appliances they cannot live without to individual pots, serving platters, and utensils that they may use only once a year. Well-planned storage will allow you to easily find and use the items you need and to keep them in a sensible place.

A well-planned kitchen not only provides *enough* storage space to house all the items you have *or would like to acquire* but also places that storage so that any item you need is readily available. Saving time is a major consideration in our lives. Proper storage cuts down on cooking time because it saves extra trips around the kitchen to gather what you need to perform various tasks.

Good storage planning also recognizes that the items you use most frequently should be stored between knee and shoulder level for a minimum of stooping, squatting, or bending in base cabinets, or reaching or climbing up to wall cabinets.

Fortunately, designers and manufacturers have now devised many storage options that maximize the potential of cabinet and counter space. Some examples include deep pull-out drawers for base cabinets; lazy Susans and swing-out shelves for corner cabinets; tilt-out bins for flour, onions, and potatoes; under-sink tilt-outs for soap and sponges; built-in spice racks; and built-in utensil racks.

Reviewing your kitchen inventory (see chapter 1) is the first step toward developing a storage plan for your new kitchen. Excluding cookbooks and collectibles, there are seven separate categories of storage inventory, all of which have their own requirements. Here are some suggestions for the size and placement of storage of each.

Cooking Equipment

Pots and pans are best stored close to where you prepare and cook meals. Unless you prefer to hang them from a rack above the cooktop, a good place to store pots and pans is in base cabinets below the cooktop. For ease of use, the drawers can be pull-outs, so that you don't have to bend over and reach back to retrieve heavy equipment. If you have a stand-alone stove, today's versions often have storage drawers included.

For cooking equipment that you use less frequently, such as a large stock pot, fish poacher, or slow cooker, storage space can be provided above the shoulder-height "comfort level." This kind of equipment can often be stored above a wall oven or over the refrigerator in a 24-inch-deep cabinet.

Pot lids, cutting boards, and trays are awkward items to store. Store them vertically, in a so-called "tray" cabinet with vertical dividers. Lids can also be stored in racks on cabinet doors if the corresponding pull-out shelves in the base cabinet are slightly recessed. If you can't accommodate lid storage in a deep cabinet drawer, consider hanging lids on a wall rack (available at hardware or kitchen specialty stores). These systems can be made of stainless steel or slatted wood with hooks. They can be used to store other small items, especially in kitchens where space is limited.

Food Preparation Equipment

Like pots and pans, the tools you use to prepare meals should be stored close to the preparation center. Drawer dividers can be used to separate long-handled tools so that they don't become hopelessly jumbled and difficult to remove when you need them. Dividers can be supplied by cabinet people, bought in hardware stores, or put together by a reasonably handy person.

Spices can be grouped and stored in a number of ways: in a base cabinet drawer adjacent to the range, tilted slightly upward on wooden slats so that you can see the labels easily; on a rack on a wall cabinet door close to where you prepare meals; or on a built-in shelf or "cubby" along the backsplash. Spices should *not* be stored so close to the cooktop that the heat will affect them.

Microwavable bowls, casseroles, lids, and wax paper or wrapping paper should be stored together, close to the microwave oven, in an easily accessible wall or base cabinet.

Small Appliances

For often-used (but not necessarily attractive) smaller appliances, such as the toaster, coffee maker, and food processor, an excellent design solution is an appliance "garage," built into the countertop (at the food preparation center). The garage fits against the standard 12-inch-deep backsplash under a wall cabinet. The door can be either a tambour or a flat garage door. If you prefer, the garage can be located in a corner. Width can range from 12 to 36 inches. Electrical outlets should be installed in the backsplash behind the appliances in a horizontal strip. There are also under-cabinet versions of many of these appliances, which can be permanently installed.

Baking Equipment

Baking equipment can be stored together close to the ovens. If you are an avid baker and plan a countertop of special height, consider installing a plastic or wood tilt-out bin for flour and sugar in the base cabinet below the countertop.

Nonperishables

Cans, jars, and boxes and bags of food are usually stored in a pantry. Ideally, the pantry should be located between the entranceway you use to bring in your groceries and the kitchen, or close to the entry to the kitchen, so that you don't have to carry heavy bags too far. An acceptable alternative location is on a wall adjacent to a planning desk, outside the work pattern.

The pantry can be either a walk-in closet or a group of cabinets arranged along a wall. The old-fashioned walk-in pantry can range from 4 by 4 feet to 6 by 6 feet, with open shelving on three interior walls. The shelving can be customized to accommodate the heights of the items stored, including pet foods and supplies. Bins can be built in.

If space is at a premium, as in an apartment or townhouse, consider pantry storage along a wall. One or more standard pantry cabinets, ranging from 18 to 36 inches wide, 84 inches high, and 12 to 24 inches deep, can be as efficient as a walk-in pantry, with the use of revolving shelves and fold-out or pull-out sections. This arrangement also takes up less floor space than a walk-in. Use door shelving to reduce the depth of the inside shelves so more of the storage will be visible at a glance.

Standard wall cabinets with shelving, which are considerably less expensive than specialized pantry cabinets, can also be used for pantry storage.

A pull-out pantry, a cabinet that has slide-out sections, can be designed for space as narrow as 7 inches wide and can be as tall as 84 inches or higher or as short as a base cabinet. This arrangement is more appropriate for smaller items. It can be adapted to hold pots and pot lids as well.

Tableware

Everyday dishes, glassware, and utensils should be easily accessible from the dining area (whether it's a separate table or a countertop snack bar) as well as from the dishwasher. Even among everyday items there are some that are used constantly—keep them on the lowest, most convenient shelves. Tablecloths, placemats, napkins, and napkin rings should be stored together, accessible from the dining area so that the table can be set easily while other activities are taking place in the kitchen.

You may want to display your fine china and crystal, or store them separately along with "special occasion" silverware in the dining room.

Cleaning and Recycling Items

A broom closet of some kind is almost a necessity. It should be a tall, narrow, and shallow space to store vertical cleaning items such as brooms, mops, and dustpans with long handles. An ironing board can be stored here, in the laundry area, or built into the sewing center.

Cleaning supplies, buckets, and twine for tying up newspapers can be stored on a shelf inside the closet or on shelves built into the closet door, depending on space availability.

Additional "hidden storage" spaces can be built into a banquette section, in small shelves or cubes between counter and wall cabinets, or under a snack counter or kneehole desk.

ISLANDS AND ANGLES: MISTAKES TO AVOID

An island can often provide an imaginative solution to the design challenge of a large kitchen. It can provide the efficient work centers of a small kitchen, create a separate work path for a second cook, and offer easy-access storage as well as visual drama in the kitchen. A very large kitchen can accommodate two separate islands, one used for food preparation and the other as a baking center or snack bar.

In a small kitchen a 36-by-24-inch island is efficient, while a larger kitchen can accommodate an island as large as 36 by 72 inches. (See chapter 11, plan II, for the use of a 15-foot "super island" in an open kitchen/family room setting.)

An island can sometimes prove to be more of a hindrance than a help if it obstructs the path between the range or ovens, refrigerator, and sink. Also, an island should not obstruct the aisles when cabinet doors or doors from appliances along an opposite wall are open.

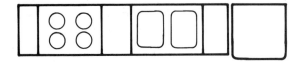

Figure 2.5   The One-wall Kitchen

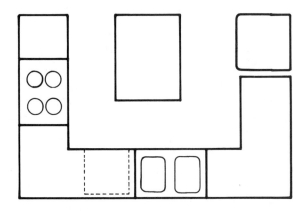

Figure 2.6   The Island Kitchen

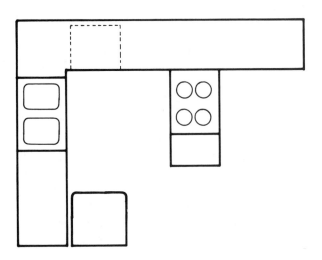

Figure 2.7   The Peninsula Kitchen

One of the most common errors in designing an island is the failure to provide sufficient countertop landing space next to a sink or cooktop. If the island is too narrow, there won't be sufficient work space either.

Be sure the path between the wall and the edges of the island is not too narrow; traffic jams will result. An aisle space of 3 to 4 feet should be provided around the island, so that the cook or cooks don't feel cramped. An island doesn't always include a snack bar, but if it does, make sure there is sufficient space between it and the kitchen's other dining area. If it's insufficient, your ability to move easily around the dining table will be impaired.

Countertop dining will also be uncomfortable if the cooktop or sink is placed too close to the dining counter. This problem can be avoided by making the dining counter higher or lower than the range or the sink, by building in a decorative barrier between the countertop areas, or by situating the snack bar at the opposite end of the island from the cooktop or sink.

Some islands include a below-countertop-level microwave oven. Such a location is both unsafe and awkward unless it includes a pull-out board on which to place food. Such a design should be considered only for the wheelchair-bound or seated cook.

Angled kitchen plans are also popular, and these include angled islands. Beware of using angles for visual pizzazz that serve no practical purpose. Avoid the following:

- Right-angled "hip punchers" that protrude into the aisle space and pose a safety hazard to the heads of kids and the hips of adults; sometimes such right angles can be cut off to ease such problems.
- Angled plans that can't function once they're executed because the cabinet doors clash, the doors don't have enough clearance to open or close, or the dishwasher placement makes it impossible to load.
- Mathematical errors that can wreak havoc with your budget if it turns out that the cabinets and countertops cannot be installed as planned. If your plan calls for angles, make sure the designer explains to you *exactly* why he or she has chosen them and how they contribute to the plan's working and/or its aesthetic appeal.

THE HOME RECYCLING CENTER

Our worldwide garbage crisis—too much trash, too few places to haul it to, too much nondegradable refuse—will have a measurable impact on all of us. Although the issue of trash handling has gotten little attention in design circles in the past, it can no longer be ignored.

Estimates vary, but we throw out some 3 to 5 pounds of trash per person per day, which amounts to approximately 1 ton per person per year. The best way to reduce this garbage glut is to reduce the amount of disposable and overly packaged materials we bring into the home; reuse as much as we can; and recycle the rest.

Either by mandate—more and more municipalities are devising recyling requirements—or by personal preference, you will want to incorporate a better system of handling trash in your new kitchen.

Recycling takes up more space than the traditional single garbage can in the kitchen but not an excessive amount of space. According to the New York State Department of Environmental Conservation, it takes a 3-by-3-foot area, enough for three boxes or bags, to store glass, cans, and newspapers for one month.

Multiple garbage cans can be housed under the sink. For added convenience, they can pull out or roll out as you sort and dispose of trash. Some designs feature lids that remain in place while the garbage can pulls out.

Alternative locations for a home recycling center are in a utility room or in a separate bank of cabinets that might be connected to pantry storage or a broom closet. An attached garage certainly makes a suitable location if it is associated with or close to the kitchen.

If you have a large family and a large home with a basement, your designer or contractor may be able to devise a chute system—much like an old-fashioned laundry chute—to handle garbage. There would be perhaps three separate chutes for plastic, glass, and cans, leading from a hatch in the wall or base cabinet in the cleanup center to separate receptacles in the basement or garage.

Instead of a 3-by-3-foot space, the recycling center can be longer and narrower to accommodate multiple cans or bags as well as a wire rack for newspapers. Separate bags and a wire rack for newspapers would take up 3 to 4 feet in width, but no more than the standard cabinet depth (24 inches).

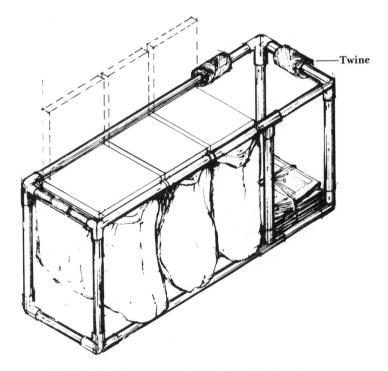

Figure 2.8   Four-compartment Recycling Center

HOUSEHOLDER'S GUIDE TO RECYCLING

Before You Recycle . . .

Reduce the amount of material requiring disposal.
- Avoid the purchase of bulky, disposable items.
- Pass on magazines, books, and catalogs to neighbors, hospitals, and nursing homes.
- Buy products in reusable containers or in simple packaging. (The average family of four pays $1 for packaging in every $11 spent for groceries.)

Reuse as much as possible.
- Plastic containers can be reused for food storage, glass jars for nails, tacks, etc.
- Reuse wrapping paper, plastic bags, boxes, and lumber.
- Give outgrown clothing to friends or donate it to a local charity.
- Buy beverages in returnable containers.
- Try to repair before you consider replacement of lawn mowers, tools, vacuum cleaners, TVs.
- Donate broken appliances to Goodwill Industries, a local rescue mission, or charity, or find out if a nearby vocational school can use them for parts or to have students practice repairing them.
- Offer furniture and household items no longer needed to college students and friends, or donate to charity.
- Join with neighbors and have a garage sale.

Preparing to Recycle

1. Ask your local government if there is a recycling center in your community, or contact your local recycling or scrap dealer to find out which recyclables they accept.
2. Decide on a storage area. To store glass, cans, and newspapers for one month, you'll need an area about 3 by 3 feet, enough for three boxes or bags—not hard to find around the house.
3. Get some tools together.

   - heavy brown bags and corrugated boxes
   - twine for tying bundles of paper and magazines
   - a magnet for testing metals
   - a can opener for removing ends of cans

Recyclable Materials

Materials	What Can Be Recycled	What Can't Be Recycled	Recycling Preparation
Glass	Glass containers: clear, amber, and green	Milk-white glass Plate glass Light bulbs Fluorescent bulbs Crystal	Rinse—labels can stay on Remove metal rings with awl, screwdriver, or needle-nose pliers Separate by color Store—do not break
Paper	Newsprint Corrugated boxes Egg cartons Junk mail Telephone books Computer paper and cards	Waxed or plastic-coated cellophane	Newspapers: keep clean and dry, stack less than 1 foot high, tie with twine or pack in brown grocery bag or box Cardboard: break down flat, stack, and tie in small bundles Office: stack in separate box
Aluminum (nonferrous metal)	All aluminum Foil food wrap, TV trays, pie tins Ice cube trays Aluminum siding, storm doors, windows, and gutters Lawn furniture		Trays, tins, foil; rinse, flatten, and store Other: remove foreign materials, cut into 3-foot lengths, tie or store separately in bags or bundles
Ferrous metal	Most ferrous metals, but separated according to type: cast iron, steel sheet metal, tin-coated cans, bimetal cans (steel and aluminum)	Nonferrous metals cannot be mixed with ferrous metal; they can be identified with a magnet, which *will not* stick to them	Tin cans: test with magnet, rinse, remove labels and ends, flatten (include ends), store in box or bag Bimetal cans: prepare same way as tin cans, but store separately Other ferrous: check with local scrap dealer about preparation and selling
Nonferrous metals	Nickel Bronze Copper Brass Lead	Ferrous metals cannot be mixed with nonferrous (test with magnet, which will stick to ferrous metals)	Check with your local scrap dealer or recycling center about preparation and sale
Plastics	All plastic containers		Rinse, remove metal caps, flatten, and store
Organic wastes	Nonanimal food scraps, yard and lawn waste	Meat and fish scraps (attract and breed pests)	Ask your local library or county agricultural extension for composting instructions
Motor oil	Oil drained from a car, motorcycle, or lawn mower	Oil contaminated by antifreeze	Drain oil into container, seal securely, and take to a Used Oil Collection Site

The hardware you need for recycling—racks that can house removable, degradable bags, and separate racks for stacking newspapers—is relatively inexpensive and easily found in a home supply store.

Smaller items you'll need to store in the recycling area are brown bags and/or corrugated boxes; twine for tying bundles of newspapers and magazines; a can opener for removing the ends of cans; a screwdriver, pliers, or awl for removing rings from bottle necks; and a magnet for testing metals.

Where do trash compactors and food waste disposers fit into the home recycling center? There is no consensus as to whether they ultimately help or harm the cause of managing the garbage glut. Some municipalities have regulations either banning *or* mandating their use, so find out your community's policy before making any decisions (see chapter 7).

SPECIAL DESIGN CHALLENGES

Whether you have a small, crowded kitchen, an average-size kitchen but one broken up into dysfunctional "compartments" by several entries, or a large kitchen that represents a "lost-in-space" approach to planning, most kitchens represent some type of design challenge. The lost-in-space kitchen has a great deal of square footage, but there is little logical flow from one work center to the next, which means extra steps and extra time.

The Small Kitchen

Small kitchens can be made to function very efficiently if they include carefully planned storage details. Built-in storage devices are especially useful, as are pull-out work counters or tables and racks for spices and pot covers. Pantry storage is usually at a premium in a small kitchen, but this can be overcome with shallow, vertical pantry storage cabinets or even shallow, open shelving along a wall.

Appliances must be placed with particular care in a small kitchen. A slip-in or drop-in range/oven combination saves considerable space and frees up wall space for storage.

The small kitchen can be made to seem larger with the use of light-colored floors, walls, cabinetry, and countertops; mirrored backsplashes; high ceilings; skylights or shaped windows; diagonal flooring; and a minimum of countertop clutter.

The Large Kitchen

When it comes to square footage in a kitchen, it is not necessarily true that "bigger is better." If you have to trudge more than several steps to move from one work station to the next, the kitchen is not functioning well. One solution to this problem is to add an island with a cooktop. This can cut down considerably on inconvenient steps for the cook. Another possibility is to create a separate desk space for household management tasks, making the kitchen into a multipurpose room.

THE TRANSGENERATIONAL KITCHEN

Much has been said about the "graying" of America. Our population is aging substantially: by 2030, one in five of us will be 65 or older. Our life expectancy is steadily increasing; more and more of us will live to see our eighty-fifth birthdays and beyond.

If current attitudes are any indication, as many as 85 percent of us who own our homes will prefer to remain there. Of the rest, many of us will live with our grown children or other relatives. For those of us who will need assistance with dressing, bathing, toileting, or housekeeping but not around-the-clock nursing care, there will probably be a more varied "menu" of home services available than there are now.

These changes will certainly affect kitchen design. Since a remodeled kitchen should serve you well for 10 or 20 years, it's important to plan now for the future. A kitchen built in the 90s should be planned to

- enable older or physically impaired people to continue living independently in their own home
- adapt to your own changing needs as you age
- serve the needs of the several generations that may be living together under one roof

Design that responds to these needs is usually referred to as "universal," "adaptable," "accessible," or "transgenerational."

Although there are many kitchen products available to serve the elderly and the physically impaired,

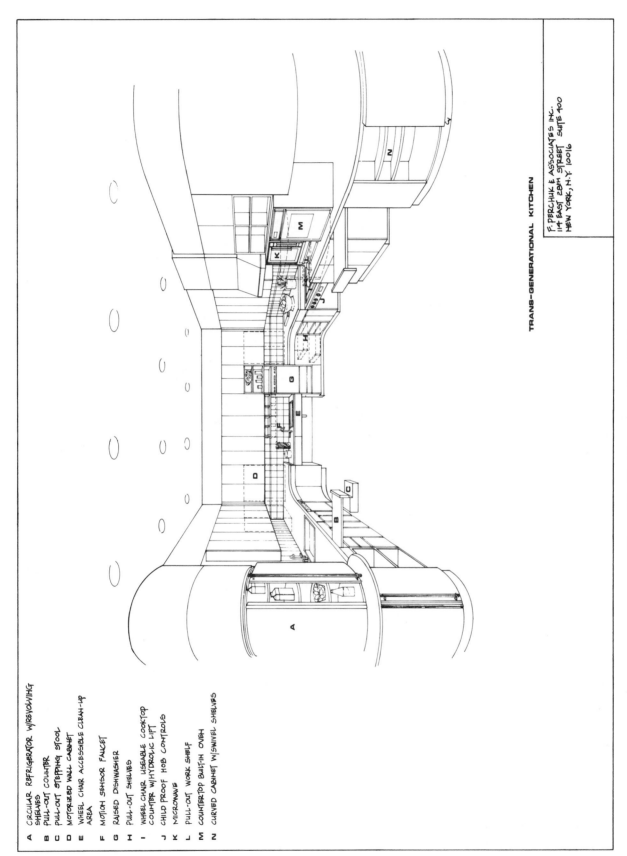

A CIRCULAR REFRIGERATOR W/REVOLVING
   SHELVES
B PULL-OUT COUNTER
C PULL-OUT STEPPING STOOL
D MOTORIZED WALL CABINET
E WHEEL CHAIR ACCESSIBLE CLEAN-UP
   AREA
F MOTION SENSOR FAUCET
G RAISED DISHWASHER
H PULL-OUT SHELVES
I WHEEL CHAIR, USEABLE COOKTOP
   COUNTER W/HYDRAULIC LIFT
J CHILD PROOF HOB CONTROLS
K MICROWAVE
L PULL-OUT WORK SHELF
M COUNTERTOP BUILT-IN OVEN
N CURVED CABINET W/SWIVEL SHELVES

TRANS-GENERATIONAL KITCHEN

F. PIRCHUK & ASSOCIATES INC.
114 EAST 28TH STREET SUITE 700
NEW YORK, N.Y. 10016

Figure 2.9   The Transgenerational Kitchen

the field is still in its infancy. The major drawbacks of some of these products and materials have been their appearance—suitable for an institutional setting rather than a warm and inviting kitchen—and their functional limitations. Labeling a product "adaptable" does not automatically make it so, and product designers will need to devote far more attention to both function and attractiveness if they are to satisfy the needs of their current and future consumers.

Products in the future are likely to rely increasingly on electronics, voice activation, and motorized operations. In the meantime, it is important to recognize precisely how the aging process affects the way we function in the kitchen and what tools are at our disposal *now* to plan the transgenerational kitchen.

How Our Needs Are Changing

Even if we are blessed with good health, the aging process takes its toll on our physical and sensory capabilities. We may not be as strong or as flexible as we might have been. We see, hear, and smell differently than we did, and we react a little more slowly to changes in the environment: floor levels and lighting, for example.

Traditional kitchen design is based on the key assumption that most tasks are performed standing up. Hence:

- Countertops are placed 36 inches high and 24 inches deep.
- Wall cabinets are usually positioned 16 to 18 inches above the counter.
- Storage for infrequently used items is often planned above a height of 7 feet.
- Conventional oven doors open from the top, not the side.

Nor is traditional kitchen design kind to the aging eye. As we get older, not only do we need more light (an 80-year-old needs three times as much light as a 20-year-old) but we perceive colors differently because the lens of the eye yellows over time.

Colors also become more difficult to distinguish as we age, particularly if they are complementary or are different intensities of the same hue. Yellows, oranges, and reds are most easily seen.

As we age, it becomes increasingly difficult to bend, stoop, and squat, and to climb and reach up high. Arthritis may make it difficult to perform fine motor tasks, or to firmly grip small cabinet pulls or traditional faucets.

Transgenerational Planning Principles

Convenience and safety, always important in kitchen design, are critical in the transgenerational kitchen. An older person should be able to move easily from task to task without a physical strain or the threat of potential danger. Products and materials should be selected for ease of maintenance. Here are a dozen important planning ideas:

1. In the transgenerational kitchen, many tasks should be able to be performed sitting down—whether on a pull-out stool, on a conventional dining chair, or in a wheelchair. A peninsula dining counter might also be designed to serve as a meal preparation area, for example.

This means that countertop height for meal preparation should be 30 to 32 inches high, depending on the individual's needs. Countertop depths can be shallower than the standard 24 inches.

2. Storage space for nonperishables, dishes, glassware, utensils, cooking equipment, and other household goods should be concentrated within the shoulder-to-knee zone. Pull-out drawers (preferably with full-extension hardware) are better than standard cabinets because they make it easier to store and retrieve larger items.

If pull-out drawers are not a realistic option for you, consider providing dual access to peninsula base cabinets. Make abundant use of swing-out shelves, and employ racks that can hang on base cabinet doors.

The depth of pantry storage should be limited so that you can easily see and retrieve what you need. Shelves can be as shallow as 6 inches. Wall cabinets can be lowered to 15 to 16 inches above countertop level. Motorized wall cabinets are already available, so that if you don't want to permanently attach cabinets at the lower level, you still have the flexibility of bringing the cabinets down to a level that is convenient for the older or physically impaired resident, at the touch of a switch.

Cabinet pulls should be shaped like a U, so that doors can be opened easily.

3. For storage of fresh foods, many design and building specialists recommend a side-by-side refrigerator/freezer because it enables the seated cook to easily reach items in either section. Many people find the side-by-side refrigerator inconvenient, however, because its freezer sections are usually too narrow to accommodate larger items, such as a twenty-pound turkey. Depending on a person's abilities, a refrigerator with a bottom freezer might be a preferable solution.

Refrigerators with automatic ice makers are a welcome amenity for those whose limited strength makes it difficult to break ice cubes out of a standard ice cube tray. The refrigerator shelves should be easy to pull out or rotate.

4. The type of sink you select will depend on whether you or a member of the household are wheelchair-bound or likely to become so. If you're not, you can work at a conventional-depth sink, using a portable plastic-coated wire dish rack in it for greater comfort. The wheelchair-bound need

- open maneuvering space of 5 by 5 feet in the center of the kitchen between the various task centers; the turning ratio should allow the wheelchair to turn in the shape of a U, not force it to trace a K
- a maximum sink depth of 5 inches
- a space under the sink at least 30 inches wide for ease of access
- countertop height of 31 inches
- insulation around the sink bowl and plumbing to prevent scalding (since insulated plumbing works are unattractive, consider covering them with a panel that matches your cabinetry and need not interfere with access). A shallow cabinet can be installed with a recess for the wheelchair.

Pay particular attention to faucets and accessories. The faucet should be a single-lever type that you can use comfortably even with arthritis or diminished strength. A good test, according to the American Association for Retired Persons (AARP), is to try to move the handle with your fist. If you can do that, it will be usable by a person who has difficulty gripping objects. Also available are antiscald devices, which eliminate the danger of accidental burns.

Certain faucets now start water flow by using an infrared light to sense a hand or other object, thereby eliminating the need for a lever. However, they are more costly than a conventional faucet. Moreover, an older person may not accept the new technology out of concern for what might happen if the electronics break down.

Installing a secondary water source at the sink—for example, a portable spray with a flexible hose—can make it easier to wash vegetables, pots, and a variety of other items. If there is a continuous countertop between the sink and the cooktop, the hose will provide the option of filling a pot with water at the cooktop or filling it at the sink and sliding it to the cooktop. Another possibility is a wall-mounted commercial faucet with a long hose.

5. A cooktop should minimize the possibility of burns or fires, and should be easy to operate. Controls at the front of the range are easier for an older person to use than those that are side- or center-mounted, but they should be chosen with caution if there are young children in the house. If yours is a multigenerational household, side- or center-mounted controls are acceptable as long as you don't have to reach across burners to use them.

Staggered burners, a safety feature, allow you to cook without having to reach across another burner. On the other hand, many cooks like to slide a pot from the front to the back burner for simmering, which a parallel configuration allows. Consider your individual style as well as your physical limitations before deciding which configuration of burners to choose.

Consider buying an induction-heat range, which transfers magnetic energy to ferrous pots and pans through a glass surface and diminishes the possibility of burns because the cooktop is never hot on the surface. It is also easy to clean because of its continuous surface. Some older people, long accustomed to using gas burners or electric ranges, may be uncomfortable about using such a cooktop, however. Other drawbacks are the difficulty in distinguishing visually between the induction-heat burners and the rest of the cooktop and the high cost of this appliance.

6. A wall oven is preferable to a slip-in, below-rangetop oven. The dials and indicators should be easy to read and to operate. Some manufacturers provide for what's called "redundant cueing," which

means that the appliance has more than one way to indicate a change in its setting or to alert you to its task's completion; if you have trouble seeing, for example, you can depend on your hearing for the cues.

Side-opening ovens are available for the wheelchair-bound. These should be used in conjunction with a pull-out shelf underneath them, so that the cook has safe and convenient landing space for food before and after baking or broiling.

7. Other built-ins in the food preparation area can ease an older person's tasks, such as

- an automatic can opener and a separate jar-opening device mounted under the bottom of a wall cabinet
- a removable mixing bowl built into a below-counter pull-out drawer so extra strength need not be used to steady a bowl at the countertop when preparing salads, dressing, sauces, or batter
- shelving at the backsplash for storing frequently used utensils, spices, and condiments
- a chopping board built into the counter to eliminate the need to carry one from one area to another
- drawers fitted for spices

8. A dishwasher need not be installed at floor level. It can be at counter height or raised on a 6-inch platform to eliminate much of the stooping usually necessary to load and unload. For aesthetic purposes, the raised dishwasher might be part of a larger countertop section, used as a snack bar or as a "shield" to hide a sink in an island or peninsula setting.

9. Use contrasting colors. In addition to lending aesthetic appeal to the kitchen, color can also provide visual cues to the aging eye. Because many older people have difficulty distinguishing different surfaces, contrasting colors should be employed to distinguish countertop from floor and countertop from cabinetry edges. Neutral colors, pastels, and complementary colors are less helpful in distinguishing forms than brighter colors in yellows, oranges, and reds.

High-gloss, lacquered surfaces should not be selected because they contribute to glare, to which the aging eye is sensitive. A matte surface increases light reflectance and reduces glare.

10. Because the aging eye requires more light than the young adult's, provide extra task lighting at the sink and under the wall cabinets at food preparation and cleanup areas. General room lighting should be indirect; lighting from recessed cans in the ceiling may be too intense.

11. Electrical outlets and light switches must be planned with care so that the seated or wheelchair-bound cook can easily reach them. Outlets should be located no higher than 48 inches off the floor and no deeper than 16 inches along the wall from the edge of the countertop.

Light switches that are wider than standard-width switches are easier to use. "Rocker" switches are easier to use than conventional switches.

12. A number of safety-oriented devices now on the market should be considered essential in planning a transgenerational kitchen. They include a smoke detector, a fire extinguisher, devices that detect gas leaks, and automatic appliance shutoffs when appliances are not in use.

Catering to the needs of an older population need not mean dull or institutional design. Carefully planned, the transgenerational kitchen can provide outstanding functional and aesthetic appeal to *all* members of the household.

If yours is a multigenerational household, consider "zoning" the kitchen plan to accommodate children, adults, and the elderly. For example, an island can be built using two or even three different heights. Knee-holes should be provided at a counter work center so that an older person, even though not in a wheelchair, can perform his or her tasks sitting down.

All kitchen remodeling projects are individual and customized. They are even more customized for people with specific physical disabilities. If you are planning to redo your kitchen to accommodate a specific handicap, you must play a very active role in the design of the kitchen.

You know your capabilities and limitations best, and your kitchen designer must have as much specific information as possible to create a plan that will work for you. It is also wise to ask your physical therapist to provide information for the designer. Physical therapists are in the front lines for the handicapped and often can suggest simple, creative, and practical solutions for specific problems.

(See appendix B for product resources and for

additional information on design geared to the elderly and the handicapped.)

DESIGNING WITH CHILDREN IN MIND

If you have very young children, the kitchen must be planned with their comfort, safety, and protection in mind. At the same time, it should be planned to withstand the inevitable abuse that children can inflict on it.

Since the kitchen serves as the family gathering place, it's likely that your kids will play there and want to help you cook and bake. Your aim is to allow them to play, grow, and explore while still supervising their activities. You all want to be together but still have enough room so everyone can carry on individual pursuits.

For this reason, an open kitchen that flows into a family room or a media room is a great boon for parents of young children. A typical plan might include a TV housed in base cabinets on the outer side of a kitchen island or peninsula. A small movable table in the kitchen makes a comfortable dining and playing spot for children who are too small to use the family table or snack counter.

Unfortunately, the kitchen can pose serious safety hazards for young children. Burns are a particular danger for kids convinced they are old enough to handle heavy, filled pots themselves. Packaged foods and snacks heated in the microwave can scald a child, as can hot water from a tap if the water heater is set too high.

Children should never work in the kitchen unsupervised, of course, and you can lessen the danger of burns by cooking with pot handles turned away from the edge of the stove, so pots won't tip over as children career by them.

If the children are old enough to begin exploring the insides of your cabinets but still too young to understand hidden dangers, you can use safety catches to thwart their efforts. (Latches are also available for refrigerator doors.) Another alternative, however, is to plan for storage of household cleaning items, liquor, breakable dishes, glasses, and tableware at a level beyond their reach.

You can provide for toy and pot storage at a toddler's level, including a place for water toys under the sink. You can also cover unused electrical outlets with plastic plugs. Below-countertop shelving or a special cabinet fitted out for "kids-only" storage, utensils, and cookware is a helpful touch.

For the comfort and safety of your children, consider

- installing a pull-out stepstool under the sink or cooktop to make it easier for children to reach these areas
- using rounded edges on countertops to cut down on bumps and bruises
- selecting a cooktop with controls on top, not on the side
- using an induction cooktop, which lessens the danger of burns because the cooking equipment (pots and pans) heats up, not the cooking surface (by contrast, a solid disk cooktop poses more of a hazard because it takes the disks a while to cool down after the heat has been shut off)
- setting countertops at different heights to accommodate the needs of all family members
- choosing cabinetry with knobs large enough that a small child will not be able to swallow them

All these measures will help protect kids in the kitchen, but what about protecting the kitchen from the hazard of kids? Most materials on the market today are designed with durability and ease of maintenance in mind, so your kitchen will survive your children's infancy, toddler years, and beyond. Some products and materials are less child-friendly than others, however. Highly glossed cabinetry, for example, is a likely candidate for nicks and scratches, while the pristine look of white or bleached flooring can be quickly altered by scuff marks.

Spills of all types and sticky fingerprints are inevitable when you have children. That means that all surfaces, including cabinets, countertops, and walls, should be easy to wipe down. And wallpaper should be washable.

AESTHETIC CONSIDERATIONS

All the tools in the designer's arsenal—color, texture, line, shape, and material—should be used to create a kitchen that is unified, functional, and interesting without being monotonous. Moreover, it should be harmonious with the adjacent areas of your home and in accord with the style you prefer.

It is entirely possible to take one kitchen layout and create such a variety of looks that the resulting kitchens would bear little resemblance to one another—without changing the layout at all. A kitchen can look like a laboratory: white, sleek, and ultracontemporary, with high-gloss materials, fixtures, and appliances and nary an accessory to be found on the countertop. Or it can have a cluttered, country look, with wood cabinets, wood floors, open shelving that displays baskets and other collectibles, and plants galore. Or it can express a variety of styles in between these two extremes, projecting a sense of warmth, sophistication, wit, serenity, or drama.

Appliances play a major role in the kitchen's appearance. Some people prefer built-in appliances because they seem to "disappear" in the room, thus contributing to a sleeker look. Others choose appliances that serve as focal points in the room: an old-fashioned stove, for example, or a commercial-grade refrigerator or wine cooler.

The better kitchen designs draw your eye to a major focal point, which might be a center island with dramatic soffit overhead or a particular work area such as a cooktop with a handsome handpainted tile mural above it. Your eye can also be drawn by the use of vertical or horizontal lines. Plans that sprinkle vertical elements, such as the refrigerator and wall ovens, virtually at random create a jarring lack of harmony.

The texture of the materials selected—such as a cool and smooth granite, very high-gloss cabinetry, nubby and "tactile" wallcoverings and window treatments—also has a major impact on the overall impression the kitchen creates.

Details Make a Difference

Good kitchen design pays very close attention to detailing: to edge treatments for countertops, to molding treatments that tie in a run of wall cabinets, to tiling details that achieve a unified effect by repeating patterns in the floor and the backsplash. Such details need not be expensive to build in, but they make a big difference. An exposed plumbing line can

be disguised by an oak mantel. An existing niche in a brick wall can be converted into a microwave center. Glass mullion cabinet doors can add charm to the area.

Arched openings and decorative wood moldings that are found throughout the house can be brought into the kitchen. A niche with concealed lighting and glass shelves can be made to look more like a display case than a storage cabinet.

The Uses of Color

Color has a tremendous impact on the look of a kitchen. We respond emotionally to colors: from the cooler, more soothing blues and greens to the warmer, more exciting and vibrant yellows, reds, and oranges. Black and white, used alone or in combination, also can be highly dramatic.

Bright accent colors, such as the rich jewel tones, can be used to draw the eye to a design detail that might otherwise be missed in the room. They can also be employed judiciously to add visual interest in a room predominated by neutral colors.

Color can also play tricks on our eyes, to good effect. For example, if you want a smaller kitchen to appear larger, you can use light, matte, and cool colors; avoid color contrasts; and use a color path to direct the eye to a larger space.

If you want to make a larger space seem more intimate, you can use dark, bright, and warm colors and color contrasts. A darker ceiling will make a room seem smaller. Conversely, a lighter ceiling will make it seem larger.

Color should reflect the overall mood that you want to achieve in the kitchen. Remember that colors will be affected by the amount of light that streams into the room from the window(s), skylight, patio, or transom as well as from the lighting fixtures.

Remember, too, that color has historical connotations: These include the grayed Colonial blues and greens, English white or sun yellow, French country, and the Scandinavian washed colors.

Many people are fearful of making choices about colors. Either they are unsure of their own taste, or they're stymied by the variety of choices available. They may also fear that this year's "fashionable" colors will be hopelessly out of fashion within a year's time. To make your decision easier, some manufacturers offer their own guidelines on which colors and patterns match well with others. You can even "paint" the room any number of ways by computer in a home supply or paint store: You select a setting that resembles yours and then change the color of furniture, accessories, walls, ceilings, trim, and doors until you're satisfied.

To take some of the guesswork out of selecting colors, seven manufacturers cooperate in a color coordination program comprised of a number of different color groupings for both the kitchen and the bathroom. Each color grouping consists of a half-dozen colors. Known as Kohler Color Coordinates, the program offers products designed to match Kohler bath and kitchen fixtures. Participants include Amana (major appliances), Armstrong World Industries (vinyl flooring), Broan/Nautilus (range hoods, trash compactors, and bath cabinets), Dal-Tile (ceramic tile), Kohler (plumbing fixtures), Nevamar (surfacing materials), and Village Wallcovering (wallpaper).

It's certainly true that color preferences come in and out of fashion. If you want to know what the "hot" colors will be in the next couple of years, here's a hint from designers: Follow clothing fashion trends, because they tend to filter down to the home furnishings market two or three years later. Some trade and consumer magazines also publish forecasts about color trends from various groups of manufacturers and designers, and they have been fairly accurate in the past if only because of the self-fulfilling prophecy element inherent in the predictions.

Color-watchers point out that general preferences tend to swing back and forth over 10-year intervals, resulting in the current preferences for light and airy colors and materials: whitewashed woods and light or neutral colors.

You should certainly not be a slave to fashion, particularly in your kitchen. At the same time, it's wise to be aware of the trends if you're concerned, for example, about the resale value of your home. When in doubt, select neutrals for major design elements and use brightly colored accents and accessories for visual excitement.

3

Working with Professionals

The horror stories all of us hear about kitchen remodeling projects usually have to do with inept or dishonest contractors: individuals who disappear from sight after receiving a sizable down payment, or who go off in the midst of a job and are never heard from again. Stories of endless delays abound, too: jobs taking twice or three times longer than anticipated, or jobs coming to a halt because the carpenter, electrician, and plumber couldn't coordinate their schedules. Some clients also become victims of huge cost overruns, with contractors charging 50 percent more than the budget estimate, ostensibly because of "extras."

Moreover, con artists prey on older and more gullible homeowners with such scams as offers of extremely low prices proferred in exchange for the use of their homes in a supplier's brochure. Down payments received, they, too, perform a vanishing act.

It's true that the field has numerous practitioners who are less than scrupulous, skilled, and sensible business managers. On the other hand, a great many of its members are knowledgeable, creative, responsive, and dependable. Your task is to separate out the professionals. The designer and/or contractor is not—or at least doesn't start out to be—your enemy. On the contrary, these practitioners are the linchpins of your project—and their expertise can save you money, time, and headaches.

CREDENTIALS

Professionals often list a set of initials after their names. These denote certifications from one or more industry organizations that accredit members fulfilling certain requirements. Each organization also has a code of ethics, to which members are expected to adhere. Bear in mind that not all outstanding designers or contractors have these certifications; you should not automatically reject those who don't. For those professionals who do use the certifications, however, here is a brief synopsis of what each signifies:

A CGR is a Certified Graduate Remodelor. The designation is earned by qualifying in a certification/ education program sponsored by the Remodelors Council of the National Association of Home Builders. It requires a minimum of five years of general management experience in the residential and/or commercial remodeling business, and also requires its graduates to have completed a certain number of courses in general remodeling business management and specific remodeling design and construction. Certification is valid for three years. After that, the contractor must take additional educational courses to continue certification.

Remodelers may also qualify for a CR (Certified Remodeler) designation from the National Association of the Remodeling Industry (NARI). This requires passing a two-part examination; the first part consists of filling out a detailed résumé; the second part entails passing a full-day written examination that covers both business management and technical areas. The exam is prepared, graded, and evaluated by the University of Illinois, and the results are submitted to a five-member NARI certification board. To maintain the CR designation, the remodeler must be recertified every year. Once a year, he or she must submit an affidavit asserting that the primary business conditions that existed at the time of certification still exist or else provide an explanation of the changes. Continuing education is also part of the process; the remodeler must attend seminars, classes, or other educational forums every two years.

A CKD certification means Certified Kitchen Designer, the designation given by the Society of Certified Kitchen Designers, the licensing and accreditation agency of the National Kitchen and Bath Association. Certification is based on documented proof of experience, knowledge, and ability in planning and installing residential kitchens. Consumer references, samples of design work, and specifications are reviewed, and a comprehensive examination is administered. The CKD may be an independent practitioner—unaffiliated with a particular manufacturer, dealer, distributor, or remodeling company—or may be an employee of such businesses.

AIA denotes membership in the American Institute of Architects. To become a registered architect (not necessarily an AIA member), the professional will have completed one of the following:

- a four-year B.A. program followed by a three- to four-year master's program in architecture or

- a five-year undergraduate program leading to a bachelor of architecture or
- a combination six-year undergraduate/graduate program leading to a master's in architecture

To become a registered architect, a practitioner must attend a school accredited by the National Architecture Accrediting Board. The professional must also serve three years of internship with an architectural firm before he or she can take a four-day examination to become a registered architect. Every state has its own examination. No continuing education is required.

A registered architect need not be a member of the AIA. An associate AIA member is a professional who has not yet passed a state licensing examination.

ASID is a certification granted by the American Society of Interior Designers. A Professional Member will have passed an examination given by the National Council for Interior Design Qualification (NCIDQ) or will have received a state-issued license in interior design. Professional Members are required to achieve one of the following: (1) complete a five-year or four-year degree program with a major in interior design, as well as two years of full-time work experience in interior design; (2) complete a master's degree program in interior design as well as two years' work experience; (3) obtain architectural registration as well as two years' work experience; (4) complete three years of education in a professional program for interior design and three years' work experience; or (5) supplement a high school education with six years' work experience in interior design.

The designation Allied Member (Practitioner) of the ASID refers to interior designers who are in the process of fulfilling requirements for Professional Membership. Practitioners can advance to Professional Membership after they have passed the NCIDQ examination.

Some states provide for state certification of interior design professionals. New York, for example, requires the completion of a minimum of seven years of education and professional training and passing two examinations within a two-year period. One exam covers design issues; the other covers fire, safety, and building-code issues.

Most states do not require designers to seek such certification, so it is still possible for someone to designate himself/herself an interior designer without certification. Find out what your state's requirements are.

No matter what the designation, the professional should be able to show you that he or she has successfully performed work similar to the project you are contemplating. A remodeling contractor, for example, may be a whiz at construction but far less skillful in design. A designer, on the other hand, may not possess the technical expertise to be able to properly evaluate construction realities.

FINDING QUALIFIED PROFESSIONALS

Despite the importance of qualified and compatible professionals, most people do not spend as much time and attention as they should in selecting them. Checking references in more than a superficial way is certainly a time-consuming process, but the ultimate result will justify the time you spend researching the professionals who will guide the project.

To start your search, ask your friends and neighbors for recommendations and follow up on leads from articles in newspapers and magazines. Professional organizations—national, state, and local offices—can provide lists of members in your area (see appendix A). These groups include the American Institute of Architects, the Remodelors Council of the National Association of Home Builders, the National Association of the Remodeling Industry, the National Kitchen and Bath Association, the American Society of Interior Designers, the local home builders' associations, and local kitchen dealers.

If possible, use local professionals—they understand your community zoning and building codes and policies. They are also rooted in the community and stake their reputations on the work they perform for you. Moreover, they can arrange to meet with you more easily to discuss problems that might arise and can make regular visits to the job site.

Checking out a Professional

Ask for three to six references, including at least two or three from recent projects, preferably in your area. These should be residential kitchen remodeling projects; a professional's skill in small commercial projects, or in finishing basements or roof replacements, does not mean that he or she will be equally competent in the kitchen. Check these references *thoroughly* as follows.

If previous clients are pleased with the work performed for them, they usually enjoy talking about it and especially in small communities may not object to your visiting their home to take a look at it.

Start with those projects that seem most similar to your own. Seeing a project for yourself is an excellent guide. It also triggers on-the-spot questions to ask the previous client, such as

- What is the quality of the contractor's finish work? In installing cabinetry, backsplash, and appliances, did the contractor have to compensate for walls that were not level or straight? How well did he/she do it?
- How skilled were the plasterer, tile installer, and other subcontractors used?
- How long did the job take? Were there extensive delays? Scheduling problems?
- Was the contractor available to deal with the client's questions and concerns promptly? Did the contractor communicate with the client often?
- Were there any major obstacles in design or construction, and how were they overcome?
- Did the contractor clean up reasonably well each day?
- Did the final stages of the job get bogged down in delays or scheduling conflicts? Were late-stage "punch-list" items (incomplete or correctable items) handled quickly?
- How did the contractor handle inspections?
- Were any warranties provided on the contractor's work?

Ask the practitioner to see plans from "works in progress." Not all architects, designers, and contractors are equally adept at drawing plans. Some plans are easily readable and logically presented, while others are sloppier and much more difficult to follow. It's important to get an accurate sense of the professional's style, because plans are such an important method of communication between all parties involved with the project.

Find out how many projects the contractor has in

progress or is otherwise committed to. Some contractors take on more jobs than they can comfortably and competently manage, and the client suffers the consequences.

Ask for bank references. You want to be assured that the professional is stable financially. This will avoid the necessity for him or her to take on new projects to finance the completion of yours—a not-unusual tactic for contractors who run out of money because of poor planning or indebtedness elsewhere.

The professional should provide you with a business address and telephone number, proof of licensing and/or being bonded (if called for in your area), and certification of insurance covering workers' compensation, property damage, and personal liability. Verify the information.

Check with the Better Business Bureau and regional or state Consumer Affairs offices to see if there is a record of complaints and, if so, what types of complaints, against the company.

Ask for professional affiliations. Being an active member of a local Chamber of Commerce or another organization, such as the Remodelors Council of the National Association of Home Builders, the National Association of the Remodeling Industry, the National Kitchen and Bath Association, does not necessarily guarantee competence. But these organizations provide ongoing educational programs for members, and you want to work with someone who stays current on technology and design trends. Moreover, such an affiliation is a sign that the practitioner is a committed professional.

Following the initial search, you'll want to narrow your choices down to a few possibilities. The scope of the project will suggest how to proceed. If you're making structural changes and/or building an addition, you will probably need an architect's seal on the plans in order to get a building permit.

You'll have to decide whether you want

- a contractor to be responsible for building an addition or making structural alterations but not for installing kitchen cabinetry, flooring, countertops, appliances, and fixtures
- an architect, kitchen designer, or interior designer solely to draw plans
- an architect, kitchen designer, or interior designer to draw plans *and* act as contractor or construction supervisor

- a contractor to be responsible for the entire job
- to act as your own contractor by selecting subcontractors yourself, supervising them, and coordinating their scheduling
- to do some of the work yourself

Warranties

As you narrow the field of contractors, find out whether those you are interviewing are enrolled in the HOW Remodeler Program. HOW (short for Home Owners Warranty Corporation) provides five-year protection for the client against structural defects, as well as against defects in workmanship and materials. Here's how it works:

If a contractor is enrolled in the program, he or she *must* enroll every job valued at $10,000 or more. In the first year of coverage, the HOW remodeler warrants that his or her work will be free from defects in workmanship and materials according to HOW's approved standards for construction and performance.

The HOW program also covers major structural defects, as well as defects in the plumbing, heating, air-conditioning, and electrical systems that are replaced or altered.

In the second year the remodeler continues to warrant against major structural defects and defects in the wiring, piping, and ductwork of the mechanical and electrical systems.

If the remodeler fails to make repairs in compliance with the approved standards in the first two years, HOW will make those repairs over an initial $250 cost.

Coverage insures against major structural defects for the next three years.

If you sell your home during this period, the coverage is transferred to the new owner.

The HOW Remodeler Program includes these additional features:

- HOW screens its applicants. All HOW remodelers must have three years of proven remodeling experience or have been in the HOW program for new home builders for two years and have remodeling experience.
- Extra services—such as customer service training and educational materials, technical

assistance, and promotional support—are provided to remodelers in the program.

· HOW offers an expedited dispute settlement process to arbitrate serious disagreements between homeowners and remodelers during the life of the warranty. Arbitrators are experienced in the building field and are trained and licensed in arbitration.

Basic premiums to enroll in the program are based on the total value of the job. You pay for this coverage. (The current range is $175 for a $10,000 project to $369 for a $100,000 job.)

According to the latest figures available from HOW, 1,000 remodeling contractors are enrolled in the program nationwide, and they are dispersed almost evenly among urban, suburban, and rural areas. Your local home builders' association can provide a list of those who are enrolled.

Even if your contractor is not enrolled in the program, he or she may offer you a similar warranty on the work. Your state, in fact, may require contractors to warrant their work for 12 months after the job has been completed. These warranties should be included in your contract.

Manufacturers provide warranties on all appliances, and the contractor should turn these over to you if you are not purchasing them directly yourself.

WHAT THE PROFESSIONALS EXPECT FROM YOU

Most designers or contractors expect certain qualities in a prospective client. He or she wants to know that you have a real commitment to the project and that you will discuss budget considerations realistically.

Before you have your initial meeting, organize your own needs and ideas on paper so that you can clearly communicate your "must haves" as well as your "wish list" and style preferences. You should also be able to point out what you like and dislike about your present kitchen. Share all of your ideas with the professional even if you think some might be impractical or too expensive to achieve. They may not be out of the question after all.

It's especially helpful to be able to convey your ideas visually as well as verbally, showing pictures of rooms that you like, even if you think they're beyond your price range. This kind of information gives the professional a sense of your style preferences. Often, he or she can adapt similar, less costly design solutions for you.

You should discuss how much, if any, of the work you intend to do yourself, and when you're available to do it, because this will affect the contractor's construction crew.

The professional will want to review your home's plumbing, electrical, and ventilation systems to judge how best to plan the new kitchen.

Finally, if more than one person in your household will be involved in decision making, you should avoid giving the professional "mixed signals." The contractor and the crew won't be able to work efficiently if you say one thing and your spouse says another regarding the same matter. Work out your own differences first; then provide consistent guidance.

FEE STRUCTURES

When you ask professionals to bid on your kitchen, make sure they are providing estimates on the same information. Otherwise, comparisons will be meaningless.

Typically, a contractor will provide you with a total cost estimate that includes labor, materials, and his or her profit, which can be 15 to 20 percent of the total. Architects and designers will charge a similar percentage of the construction costs when their services include supervision of the total job.

If an estimate comes in at a figure that seems totally out of line—either too high or too low—ask the contractor to clarify the reasons for you. *Don't select a contractor on the basis of a low bid alone.* Quality of workmanship, reliability, creativity, and management skills are key elements, too. An intangible quality such as personal rapport can make the difference between a pleasant process and a disaster, so don't ignore it. And the impractically low bid is a lure that you should resist. In economically tight times, even otherwise responsible contractors have been known to resort to "lowballing" the competition and then charging even higher fees than their competitors by designating necessities as "extras." Beware.

Less popular than the fixed-cost approach are the "cost-plus" and the "design-build" methods of contracting. In the cost-plus project, the client pays for the materials, plus a percentage for overhead and profit, with or without a guaranteed maximum cost. This may make sense for the client who has extensive construction expertise, who has worked with the contractor previously and trusts his or her abilities, and who wants maximum flexibility regarding possible changes in the project.

In the design-build project, design and construction functions are combined, which can save time and eliminate problems that might arise concerning whether defects are design defects or related to construction. This method is more common in larger commercial developments and should be used only if the homeowner has substantial construction knowledge. Normally, if you have a designer and a contractor involved in your project, they provide a natural counterbalance to each other.

If you have decided to work with a kitchen design specialist, the fee can be structured in a number of ways:

- You pay a flat design fee (which could be several hundred dollars or more), for which the designer prepares plans that become your property. This makes sense if you plan on using a remodeling contractor (rather than the kitchen designer) to supervise the project.
- You pay the designer a consultation fee, based on an hourly rate, for initial review and guidance, and any plans remain the property of the designer.
- You pay the designer a retainer, which entitles you to ownership of the plans; if a contract for the project is signed with the designer, the retainer is applied to the cost of the project. In some cases, only a portion may be applied; the remainder is considered a design fee.

The level of detail of the plans will determine the designer's fee. If the designer is to create working drawings, on which remodeling contractors can bid, the cost can run into thousands of dollars. Generally, a contractor doesn't prepare plans, but a designer may prepare a very basic floor plan and listing of specifications and materials, and the contractor can write a proposal based on them.

There is no set standard for fee payment. Some designers and/or contractors may require you to pay it—or a major portion of it—before plans are drawn; others offer a rudimentary space study and budget review at no charge, requiring payment when full working drawings are prepared.

IF YOU'RE CONSIDERING DOING SOME OF THE WORK YOURSELF

As you are contemplating timing and budget considerations, assess realistically your willingness, expertise, and availability to tackle major elements of the project. For example:

- Are you available only at night and on weekends, or can you devote larger blocks of time to specific tasks? If you're not available, how will this affect the construction schedule?
- Does the contractor seem willing to include you in the construction crew? Can you agree on an efficient working relationship?
- If building permits and inspections are required, are you prepared to invest the time and effort needed to bring your work up to standard if it should fail to pass inspections?
- Can you rely on others to help you unload equipment and help with installations? Remember that major jobs, such as cabinet installation, must often be handled by more than one person.
- Do you have sufficient construction knowledge to judge whether walls and subfloors are level enough and in good enough condition so that cabinetry and flooring materials can be installed correctly?
- If you make mistakes in your portion of the work, how will this affect the remainder of the job? For example, if cabinets are not plumb and level, flooring installation will be a far more difficult task.
- Are you sufficiently experienced with the construction equipment needed for such tasks as countertop fabrication and cutouts or tile installation?
- Even if you're familiar enough and experienced with basic electrical and plumbing tasks,

are you prepared to make judgments when construction begins as to whether more extensive rewiring or replacement of fittings may be necessary? Your local code may specify that such work must be done by licensed electricians or plumbers.

Since you'll also be working with very costly materials, the financial consequences of making mistakes, or damaging the materials, are serious. Moreover, some manufacturers' warranties may not cover installation by a nonprofessional, so you should check on this before you decide what to do.

Kitchen remodeling is an intense process involving several different kinds of special technical skills. Unless you truly have the time and expertise to do much of the work yourself, you will save time and aggravation by having it done by others.

Even if you choose to do none of the work yourself, however, it's important to understand how the construction process works, how it should proceed, and what constitutes proper techniques that are also cost efficient.

THE CONTRACT

The contract is the legal communication of the agreement between you and your contractor. It is designed to spell out the responsibilities and expectations of both parties and should be as detailed as possible concerning the project's timing, payment schedule, workmanship, materials, and warranties.

Many of the typical problems and horror stories you hear involving remodeling projects arise because so many important details are left vague and unresolved when the job begins, or because verbal assurances are interpreted differently by the client and the contractor.

Most professionals will have their own contract forms to present to you. Some follow guidelines from trade organizations, such as the American Institute of Architects and the National Kitchen and Bath Association. Review such contracts with extreme care, because contracts tend to represent the interests of the parties who prepare them. You can also have a lawyer/friend review them. Make sure you can add provisions to cover the specifications and even-

tualities that are *not* referred to in the prepared or "boilerplate" contract.

For example, because kitchen remodeling represents a significant investment, you'll want to protect yourself from liens brought against your home in the event that your contractor does not pay his subcontractors or suppliers and they sue you to recover payment. Ask your attorney about adding a "release of lien" clause requiring the contractor and the subcontractors and suppliers to provide you with a certificate of a waiver of lien. You might also want to specify that payments be placed in an escrow account, to be released according to the payment schedule when the subcontractors and suppliers verify to you that they have been paid.

Other important contract elements include

- the contractor's name, address, phone number, and license number
- a general description of the project that has sufficient details to fairly describe its scope
- the intended commencement and completion dates, including the phrase "time is of the essence"
- a description of work to be done and the materials to be used, specifying that the project should be performed "in a workmanlike manner," meaning that it is to be executed according to accepted local standards. This section of the contract is particularly important, because it should specify the product names and model numbers of all kitchen equipment and materials. It should not simply mention "sink," for example, but should itemize an exact sink— the model number, the size, and the material. Some contracts build in flexibility by specifying a product "or the equivalent," in case that product is not available. A better alternative is to select and specify a second choice before signing the contract.
- a cancellation clause, giving you the right to cancel the contract within three days of your having signed it (should cancellation be necessary, send a written notice to the contractor, registered and return receipt requested, so you can prove the cancellation was made within the required time)
- all warranties and guarantees, specifying which

party will honor them (i.e., contractor, distributor, or manufacturer) and whether they are "full" or "limited"

- a cost and payment schedule. Most contracts call for a substantial down payment of 30 to 40 percent at the start, with progress payments continuing throughout the project and final payment to be made on completion (see the following section, "The Meaning of Completion"). You should withhold at least 10 percent of the cost as final payment and be as specific as possible regarding payments to be made on completion of various tasks
- an understanding that the contract is contingent on your arranging outside financing, if you have decided to finance the remodeling
- additional responsibilities of the contractor, such as trash removal, blocking off work areas, and daily cleanup (make sure your definition of "clean"—for example, "broom-clean"—is the same as your contractor's and construction crew's)
- any penalties required for delayed repairs of defects or completion of the project
- any interest that may be charged you for late payment
- a mediation/arbitration clause in which you both agree to seek such a resolution should it become necessary
- the responsibilities the client has agreed to take on, which might include demolition, painting, wallpapering, or purchasing appliances
- agreement that change orders will be put in writing, with a separate estimate of the additional cost provided by the contractor
- a definition of what will constitute "extras" and how their cost is to be calculated
- the contractor's responsibility to apply for and obtain any necessary building permits, to arrange for and be on hand for inspections, and to work in accordance with zoning, building-code, and/or deed restrictions

The Meaning of Completion

Remodeling contracts can be vague about the important issue of completion, which can lead to serious problems. Final payment is usually pegged to the project's completion; indeed, lenders usually require a signed completion certificate from you before they will release their last payment. It is therefore vital that you and your designer or contractor come to a meeting of the minds about precisely what constitutes completion and then include this definition in your contract.

Does *completion* mean that 90 percent of the work has been done but small, decorative finishing work has not? Or does it mean that all the work has been done and that every item in the punch list has been cleared?

It is not enough to use terms like *reasonable completion* or *substantial completion*, since they leave considerable room for different interpretations by different parties. One way of arriving at an equitable solution to this question is to stipulate that the last payment is due on final *inspection*, not completion, of the job. If problems with the job still exist, you and the contractor can decide what amount should be held back and then prepare a second, mini-contract, which outlines the specific problems and amount to be paid when they are corrected.

To protect him- or herself, your contractor may want to include an interest clause in the agreement stating that 15 percent (or another figure) per year interest will be charged for late payments. The primary reason for this clause is that just as there are unscrupulous contractors, so too are there unscrupulous clients who continue to withhold payment and to devise additional rounds of complaints about the job to justify their delay.

RESOLVING DISPUTES

If you have selected an architect, kitchen designer, or contractor wisely, you should be able to iron out any difficulties that may arise with them in a timely way. Nevertheless, problems do occur. According to the Council of Better Business Bureaus, home improvements rank among the highest categories in consumer complaints. Most of those complaints arise when the contractor "disappears" after final payment is made, with at least 5 percent of the job still to be done.

Delays are another big problem in home improvement projects. Some delays in construction are unavoidable. A cabinet manufacturer, for example, may have promised delivery by a certain date, but production requirements can change and your shipment may be delayed.

Most delays have to do with scheduling subcontractors' work, and some contractors are more adept than others at juggling the many different kinds of work that must be accomplished. An electrician, for example, may move on to a different job instead of waiting idly for a carpenter to finish his rough-in tasks. Subcontractors often become inaccessible by phone during such periods.

Some minor delays are to be expected, but when minor turns into major, seeking help is appropriate.

In addition to incomplete jobs and excessive delays, the American Arbitration Association finds that most home improvement cases involving $50,000 or less relate to issues of workmanship and construction quality. In a common scenario, you withhold payment from the contractor because you believe that certain workmanship has been shoddy, and you want the contractor to redo the job. The contractor refuses and demands payment. You're faced with the choice of living with a ripped-up kitchen or paying the contractor under circumstances you regard as blackmail.

Mediation or arbitration allows you to seek relief without a courthouse confrontation. Both involve the use of a trained, neutral third party's expertise (for a fee) in reaching an equitable solution.

For two keys reasons, these methods are preferable to suing the contractor. First, the cost of litigation could very well exceed the cost of the kitchen remodeling. Second, litigation is a highly time-consuming and tension-producing process, which means your life will remain in disarray for some time to come.

Mediation is usually a less formal and quicker process than arbitration, which may involve one or more formal hearings and a visit to the site. A drawback of mediation is that although the mediator can help you negotiate an agreeable settlement, he or she cannot make any decisions for you or enforce the terms of that settlement. An arbitrator decides the issues and makes a binding award based on those decisions. You cannot be awarded more than what you ask for.

Mediation and arbitration are available through several organizations and associations. You can even find a mediator listed under "Mediation Services" in the Yellow Pages. You can also contact the office of your state's attorney general or Better Business Bureau for suggestions.

It is important to note, however, that *because submitting to mediation and/or arbitration is voluntary, you and your contractor must agree to it, in writing, before problems arise.*

Here are some programs that are available:

The "Care Program" of the Better Business Bureau. Most of the bureaus around the country offer this service to their members at no cost. If your contractor is a member of the BBB, he or she can sign an agreement with clients that provides for arbitration to resolve disputes. Cases referred to the BBB are resolved within a 30-day period, including a hearing and rendering of a decision. Decisions are binding on both parties. The big drawback of this program is that your contractor must be a BBB member; otherwise, the case won't qualify for the program.

The American Arbitration Association (AAA) administers mediation and arbitration services in cases where both parties have agreed in advance that they will use these routes if difficulties arise. (The contractor can also file a complaint against you if he or she believes you have improperly withheld payment.)

The AAA has a special set of procedures for construction cases, developed by its National Construction Industry Arbitration Committee. It starts with mediation. If the mediation efforts fail, the next step is to submit the dispute to final and binding arbitration.

If the value of the job is under $25,000, the procedures are streamlined. The average small case can take from three to five months from the date of filing to resolution. For a job valued at $10,000 or less, the minimum fee is $300.

The *American Institute of Architects'* short-form model contract for architects and their clients includes mediation and arbitration clauses.

If your job is covered under the *Home Owners Warranty Corporation*'s remodeler program, you are automatically entitled to dispute resolution by a neutral third party if the remodeler disagrees with your written request to correct defects.

Again, if you take the time and effort to select your practitioner carefully and attend with care to the contract you sign, you'll greatly minimize the potential for any serious disagreement.

4

Turning the Plan into Reality

REVIEWING THE PLANS

A fully drawn and agreed-upon set of kitchen plans is one of the most critical tools in the remodeling project. The plans become the direct method of communication: between you and the designer and between the designer and the contractor and subcontractors. They will serve as the road map that shows you what your kitchen will look like, how it will function, and precisely how it should be built.

To develop plans that suit your needs, your style preferences, and your budget is no simple task. Don't expect the initial review process to go quickly. Be prepared to ask for revisions if any of the designer's ideas or specifications seem inappropriate for you. Try to picture the look of the total design as well as review all the details involved. Ask as many questions as necessary until you fully understand the concept and how it will be executed.

At the initial presentation, the designer should explain to you why he or she created a particular plan; how it will suit your needs; some of the key design principles used; what alternative solutions were considered and rejected and why. The designer should also be able to give you samples of suggested color schemes and materials, such as cabinet door, flooring, and countertop samples.

Here are some questions to consider as you analyze the plans:

- How does the kitchen relate to the rest of the house? Have entries, windows, or doors been changed or relocated? How easily can groceries be set down and stored?
- What is the focal point of the room?
- What are the distances between work centers?
- How much aisle space is there? Is there room for several people to work and move around comfortably?
- If there is an island, does it impede the path between the cooktop and sink? Between the refrigerator and sink?
- What provisions, if any, have been made to maximize storage space in corner cabinets?
- Is the storage planned to relate to separate work centers?
- What type of storage has been planned for canned and packaged foods?

- If the sink and dishwasher are angled, is there enough room to stand comfortably while loading and unloading the dishwasher?
- Is the refrigerator located close to the snack bar, banquette, or dining table? Can household members reach the refrigerator without getting in the cook's way?
- When appliance and cabinet doors are opened, do they impede anyone's path? Do they abut each other?
- If the ovens and/or microwave are located next to the refrigerator for aesthetic purposes (for example, to keep vertical elements together), is there enough landing space around each of these appliances?
- If countertops are to be higher or lower than standard height, will they be suitable for your individual needs?
- Is there sufficient continuous counter space around work centers?
- Does the plan depend too much on storage placed above the wall cabinets and refrigerator?
- How does the lighting plan relate to the layout? Where are outlets located? Can they be located under cabinets?
- How will heating, air-conditioning, and ventilation work?
- What provisions have been made for garbage handling and recycling?
- Are any special decorative elements included to unify the room plan?
- Has any existing architectural asset or liability been highlighted or minimized accordingly?

Understanding Floor Plans

The set of plans presented to you should constitute a complete visual representation of the designer's ideas for your kitchen. It should include an overall floor plan, an artist's rendering of what the room will look like, electrical and plumbing plans, and perhaps renderings of certain details, such as special countertop treatments and cabinetry design.

Don't expect to be able to absorb all the information presented to you in one sitting. After the designer's presentation, during which you have an oppor-

tunity to ask some preliminary questions, take some time to study the plans alone.

If the floor plan is drawn clearly and professionally, it should numerically list specifications: the location, dimensions, and type of base and wall cabinets, all appliances, sinks, countertops, windows, and, if appropriate, skylights (which are usually indicated by dashed, or "phantom," lines). Plans may also show door swings for dishwashers, refrigerators, and/or entry doors.

Some floor plans depict the various appliances very clearly, whereas others can be confusing. If you can't tell which appliance is the refrigerator and which is the cooktop, don't hesitate to ask the designer to clarify it for you.

All plans are drawn to scale; the most common show ¼ inch equaling one foot, or ½ inch equaling one foot.

To better understand the designer's language, here are some letter designations you'll find in your set of kitchen plans:

W = Wall cabinet
WC = Corner wall cabinet
B = Base cabinet
D or DB = Draw base cabinet
BC = Base corner cabinet
RC = Revolving corner cabinet
SF = Sink front (also for cooktop)
SB = Sink base (also for cooktop)
U = Utility or broom closet
OV = Oven cabinet
SOS = Swing-out shelf cabinet
WBRO = Wastebasket roll-out
FO = File drawer
BB = Bread board
AG = Appliance garage
SO = Spice drawer
SR = Spice rack
ROS = Roll-out shelves
TB = Tray base
CT = Cutting drawer

The numbers you find next to cabinetry symbols indicate the dimensions of the components. Not all plans follow the same format for delineating these dimensions, however, so ask your designer to explain the system your plan uses.

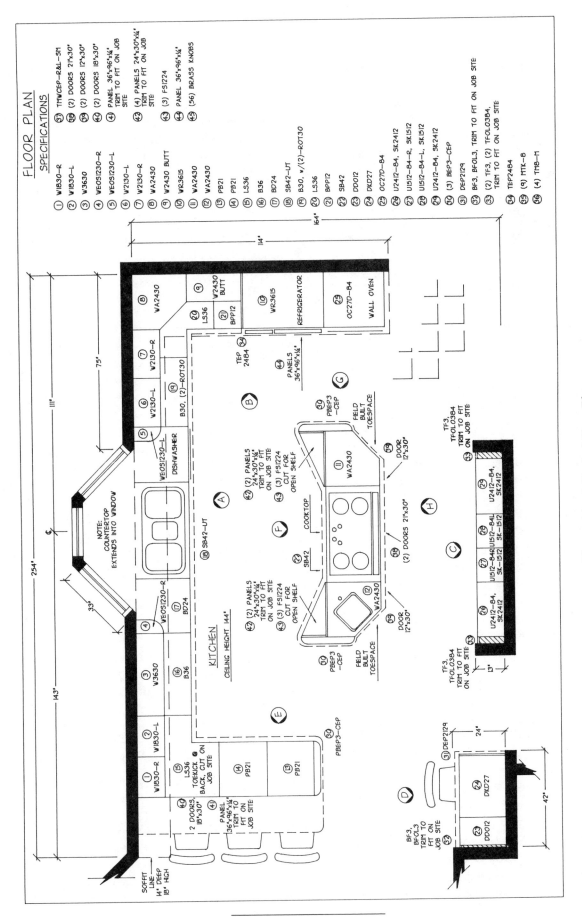

Figure 4.1 A Typical Floor Plan

FLOOR PLAN

SPECIFICATIONS

① W1B30-R
② W1B30-L
③ W3630
④ WEOS1230-R
⑤ WEOS1230-L
⑥ W2130-L
⑦ W2130-R
⑧ WA2430
⑨ W2430 BUTT
⑩ WR3615
⑪ WA2430
⑫ WA2430
⑬ PB21
⑭ PB21
⑮ LS36
⑯ B36
⑰ BD24
⑱ SB42-UT
⑲ B30, w/(2)-ROT130
⑳ LS36
㉑ BPP12
㉒ SB42
㉓ DDO12
㉔ DKD27
㉕ OC27D-84
㉖ U2412-84, SK2412
㉗ U1512-84-R, SK1512
㉘ U1512-84-L, SK1512
㉙ U2412-84, SK2412
㉚ (3) BEP3-CEP
㉛ DEP2129
㉜ BF3, BFOL3, TRIM TO FIT ON JOB SITE
㉝ (2) TF3, (2) TF-OLO3B4, TRIM TO FIT ON JOB SITE
㉞ TEP2484
㉟ (9) MTK-8
㊱ (4) TMB-M
㊲ TMWCEP-R&L-SM
㊳ (2) DOORS 21"x30"
㊴ (2) DOORS 12"x30"
㊵ (2) DOORS 18"x30"
㊶ (4) PANEL 36"x96"x¼" TRIM TO FIT ON JOB SITE
㊷ (4) PANELS 24"x30"x¼" TRIM TO FIT ON JOB SITE
㊸ (3) FS1224
㊹ (3) PANEL 36"x96"x¼"
㊺ (56) BRASS KNOBS

43

PRACTICAL CONSIDERATIONS

Every experienced design and construction practitioner knows that the most exquisitely drawn plan means very little if it cannot be turned into reality. A number of practical elements must be taken into account. The structure of your home or apartment may prevent certain design elements from being added, for example, or the cost of changing from gas to electric, or vice versa, or of relocating windows and doors may be so high that the plan will far exceed your budget.

Before creating the plan, your designer or contractor should have become familiar not only with your home or apartment's general structural conditions but also with relevant local building codes, a condominium or homeowners' association's bylaws, or a co-op board's approval process.

Some basic construction considerations include:

Identifying Load-bearing Walls. Since so many kitchens in older homes are little "complexes" of small, separated spaces, remodeling plans often call for removing walls or partitions to create a single, larger open space. But if the partition is *load bearing*—that is, if it supports the weight of the home's structure—it cannot be removed without compensating in another way for its loss.

Typically, exterior walls running perpendicular to the ceiling and floor joists are load bearing, as is at least one main interior wall. If a wall runs the entire length (or width) of the house, chances are it's load bearing too.

Your designer or contractor should inspect the roof line above the kitchen as well as the attic or crawl space to check ceiling joists. (If ceiling joists are connected over any wall, the wall is load bearing.)

If a load-bearing wall is removed, some type of stronger beam can probably be used to support the span where the load-bearing wall has been. Your local construction code will specify what length and type of material should be used for spans of varying lengths. Wood beams can sometimes be used for short spans, whereas long spans may require a steel "I-beam" or a beam made of structural glue-laminated timber.

Locating Existing Mechanical System Ducts. Many surprises await the designer behind the walls of older homes and apartments. Heating and air-conditioning ducts and cold-air returns are often hidden behind the walls and will need to be rerouted if the wall is removed.

Remember that in an apartment building, you cannot move a load-bearing wall or column or drill into it. If you are contemplating removing walls or moving the kitchen to another part of the apartment, the plan must still maintain the existing load-bearing elements. In most communities, cutting into the exterior will require a building permit. If you live in a co-op, you'll need to get approval from your board; if you live in a building that is designated a historic landmark, you won't be permitted to cut into the exterior wall at all.

Plumbing supply, drain, and vent pipes may also be hidden behind walls. Your designer or contractor should be able to determine their location by inspecting the roof line, basement, or crawl space. The main stack, branch drains, and secondary stacks must be identified. Local codes will determine what size, length, and type of piping can be used to accommodate the remodeled kitchen.

In an apartment building, plumbing lines have to be routed from a branch line. Although piping can be moved across a floor, ideally it should be close to the branch line because the building may have water back-up problems. (See chapter 8 for more details on the plumbing system.) If piping is to run under the finished floor, you'll need to determine whether the subfloor is going to be removed, retained, or replaced. Gas lines are easier to move than plumbing lines.

Determining Your Home's Existing Electrical Load. The electrical system is your home's central nervous system and functions like the human system: It reacts negatively to being stressed or overloaded. Today's kitchens require far more electricity than kitchens of the past. Lighting fixtures, appliances with electronic controls or plug-in modules, and ventilation equipment demand considerable electric power. Even if gas is your energy source, electrical hookups are needed for the electronic timers, clocks, and programming controls that add so much to a modern appliance's usefulness and convenience.

Your present electrical system, then, should be checked to make sure that it will be able to handle the additional load called for in the plan. If your home's existing load is already causing problems—for example, blown fuses or circuit breakers going off, lights flicker or dim when appliances are being used, appliances give shocks, or motors either overheat or heat slowly—then remodeling the kitchen presents an excellent opportunity to upgrade your system.

The "brain" of the electrical system consists of a service head (to which service conductors bring electricity into the home), the watt-hour meter (through which the conductors must pass), the electrical panel board (which distributes electricity throughout the home), the main disconnect (main circuit breaker or main fuses), and the system's grounding connection.

The grounding connection is especially important. Although codes vary from community to community, the National Electrical Code® wisely requires that all circuits have a grounding system. In the event of a short circuit, the grounding wire carries current back to the service entrance panel; the fuse or circuit breaker will open, shutting off the flow of current.

An older home that has 60-amp or even 100-amp service may not be able to support additional appliances and equipment. Service of 150 or 200 amps would be more appropriate.

Check your meter to see if you have sufficient service. The *service rating* (the maximum amount of amps) should be stamped on the main fuses or circuit breaker. If you are not individually metered (in an apartment building, for example), check with your building management company, utility company, or local building department for assistance. Although you may be able to add a circuit or a subpanel, that does not mean that the total electrical load can exceed your home's service rating.

Your meter will also tell you whether you have a two-wire service or three-wire service. If it says 120V, it is a two-wire service; 240V means that it is a three-wire service that provides 120- and 240-volt capabilities.

In a three-wire service, there are three wires connected to the service entrance panel. Two are "hot" wires, and the third is neutral, maintained at zero voltage. One hot wire and the neutral combine to supply 120 volts, while both hot wires and the neutral complete a 120/240-volt circuit.

A "circuit" is the path that current travels from the service entrance panel to appliances and lighting fixtures and back to the panel. If you are extending a circuit, your electrician, adhering to local code requirements, will determine whether to tap into a switch box, outlet box, fixture box, or junction box; what type of wiring to use; and how to route the path.

Typical routes may run behind walls, under floors, or above ceilings.

Your local code will also dictate the types of circuits appropriate for a variety of appliances and fixtures. As a guideline, however, the National Electrical Code specifies that plug-in outlets and switches for small appliances and the refrigerator must be served by at least two 20-amp circuits.

Generally, wall ovens and cooktop can share a 50-amp circuit. Light fixtures cannot be connected to circuits serving appliances. Some appliances, such as an electric range and microwave, require their own circuits. Dishwashers and/or disposers each require a separate 20-amp circuit.

Don't forget that the telephone is an important kitchen "appliance" too. Electricians can wire for telephones, a provision that should be planned at the beginning of the project. The phone should be central to the cook—cordless or with a long cord—and accessible to people in the breakfast area as well.

The Importance of Ground Fault Circuit Interrupters. Three-wire grounded outlets do not always ensure shock protection in the home. Even if all the system's ground connections are good, a ground fault can occur in which a dangerous voltage is present for a time at the grounding connection of a receptacle.

According to the U.S. Consumer Product Safety Commission, a ground fault circuit interrupter (GFCI), installed in selected branch circuits, could prevent more than two-thirds of the electrocutions that take place each year in and around the home. It can also prevent burns and other injuries from electric shocks. Some communities, in fact, require GFCI outlets in the kitchen.

A *ground fault* is an unintentional electric path between a current source and a grounded surface. Electrocution or shock occur when your body provides a path for the electric current to return to the ground.

A GFCI constantly monitors electricity flowing in a circuit to "sense" any loss of current. If the current flowing through the hot wire differs from that returning in the neutral wire by a small predetermined amount, the GFCI quickly switches off power to that circuit. Although you can still receive a shock between the time that a GFCI detects and interrupts a hazardous ground fault current, you won't be electrocuted or seriously injured.

Since water and electricity do not mix, the GFCI is invaluable in the kitchen, where electrical appliances are used near the sink. Three types are available: a wall receptacle, circuit breaker, and portable.

The wall receptacle can be used in place of the standard duplex electrical receptacle found throughout the house. If the GFCI shuts off the power, it must be reset after the problem has been corrected, to restore power.

A dual-purpose circuit breaker GFCI can be installed to give protection at all or selected circuit breakers. It not only will terminate electricity in the event of a ground fault but will also trip on overload currents. Here, too, you reset the GFCI in the panel box to restore power to the circuit.

If a permanent GFCI is not practical, a portable device can be installed. It is plugged into a receptacle, and then the electrical product is plugged into the GFCI.

These devices should be installed by a licensed electrician. You should test them once a month to make sure they are fully operational.

Heating and Air-Conditioning Equipment.

Many older homes and apartments have bulky radiators under windows or against walls. Since you want to use every possible square inch of space in the kitchen, discuss with your designer, contractor, or plumber and electrician the possibility of baseboard or floor heating, where the registers are in the floor.

If you don't have central air-conditioning, consider installing an air-conditioning unit through the wall or above a window. Placing a unit low in a window or wall will not be as efficient, since heat rises. If you're placing the unit high up, you'll need a switch you can easily reach.

Your contractor or electrician should be able to advise you about the size and power of the unit you'll need, depending on the number of people in your household, how often and how many people you entertain in the kitchen, and the heat generated by your appliances.

PREPARING FOR CONSTRUCTION

After you have reached agreement on the plans and arranged for any financing and building permits (if needed), you can prepare for construction.

Kitchen remodeling will disrupt your life pro-

foundly, even under the best of circumstances. For a period of up to several months, you will have to deal with

- workers arriving at your home early in the morning and, from time to time, staying through what ordinarily might have been your dinnertime
- loss of privacy
- noise of construction equipment
- frustration of waiting for workers who may have scheduling conflicts, or who have to leave the job in search of materials or equipment they don't have on hand
- plaster dust that settles beyond the work area, no matter how meticulous the workers are, and its constant presence regardless of your attempts to banish it
- chaotic mealtimes
- the nagging feeling that no one understands—much less, sympathizes with—what you're going through

First and foremost, try to maintain your sense of humor, since that and a flexible attitude will be the biggest help in weathering the adventure you are undertaking. The following preparations can help make the process less disruptive.

Although you will be eating out much of the time or bringing in various kinds of take-out food, try to set up a temporary kitchen, if possible, in the den, on the porch, in the basement, or in another room. It should be able to house the refrigerator and have enough power for your existing microwave or toaster/oven and perhaps an electric fry pan. Your contractor should help you set this up.

Stock up on disposables: plates, napkins, and utensils. Washing dishes will be problematic during the construction period, so you'll want to keep it to a minimum.

If necessary, set up temporary tables in the basement, den, living room, or dining room, to store boxes of dishes, small appliances, dry goods, and so on. Label the boxes so that their contents won't be a mystery when it's time to move the contents into the new cabinetry.

Before construction can begin, you have to clean out your existing kitchen. It is very dismaying to contractors to arrive at a job site and find that it is not ready for construction, and loyalties are often forged or weakened at this crucial starting point.

If you are doing extensive remodeling, cleaning out includes removing foodstuffs, dishes, utensils, glassware, tablecloths and towels, and other items in cabinets, closets, and shelves; storing away accessories and small decorative items; finding space elsewhere for the table, chairs, and other freestanding furniture. When it comes to appliances, countertops, cabinetry, flooring, light fixtures, and wallcoverings, these are normally taken out by the contractor, unless you have agreed otherwise.

You can do much of the dismantling yourself. You may need assistance with the more complicated tasks involving appliances, countertops, cabinetry, flooring, and light fixtures. Demolition can take one day to one week, depending on the scope of the project. Prepare carefully for it so that you won't have to snatch something from under a worker's hammer at the last moment.

If you are planning to use the old appliances in your new kitchen, be sure to

- empty the contents, packing all loose parts in a box; defrost the refrigerator, let it dry completely with the door open, then strap the door shut
- disconnect the electrical power, and if you have a gas range, contact the utility company for any special requirements—there may be a shutoff valve at the end of the gas line
- clean the appliances inside and out
- tape the power cords to the backs of the appliances
- store the appliances in a place that is protected against construction debris and dust; keep them in a dry place to prevent moisture damage

Create a traffic zone for workers to use during construction; the contractor should provide large garbage cans in the kitchen. This will help control debris and slightly reduce the sense of invaded privacy. Establish "ground rules" with your contractor regarding which bathroom the crew should use, which telephone they can use, and under what circumstance they can use it.

If you have young children, establish "ground rules" for their behavior during the construction period. Some workers are extraordinarily patient and friendly with children, a great bonus that many homeowners come to appreciate as the job progresses. But workers cannot be expected to entertain your kids or teach them about construction. Try to keep them away from the kitchen so that the workers can proceed undisturbed. The same holds true for your pets.

Cover all floor surfaces adjacent to the kitchen area with sheets of Masonite boards. Install plastic sheets over doorways, bookshelves, record collections, paintings or murals that cannot be removed, and furniture. Change these sheets often to combat the films of plaster dust that settle everywhere.

At the end of each day, you'll want to check what work has been done. Then, arrange for a walkthrough of the project with your contractor at least once a week, so that you'll understand how the work is proceeding and what lies ahead. This meeting also represents an opportunity to solve small problems before they become big ones and to apprise the contractor of any difficulties you may be encountering with the construction crew. Managing and/or disciplining the crew is the contractor's responsibility, not yours.

Remember that a kitchen remodeling project is highly labor-intensive, so you'll be dealing with many individuals whose personalities and skills can vary widely. Don't expect to relate equally well to all the workers who enter your home. Remember that if you have questions regarding any of the crew's quality of workmanship, attitude, or work habits, discuss them promptly with your contractor.

Expect to have to make many on-the-spot decisions. As we've noted, older homes often present surprises once a wall is broken through.

In establishing the "ground rules" with your contractor before construction begins, stress the importance of alerting you to any minor adjustments that have been made in your absence. If major adjustments—such as unexpected rewiring or refitting of pipes—become necessary, be firm about wanting to be consulted before work proceeds.

Finally, build in enough time for the project so that in case there are unforeseen delays—in obtaining permits, materials, or in scheduling—you won't have the added anxiety of worrying whether the kitchen will be ready in time for Thanksgiving dinner.

Be prepared, too, for the rapid progress of the initial rough stages of construction and what seems like the slower pace for the finishing details. Toward the end of the job, when your patience and emotional resilience are wearing thin and the crew is eager to get started on the next major project, the detailed finishing work can seem to drag on forever.

The best way to avoid this situation, as discussed earlier, is to spell out the definition of "completion," and its payment implications, in your contract.

THE "CRITICAL PATH" IN CONSTRUCTION

Kitchen remodeling follows a logical series of steps over a period that may take from a few weeks to several months. The sequence for an extensive project includes

1. Demolition and removal of the old kitchen
   TIME: 1 day to 1 week

2. Demolition of walls and removal of debris
   TIME: 2 or 3 days to 1 week

3. Removal of existing flooring to be replaced
   TIME: 1 to 3 days

4. Construction of addition:
   Excavation of new foundation
   TIME: 1 week, depending on size; inspection of space must be done before pouring of new foundation; timing is dependent on inspector's schedule

   Pouring of new foundation
   TIME: 1 week; foundation must dry, so timing for drying depends on weather conditions: approximately 2 to 4 weeks

   Demolition of all areas including side wall of existing house and section of roof
   TIME: 1 week

   Framing out of new walls and roof; insulation of roof and walls; installation of windows, roofing, and exterior doors
   TIME: 3 to 4 weeks

5. Roughing-in plumbing and electrical work
   TIME: 2 to 3 days; if rewiring totally, 6 to 7 days for small kitchen, up to 2 weeks for room extensions; rough plumbing and electrical must be inspected

6. Sheetrocking for all new walls; installation of interior doors
   Taping and plastering (If floors are bowed, sagging, or sloped, or if walls are damaged and/or out of plumb, this is the time to correct deficiencies.)
   TIME: 2 to 3 weeks

7. Installation of new flooring
   Wood: 3 to 6 days
   Ceramic: 3 to 4 days
   Vinyl: 1 to 2 days (can be installed after cabinets)

8. Delivery and installation of kitchen cabinets
   Preparation of countertop cutouts; delivery of appliances
   TIME: 3 days to 2 weeks

9. Installation of countertops
   TIME: 2 to 5 days

10. Finishing of plumbing and electric
    Hooking up of appliances
    TIME: 3 to 5 days

    Connecting and hooking up of recessed or ceiling-mounted lighting
    TIME: 2 days

    Installation of tile backsplash
    TIME: 2 to 3 days

    Installation of backsplash outlets
    TIME: 1 day

    Installation of under-cabinet lighting
    TIME: 1 day

    Final plumbing and electrical inspections

11. Trimming of all windows and doors
    TIME: 2 days to 1 week

12. Installation of wallcovering
    TIME: 1 week (If walls are simply to be painted without installing wallpaper,

painting can be done before cabinets are installed. Touch-ups may be necessary, however.)

13. Massive cleanup
    TIME: 1 to 3 days

14. Final walk-through and preparation and review of final-stage punch list with contractor; punch-list items corrected
    TIME: 2 to 3 days, depending on scope of work, logistics, and scheduling

15. Installation of furniture and accessories, including decorative light fixtures
    TIME: 1 to 2 days

Maintaining the Schedule

If you live in an apartment building, access to the building entrance and the elevator for delivery of materials may be limited to a certain number of hours during the day or expressly forbidden on certain days (such as weekends). Since this can affect the construction schedule, your contractor should coordinate deliveries with the building's management.

You'll also need to know whether the building itself might be installing new elevators or undergoing other renovations when your project is scheduled, since that will mean delays for your project.

Very often, deliveries can be brought up only on service elevators, and these can be frustratingly small. If your deliveries don't fit into the elevators specified, the contractor may need to bring material up on top of the elevator cab or carry it up many flights of stairs. Besides damaging controls and finishes of new equipment and delaying the project, this will not endear you to the contractor, which is why it's essential to anticipate such problems in the planning stages of your remodeling job.

Keeping a job on schedule is no easy task. You can achieve this goal, however, by starting with a clear schedule that is *written into your contract*. The contract can also specify that the contractor must discuss with you delays of two days or more. Whether or not you wish to include penalties for construction delays is another matter. A better strategy is to avoid working with a contractor you feel you cannot trust.

How smoothly the job progresses from one step to another depends greatly on the scheduling, construction, and communication skills of your contractor. You can help prevent delays by keeping change orders to a minimum. If a change order is necessary, it should be made only in writing and described in detail so that you and the contractor can sign it for the record.

Occasionally there will be an element of the plan that is properly executed but you decide you don't like. The project will be delayed as the changes you request are made. The contractor probably will want to be paid for the extra work at the time these changes are made, so that there's no chance the payment will be overlooked later on. On the other hand, you may prefer to make this payment at the end of the job. You and your contractor should iron out a procedure for this eventuality *before* it arises and write it into the contract.

You can also prevent delays and misunderstandings by being a respectful client, which includes not asking the crew to do additional work for you simply because they are on site.

The project will proceed more smoothly if all necessary materials are ordered and delivered to the job site on time and, most important, are checked thoroughly on delivery. The contractor should check that all sizes, colors, and styles are exactly as ordered, that the materials are undamaged, and that *each* package is complete and ready for installation. It can happen, unfortunately, that what is marked on a box is not what is found inside or that components essential for construction are missing.

The danger of *not* checking every delivery thoroughly is that errors discovered only when installation is about to begin can bring the project to a halt while replacements are ordered and delivered. Because this process can take weeks, every major component of the kitchen should be on the job site a week before the starting date.

Once the materials are in place, refrain from "rearranging" their storage. Construction equipment and materials are heavy and unwieldy; you should not try to deal with them.

If you are acting as your own general contractor, make sure that there are very clearly defined areas of responsibilities among the subcontractors. This understanding will keep subcontractors from shifting blame if problems occur later on. If you are working with one or two key trades, ask the workers if they can refer you to competent people to perform the subcontracting work. The job is likely to proceed more smoothly if you employ several individuals who have worked together successfully in the past and have a rapport with one another.

GUARDING AGAINST MISTAKES

Although contractors appear to exercise a wide range of choices in construction style and technique, in reality the building business is characterized by a good deal of standardization and governed by a considerable number of regulations.

First and foremost, of course, your plan and its execution must conform to local building and zoning codes. In addition, a plethora of model codes developed by organizations such as the Building Officials and Code Administrators International and the National Fire Protection Association provide guidelines for construction, plumbing, and electrical work.

Furthermore, the American National Standards Institute has developed more than 11,000 product standards, many of which relate directly to the kitchen. These range from microwave ovens, ceramic tiles, dishwashers, water pipes, and windows to specifications for accessibility and usability for handicapped people. You can contact these groups for copies of specific codes and standards, which are usually available for a nominal sum (see appendix A).

Even if you are planning on doing none of the construction work yourself, you should understand some basic procedures so that you'll know when to question the contractor if anything seems awry. Specific guidelines are found in subsequent chapters. Here are some general considerations:

Cabinetry

How the cabinetry is installed is probably most critical to the quality of your kitchen. If cabinets are not hung properly, for example, it will be impossible to install flooring correctly as well. Since cabinet installation is a complex task and the materials represent a significant expense, even the hardiest do-it-yourselfers might be better advised to have it done professionally.

Replacing cabinetry components can be costly in money and time. Even the simplest errors can take a half day to correct.

Some problems may be the manufacturer's or supplier's fault. Doors may be warped, or cabinet colors may not match. Perhaps the delivery is not complete or includes the wrong components. Your contractor should not begin to install new cabinetry until it has been carefully checked to make sure that the pieces delivered match the order.

Cabinets should be installed by first marking off dimensions on walls, then lining up cabinets on the floor and attaching them together. Finally, they are ready to be attached to the walls and must sit or hang plumb and level.

If cabinet drawers won't close properly after installation, it could be because the base cabinet has been pushed out of line by an irregularity in the wall or floor. The same kind of irregularity can make cabinet doors hang crookedly.

A different kind of problem arises when installers don't mark cabinet locations on the walls. Or when, instead of starting installation in an inside corner and working out, they start installing from the sink or from another center. As a result, there may not be sufficient space to install the last cabinet.

Frameless European cabinetry requires even more precision than face-frame cabinetry (see chapter 6 for cabinetry specifics). Be wary if you notice that your installers are using many kinds of adjusting hardware (hinges and leg levelers) as they proceed. Watch out for insufficient corner clearances (for example, a drawer on one side of a corner that can't be opened because it hits the range handle or another drawer). Frameless cabinets have zero clearance, so a corner filler of at least 4 inches is necessary to allow for drawer movement.

Make sure installers remove cabinet doors before they install European hinged cabinets; the doors can be adjusted after the cabinets are installed.

Flooring

Key problems include unevenness, squeaking, or loose subfloors. Floors should have no more than a ¼-inch ridge or depression within any 32-inch measurement, when measured parallel to the joists. Squeaking and loose subfloors may prove to be a temporary condition, but you should voice your concern about it.

If the flooring is wood, there should be no cracks wider than ⅛ inch between floorboards. Nail pops may appear on the surface if the flooring is resilient, and they should be repaired. Discuss in advance with your contractor how he or she will deal with the possibility of nail pops breaking through the surface.

Seams or shrinkage gaps may also show at resilient flooring joints. These gaps should not be wider than ¹⁄₁₆ inch unless the flooring abuts a different material.

Ceramic Tile

Watch for cracks in the tile, tiles that become loose, or cracks appearing in the grouting of tile joints. The contractor should replace cracked tiles and resecure loose ones. Cracks in grouting may be due to normal shrinkage, but you and your contractor should agree in advance what is to be considered "normal."

Additional Items

Before final payment is made, a walk-through with your contractor should resolve questions concerning

- surface cracks, joint delaminations, and chips in laminate countertops
- walls that seem bowed or out-of-plumb
- leaky faucets or pipes
- defective plumbing fixtures, appliances, or trim fittings
- cracked or chipped sink surfaces
- defective electrical outlets, switches, or fixtures
- separating ductwork
- installation of any material that may have been delayed in delivery, damaged and returned, and so forth

5

Bringing in Light and Air

Light and air—fresh air—are fundamental elements of kitchen design. Lighting affects more than the way you'll be able to function in the kitchen. Proper light for kitchen tasks is obviously essential, but light is also a potent design tool that can highlight the pleasing architectural features of the room, enhance the conviviality of the occasions that take place there, and affect your mood.

At the same time, the kitchen also needs to "breathe." Its respiratory system should be able to remove smoke, heat, moisture, grease, and odors from cooking. Windows, operable skylights, a greenhouse, and even an exterior door can provide natural assistance for this important task. Your kitchen's mechanical systems, such as exhaust fans and hoods or the newer downdraft systems, are particularly important, especially in rooms that don't have windows.

COMBINING NATURAL AND ELECTRICAL ILLUMINATION

Ideally, the kitchen should mix natural light, sufficient general illumination, task lighting, and accent lighting so that you can work comfortably, without being in your own shadow. The lighting plan should be flexible enough to accommodate preparations for a buffet dinner for fifty as well as an intimate late-night supper for two.

Most important, perhaps, is that the lighting plan match your needs and habits. In many dual-career households, for example, the kitchen may be unoccupied during the day but is a hub of activity for several hours from dinnertime on. A plan that relies heavily on natural light for this kitchen, then, would be woefully inadequate.

The lighting plan should avoid sharp contrasts between various areas of the kitchen. That is, you should not be bathed in light at the sink while the rest of the cleanup area is in shadows. This kind of contrast is particularly hard on older eyes.

The plan should also be zoned to enable you to create an illuminated path for yourself: turning on lights when you enter the kitchen and turning them off when you leave to go to another room in the house. One switch should govern no more than six bulbs.

Maximizing Available Natural Light: Skylights

Adding a skylight, a bay window, half-rounds, a clerestory window, or other dramatic windows brings welcome light into the kitchen and makes the room seem larger than it is.

Changing existing windows, like moving existing lighting fixtures, isn't simple. It is far easier to plan new windows, a skylight, and/or a greenhouse if you are building an entirely new room addition. Any time you break the "skin" of a house—that is, the walls to the exterior—you must have three key concerns: air infiltration, heat retention, and potential water leakage.

In selecting skylights and windows, look for test reports from manufacturers on air-leakage ratings. The maximum allowable is .07 cubic feet per minute per foot of perimeter.

Skylights provide about five times as much light in kitchens as a comparably sized wall window. There are two basic types of skylights: those that open, with a hinged frame, and those that are fixed. Skylights that open can provide ventilation as well as light, but they cost more than the fixed types. A variety of accessories, such as sun shades, insect screens, and electric controls, boost the price of the skylight but increase its convenience.

A fixed "bubble" skylight is ideal for flat roofs as well as for those that ice up, collect snow, or drain slowly. Because of its domed surface, relatively more of it is exposed to natural light than skylights of other shapes, so it is an apt choice for a northern exposure.

The simplest way to install a skylight is to use the space between existing rafters or trusses, so that you can avoid the extra expense of construction changes in the roof-support system. Skylights come in standard sizes, such as 14½-by-14½-inch squares, or rectangles. Larger windows, such as 52 by 52 inches, are also available.

The glass size of the skylight should be 10 to 15 percent of the kitchen's floor area. Skylights installed adjacent to one another vertically or horizontally provide even more natural light than a single unit.

If the ceiling is not at the roof line, the installation must include a light shaft, an opening cut in the ceiling framed with plywood or plasterboard, and finished—usually painted white to reflect light. Light shafts can be straight, angled, or wider at the ceiling line. If the skylight is installed in a ceiling at the roof line—in a low-slope or flat-roofed house—the opening is simply framed in and finished.

Incandescent or fluorescent lights can be installed in the light shaft, so that the area illuminated by the skylight during the day can be lighted after sundown, too.

If there is air space between the interior and exterior skylight materials, a manufacturer may provide "weep holes" to prevent condensation problems. If the air space is sealed, it will improve insulation and ward off potential condensation.

The type of material you choose for the skylight will be determined by a combination of the climate and your personal preferences. If you live in the South or Southwest, for example, you'll want to minimize heat instrusion during the hottest months. Bronze- or gray-tinted acrylics would be appropriate here.

If heat transmittance is not a problem, a clear, colorless acrylic is appropriate, providing the maximum amount of light. To reduce glare, and ultraviolet and infrared transmittance, white translucent materials are appropriate.

If you live in the Midwest or the Rockies, on the other hand, you will need to think about the load capability of the skylight materials so that heavy snowfalls won't damage it.

Great improvements have been made in skylight materials and features since the 1970s. You can buy self-flashing units (which help prevent water leakage) or double-glazed and double-insulated units, as well as skylights that have their own shade screens and storm panels to prevent ill effects from extreme temperature and weather conditions.

Adding On: Sunspaces

If your climate is temperate, adding a greenhouse as an extension of the kitchen can be an effective way of bringing the outdoors "indoors." Besides contributing a wonderful sense of light, air, and view, the sunroom easily becomes a setting for multiple informal uses—a place where children can play under their parents' supervision or where the family can gather both before and after meals.

Like skylights, greenhouses must be installed properly—level, square, and plumb—to avoid subse-

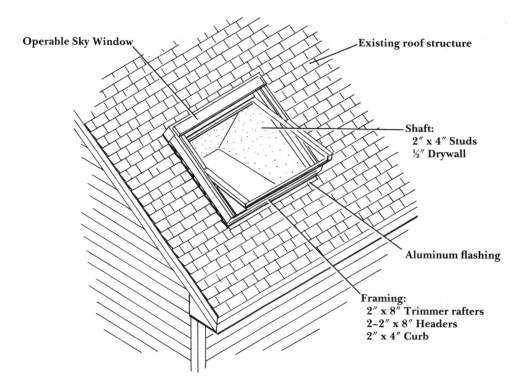

Operable Sky Window

Existing roof structure

Shaft:
2″ x 4″ Studs
½″ Drywall

Aluminum flashing

Framing:
2″ x 8″ Trimmer rafters
2–2″ x 8″ Headers
2″ x 4″ Curb

Figure 5.1 Sky Window, Operable

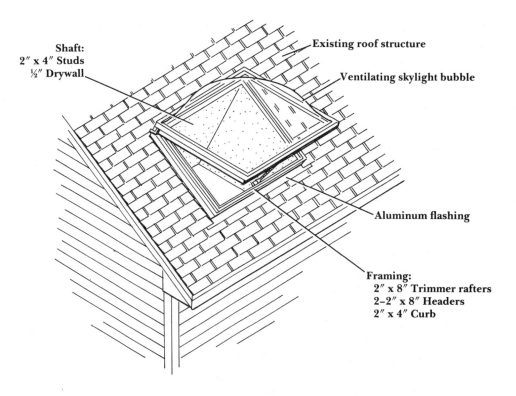

Shaft:
2″ x 4″ Studs
½″ Drywall

Existing roof structure

Ventilating skylight bubble

Aluminum flashing

Framing:
2″ x 8″ Trimmer rafters
2–2″ x 8″ Headers
2″ x 4″ Curb

Figure 5.2 Bubble Skylight, Ventilating

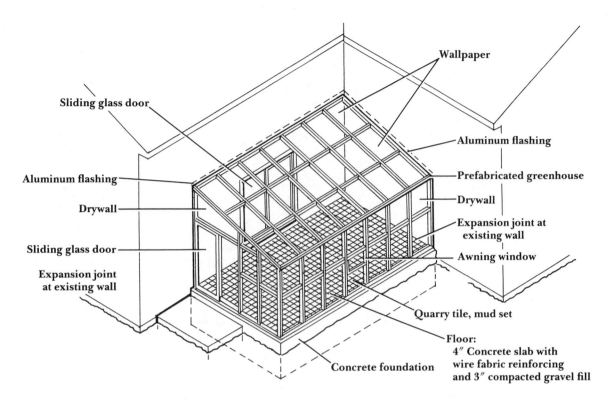

Wallpaper

Sliding glass door

Aluminum flashing

Aluminum flashing

Prefabricated greenhouse

Drywall

Drywall

Sliding glass door

Expansion joint at existing wall

Awning window

Expansion joint at existing wall

Quarry tile, mud set

Concrete foundation

Floor:
4″ Concrete slab with wire fabric reinforcing and 3″ compacted gravel fill

Figure 5.3   Sunroom-Greenhouse, Large

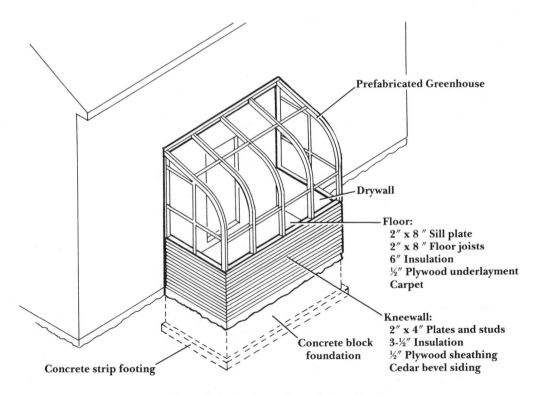

Prefabricated Greenhouse

Drywall

Floor:
2″ x 8 ″ Sill plate
2″ x 8 ″ Floor joists
6″ Insulation
½″ Plywood underlayment
Carpet

Kneewall:
2″ x 4″ Plates and studs
3-½″ Insulation
½″ Plywood sheathing
Cedar bevel siding

Concrete block foundation

Concrete strip footing

Figure 5.4   Sunroom-Greenhouse, Small

quent problems with drafts, water leakage, heat loss in winter, and heat buildup in summer. It's critical, then, that the foundation and floor systems be installed with particular care. Your climate, the slope of your property, and your local building code will guide you to the proper methods.

During greenhouse installation, be wary of a contractor's relying too heavily on the use of shims under sills (a procedure that indicates a problem with leveling) and subjecting the glazing bars to extensive adjustment (a practice that indicates a problem with installing the glass itself).

Greenhouses are available in a variety of standard-size "kits," and using one of these is a far less costly alternative than purchasing custom-designed units; the premade types also can be installed more quickly. Generally, a "kit" consists of an insulated aluminum framing system, tempered glass panels, and the hardware needed to put the sunroom together.

If the greenhouse is to be an integral part of the kitchen (that is, opening to the kitchen or to a family room without a door to close it off), you will need to consider electrical outlets, a lighting fixture, a heating system such as baseboard heating to make it more comfortable in colder months, and perhaps a fan to cool it off during warmer weather. Flagstone or another type of stone flooring for the greenhouse will tend to keep the space cool and easy to maintain. In keeping with its informal style, the room can be furnished with semi-outdoor or outdoor furniture.

Special attention must be paid to weather stripping, flashing, insulation, and how the unit is attached to the side of the house. A poorly installed sunroom will provide a drafty or stifling setting for people and plants alike. You should be able to open sections of the sunroom for ventilation, for example.

Greenhouses can be very expensive to install. Even if the price of the kit itself is less than $10,000, that cost can easily double after the price of labor is figured in.

Other Alternatives

Less costly techniques for providing additional natural light include adding "ribbons" of windows, either clerestory windows close to the ceiling or in the space normally devoted to a backsplash, between the countertop and wall cabinets. As a design element,

these types of windows make the wall cabinets seem to "float" in their space. The drawback of ribbon windows is that they reduce the backsplash space available for small appliance storage, wall outlets, and additional built-in shelving.

Another alternative is a greenhouse window, designed to increase natural light and to contain plants. If you are installing a greenhouse window abutting a countertop at the sink, be sure that the countertop material is installed to slant away from the window, so that when you water your plants, the excess water won't collect on the countertop.

Energy Considerations

Even if your remodeling project doesn't include changing window locations or adding windows to the kitchen, it provides the opportunity to replace existing kitchen windows. If your old window is inefficient and cold air seeps through it, your heating system has to work that much harder to compensate for heat loss and your energy bills will be notably higher. Replacement makes sense if your kitchen windows are single-glazed, have become difficult to operate, are improperly insulated and weather stripped, or create drafts in the room.

Most manufacturers label their products to show you that they have complied with voluntary industry standards established by the American Architectural Manufacturers Association (AAMA). Some manufacturers also test their products for thermal performance.

Double and triple glazing save energy and money by reducing "U-values." U-value, measured by the BTUs per hour per square foot per degree of temperature difference, tells you about overall heat transfer (heat loss through the window). The lower the U-value, the lower the heat transfer rate.

You should also check the R-value listed for these units. The higher the R-value, the better the unit will insulate against heat and cold. Recently, the American Society of Heating, Refrigerating, and Air-Conditioning Engineers (ASHRAE) has revised its calculation procedures for R- and U-values to better reflect the impact of heat loss through the edge of glass and frame material. As a result, while window products may not themselves be undergoing changes, the method of calculating their performance is.

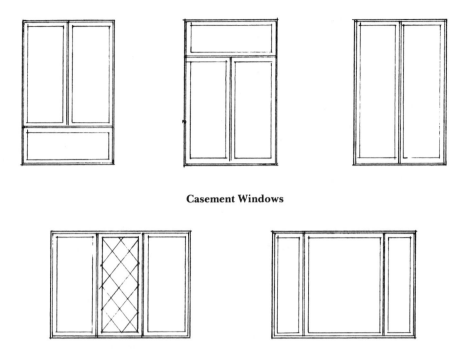

Casement Windows

Figure 5.5   Window Configurations

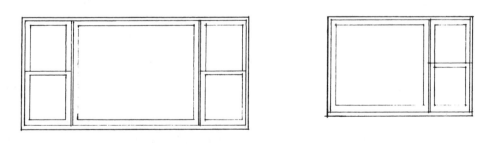

Double   Triple

Double-hung Windows

Double flanker   Single flanker

Figure 5.6   Window Configurations

However, all manufacturers may not calculate R-values the same way, which can make an "apples-to-apples" comparison of technical specifications difficult. So when comparing various products, if you notice a significant difference between the R- and U-values listed for those that are otherwise comparable, find out what methods were used to determine the values.

"Low-E," or "low-emissivity," glass is more expensive than conventional glass, but it offers the additional benefits of deflecting ultraviolet rays, keeping warmth in the room during the colder months, and reducing the heat flow in warmer months. This is accomplished by means of a metal oxide coating that is either applied to the glass or suspended between two layers of glass.

Because heat is also lost through cracks in brick and other walls, remodeling might also give you the opportunity to have such cracks sealed.

ADDING ARTIFICIAL LIGHT

Because so much activity in the kitchen takes place in the evening, after members of the household have returned home from work and school, artificial lighting is particularly important there. Many apartments and town houses feature windowless kitchens, and creating a sense of light and air in them is even more of a challenge.

Lighting serves three major purposes: providing general illumination, furnishing specific illumination for task work, and offering visual interest for specific objects or areas in the room. Most well-designed kitchens mix fluorescent and incandescent lighting to provide general illumination, brighten task areas, and set a warm mood. *All lighting with exposed metal parts should be grounded.*

General Illumination

Much will depend on the size of the room; its orientation (the direction it faces); the availability of natural lighting, windows, and skylights; the ages of household members; and the color and texture of cabinetry, countertops, walls, and floor. A darker color scheme, or a kitchen facing north, will require more actual light than a south-facing kitchen with a lighter color scheme, for example.

According to the American Home Lighting Institute, you should allow at least ¾ watt of fluorescent or 1½ watts of incandescent lighting for each square foot of space.

Specifically, for a 75- to 120-square-foot kitchen, the organization recommends one to four incandescent bulbs totaling 150 to 200 watts or 60 to 80 watts in fluorescent bulbs. For a kitchen larger than 120 square feet, 2 watts per square foot for incandescent bulbs or ¾ watt per square foot for fluorescent bulbs are minimum requirements. Other design sources and organizations call for higher amounts, up to 5 watts per square foot of incandescent and 2 watts per square foot of fluorescent lighting for general illumination.

General lighting should be indirect. It is usually provided by a ceiling fixture centered in the main working area, but it could be provided in the form of a fluorescent luminous ceiling, a single fluorescent or incandescent fixture, or by recessed incandescent "can" or "high-hat" lighting.

Several words of caution should be added about recessed incandescent can lighting. Although these fixtures are widely used because they are attractive and unobtrusive, they have certain drawbacks:

· Because their light is directed downward, you must provide for greater wattage per square foot: perhaps a total of 3 watts per square foot. As a result, they will be costly to use.
· Because they produce heat, certain building-code requirements must be followed to prevent fires: these will determine how far the fixtures must be from combustible materials and insulation as well as how to provide for a flow of air around the fixture enclosures. Low voltage illumination may be the answer when heat generated by recessed lights would be a problem (see below).
· To avoid discomfort from heat, the fixtures should never be placed directly above where people dine at a table or at a countertop.

In the dining area, a chandelier can also provide general lighting. The chandelier should not extend to lower than 25 to 30 inches above the table surface so that people have an unobstructed view of one another while dining. It should not be larger than the width of the table, less 12 inches, to allow people to rise without bumping their heads. The exact placement of the chandelier will depend on its size, appearance, and weight.

Task Lighting

Working comfortably without shadows requires supplemental lighting in the areas where you prepare food, cook, and clean up.

At the sink and range, this can be accomplished with two recessed or track downlights that are 15 to 18 inches apart, with 75-watt "R" flood blubs. As an alternative, compact fluorescents totaling 60 watts can be used, either recessed, surface-mounted, or behind a faceboard. If you don't have a built-in light in the range hood, use an incandescent bulb of at least 40 watts.

For countertop work surfaces that are 30 inches or longer, task lighting can be provided with fluorescent fixtures mounted under wall cabinets. The fixtures should be mounted close to the front of the cabinets, and the tubes should cover at least two-thirds of the length of the counter. A rule of thumb from the American Home Lighting Institute is to provide 8 watts for every 1 foot of counter length. Use a plastic diffuser to shield the fluorescent bulb; it will soften the light. Incandescent tubes are available, but their light doesn't spread as far as fluorescent, and they don't last as long.

Caution: To avoid warpage, don't place an under-cabinet fixture with a plastic diffuser above built-in backsplash appliances that produce heat, such as toasters or toaster-ovens.

Incandescent low-voltage strip lighting and halogen lighting can also be used under cabinets, but they require transformers—small devices that reduce the electric current. While these are small, they must be accessible in an open soffit area or behind a base cabinet drawer. These strip lights can also be used in the toe-kick space, where they serve not only to provide a dramatic visual effect but as a useful "pathfinding" aid at night.

Islands pose unique lighting challenges. In a smaller kitchen, the general lighting fixture can also serve as task lighting for an island or peninsula. But a pot rack, for example, should not interfere aesthetically or functionally with a general ceiling-mounted lighting system or a soffit-based task lighting system.

Accent Lighting

This type of lighting is used to draw attention to some wall-mounted work of art, to the texture of the wall itself, to collectibles on shelves, or to kitchen plants. Accent lighting can be mounted on a track, recessed, wall-mounted, or, in rare instances, placed on the floor.

To light an object on a wall, aim the fixtures at a 30-degree angle to prevent the light from shining in your eyes and creating reflections on the object's surface. On ceilings up to 9 feet in height, the fittings should be placed 2 to 3 feet from the wall. For higher ceilings, they should be 3 to 4 feet from the wall. The distance between individual fixtures should be the same as their distance from the wall.

Walls can also be accented with lighted cornices, which direct light downward, or with lighted, low wall brackets.

Window treatments can be accented with a lighted valance above a window, which also provides up-light that reflects off the ceiling for overall room lighting. These lights should not be closer than 10 inches to the ceiling.

To provide dramatic up-lighting for large plants or sculptures, spotlights can be anchored on a weighted base on the floor and aimed upward. Such a fixture may be a hazard, however, for active young children and pets.

To add to the visual drama of a kitchen, or to make the ceiling appear higher, lighting can be mounted above cabinets. Controlled by their own switch, these incandescent or fluorescent strips create the illusion of volume and provide an additional lighting source.

You can employ multiple lighting systems in the kitchen and have them custom-designed, if you like. A light box can be designed to house both incandescent and fluorescent lighting, which you alternate, depending on the activity at hand. The fluorescent might be used during meal preparation, for example, while incandescent lighting would be chosen for creating atmosphere during the meal.

EVALUATING LIGHTING FIXTURES AND BULBS

What we see is not light itself but, rather, reflected light, and this is partly why colors, materials, and the textures of the environment play such a key role in determining lighting plans.

Light is measured several ways, and contrary to popular opinion, the amount of *wattage,* in and of itself, is not the critical figure; the more important one is *lumens*: a measurement of the amount of light produced from a given light source. A candle, for example, produces about 12 lumens, a 75-watt incandescent bulb produces about 1,180 lumens, and a 40-watt warm-white fluorescent tube produces about 2,000 or 3,150 lumens.

Wattage indicates how much electricity is being used by a bulb. Foot-candles measure the light that reaches an object, all parts of which are located 1 foot from the candle. Foot-lamberts measure the amount of light reflected from the object. Different surfaces—ceilings, walls, floors, countertops, and cabinets—can have widely divergent reflectance levels.

Fluorescent Lighting Fixtures

Although in the short run fluorescent lighting is more expensive to install than incandescent lighting, it is generally more energy efficient. It provides considerably more light at a lower cost over a longer period than incandescent lighting—10,000 hours or more versus approximately 1,000 hours for a standard incandescent. Many people object to fluorescents, however, because their light is not as flattering to people, materials, or food as incandescent light and because of the soft "hum" that the fixtures emit.

Great improvements have been made in fluorescents, however. Compact fluorescents, for example, now come in varying lengths measuring 5¼ to 7 inches long and in an increased number of rounded shapes as well. They also have a screw base that can fit into regular incandescent sockets. And more fluorescents can be controlled by dimmer switches now than was the case several years ago.

Ballasts have been improved to reduce the "hum" and are available in a number of improved color-tone renditions. White, for example, blends with daylight, and "deluxe cool white" simulates natural daylight. "Warm white" and "deluxe warm white" blend with or simulate incandescent light. Standard fluorescents produce 40 to 100 lumens of light per watt, versus incandescents, which produce 12 to 21.

Wattage equivalencies, according to the American Home Lighting Institute are the following:

Compact Fluorescent		Incandescent
1–7 watts	=	40 watts
1–13 watts	=	60 watts
2–9 watts	=	75 watts

Remember that higher-wattage bulbs, whether fluorescent or incandescent, produce more lumens per watt.

Incandescent Lighting

Although they are demonstrably less efficient than fluorescents, incandescents play a prominent role in kitchen design because of their versatility, aesthetic appeal, and flattering color rendition.

There are three types of incandescent bulbs. The first category, general service bulbs, provides illumination in all directions. An *A* bulb is the typical, pear-shaped bulb; a *G* is globe-shaped; and a *D* is shaped like a teardrop, a flame, or another decorative configuration.

The second category, reflector bulbs, provides illumination in one direction. An *R* provides about twice as much light on an object as an *A* bulb of the same wattage. A *PAR*, or *parabolic reflector*, produces about four times as much light as an *A* bulb of the same wattage. A floodlight spreads light, whereas a spot light concentrates it. Recessed incandescents can use baffles, diffusers, and apertures such as "eyeball" and "barndoor" fixtures to control the path of light, shield the light source, and avoid glare.

The third category, low-voltage incandescents, is available in small sizes (*MR-16*) for smaller fixtures, while *PAR-36* is employed for longer distances and is appropriate for both indoor and outdoor use. These bulbs require a transformer.

Within these categories the market offers such a plethora of choices that a certain amount of initial confusion is inevitable. Is a longer-life bulb worth the extra cost? Is a 55-watt bulb as effective as a 60-watt bulb?

To determine how efficient a bulb is, divide the amount of lumens it produces by the wattage listed. For example, if a 60-watt bulb produces 870 lumens, it yields 14.5 lumens per watt. A 55-watt bulb that produces 810 lumens yields 14.7 lumens per watt, which is not much of a gain, and therefore would be a less sensible choice if the price for the 55-watt bulb is higher than for the 60-watt.

Whether or not to choose a "long-life" bulb is a tricky question, too. First, you need to determine a "cost per hour" by dividing the advertised life of the bulb (for example, 1,500 hours for a long-life versus 1,000 for a standard). Remember, too, that a bulb's life expectancy is not set in stone; some will last longer than others labeled with the same life expectancy.

The long-life bulbs are more costly than their standard counterparts, but generally produce fewer lumens per watt and cost more to use per hour.

The chief advantage of a long-life bulb is convenience. Using them in a high ceiling, for example, will mean fewer trips up and down a stepladder for replacements.

Halogen Light Fixtures

Halogen is the most efficient type of lighting. Along with mercury vapor and high-pressure sodium lamps, which are generally used only outdoors, halogen bulbs are categorized as *High Intensity Discharge* light sources.

Halogen bulbs are small and thin, but they can produce as much light as an incandescent bulb 10 times their size. The light quality is not as yellowish as in incandescent lighting.

Halogen lighting systems are low-voltage, requiring only 12 volts of electrical power, as opposed to the 110 volts required by incandescent lighting, and thus need a transformer and special dimmers.

These bulbs take some getting used to. When they are first used, they "smoke" as the protective coating burns off. Children should be cautioned against touching the bulbs, too, for this can cause painful burns. Not only do halogen bulbs burn hotter than incandescents, but their longevity suffers when the oil from your skin rubs off onto the bulb.

Halogen bulbs are three to five times more expensive than incandescents, but less costly than compact fluorescents. They may last slightly longer than incandescents, but not as long as fluorescents.

VENTILATION: THE "RESPIRATORY" SYSTEM

It is important to insulate and use proper construction techniques to prevent drafts, heat loss in winter, and heat gain in summer. But there is a negative side to a superinsulated, or "tight," remodeled kitchen or any room addition, for that matter: the potential buildup of indoor pollutants. Particularly in open kitchen plans that flow freely into other areas of the home, and in apartment kitchens where you cannot vent to the outside, indoor pollution from smoke, odors, and grease can ultimately contribute to a health problem. It can certainly detract from the kitchen's appearance over time and make floors, walls, windows, and window treatments difficult to clean. At the same time, the heat and steam generated at the range can make cooking an uncomfortable, unpleasant task. The potential problems of indoor pollution have also increased with the rising popularity of indoor grilling. The solution to these problems lies in the mechanical ventilation system planned for your kitchen.

A ventilating system collects cooking vapors, removes them with a fan or blower, and generally vents them to the outside. A ductless system filters the air with an activated carbon filter and an aluminum filter, then recirculates the air through louvers in the front of the hood. Ductless systems obviously cannot be as efficient as updraft and downdraft systems.

In an *updraft* system, the blowers are set above the cooking unit. The fan pushes air in a circular motion, forcing smoke and grease up into the filter system and then ducting them to the outside. Unless the total cooking area is covered by a hood and a powerful roof fan is used, at least some smoke will escape into the room with this type of system. Ductless updraft systems are designed for kitchens that cannot vent to the outside, such as apartment kitchens. Their biggest drawback is that the filters must be cleaned regularly and changed approximately every three months.

In a *downdraft* system, the blowers are set below the cooking unit. Smoke and grease are sucked downward, with filters on one or both sides of the cooking unit, and then ducted to the outside.

In some special instances, where there may be a lineup of several different types of cooking surfaces, it may be appropriate to include both types of ventilation systems.

Although an updraft system's work to capture vapors is aided by the natural rise in hot air, you'll need more ventilation capacity than you would with a downdraft system because the downdraft system

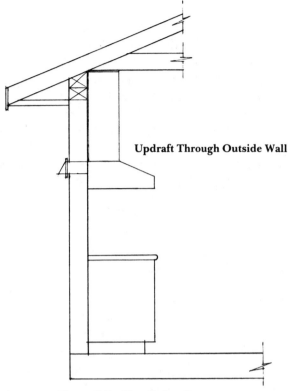

Updraft Through Outside Wall

Figure 5.7   Ventilation Systems

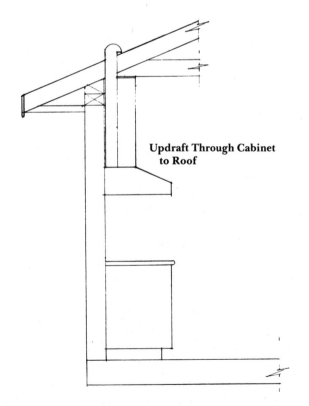

**Updraft Through Cabinet
to Roof**

Figure 5.8   Ventilation Systems

captures vapors closer to the source. Updraft systems can be vented over a longer distance than some downdraft systems and are the only alternative for ductless systems and commercial-style ranges. An updraft system is necessary if your house is built on slab.

The range hood in an updraft system can be a focal point of the room, but it can also be an eyesore, and for tall cooks it can be more of a hindrance than a help. Several imported and European-style systems offer range hoods that are sleek and unobtrusive. Some systems, both updraft and downdraft, are retractable, so they are literally out of your sight when you're not cooking.

Getting Adequate Ventilation

The capacity of ventilation systems is described by the *cubic feet per minute (CFM)*. Standards developed by the Department of Housing and Urban Development call for a minimum of 150 to 160 CFM at the range.

According to the Home Ventilating Institute, an industry organization, an effective ventilating system for a range hood installed against a wall would have a rating of 40 CFM per linear foot and for a peninsula or island range hood, a rating of 50 CFM per linear foot. Based on these calculations, a 36-inch range at the wall would require a 120 CFM rating, while the same size range in an island or peninsula would require a rating of 150 CFM.

If you're installing an indoor grill, however, ventilation capacity must be greater. An updraft system would need at least 400 CFM, and a downdraft system 270 to 300 CFM. If you're installing a commercial-grade range, plan on an updraft system with a 600 CFM rating.

A range hood should be at least the same width as the range. It should extend from the wall at least 17 inches and should be no higher than 30 inches above the cooktop surface; the closer it is to the surface, the more effective it will be.

While you are minimizing air pollution, you don't want to add to the noise pollution in the kitchen. For that reason, check the "sone rating" of a ventilating system before you choose one. The lower the number, the quieter the blower. One sone is comparable to the sound level of a quiet refrigerator. Some sys-

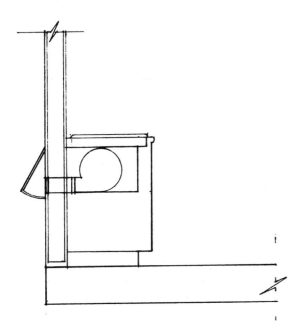

Downdraft Through Outside Wall

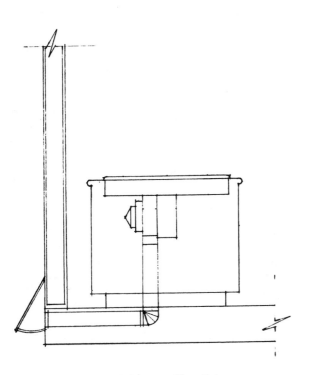

Downdraft Between Floor Joists

Figure 5.9   Ventilation Systems

tems are available with two-speed or three-speed controls, so that you can better moderate the noise.

Kitchen exhaust fans can serve as an adjunct ventilating system and should be mounted as close to the range as possible and vented to the outside. The Home Ventilating Institute recommends a fan or hood capable of 15 air changes per hour. For a wall or ceiling fan, its formula calls for multiplying the square footage of the kitchen floor by two to determine the proper CFM. Thus a 130-square-foot kitchen would require an exhaust fan with a 260 CFM rating.

Ducting Dos and Don'ts

A ventilating system will function most efficiently when the ducting is properly planned and installed. Generally, the shortest and straightest duct "paths" are best.

For updraft systems, five duct paths are possible:

1. through the attic, to roof or eave (this can work if the range is located on an inside wall, with attic space above it)
2. through a soffit to an outside wall (this can work if the range is against an inside wall of a two-story home)
3. through an outside wall (this can work if the range is located on an exterior wall)
4. between joists, to an outside wall or eave
5. under the ceiling (this is the least desirable path, but it is necessary when structural problems preclude any other method; ducts can be attached to the ceiling and covered with a false wood beam or other camouflaging design element)

There are four ways to install a downdraft system:

1. through a wall directly
2. between floor joists or through crawl space or basement
3. through cabinet toe space
4. up inside a wall, or a cabinet, to the roof

Ventilating systems should *never* be vented indoors—for example, to an attic or unused second- or third-floor room.

If the installation requires more than two "elbows"—the joints that allow the ducting path to "bend" where necessary—a larger duct size may be more appropriate. All duct connections should be taped, and dampers must operate freely. The duct size should not be restricted at any point along the ductwork.

Manufacturers include recommended maximum duct lengths and diameters in their installation specifications. If you exceed the lengths or reduce the diameter, you will reduce the system's effectiveness. You should also follow the manufacturer's recommendations on wall or roof vent caps.

PART TWO

Products
and Installation

6

Setting the Style: Selecting Cabinetry

COST CONSIDERATIONS

Cabinetry is the biggest single design element in the kitchen, not to mention the biggest single expense (aside from labor costs). Because it will set the style and tone of your kitchen, as well as fulfill your storage needs, the cabinets must be chosen and planned with great care.

Traditionally, three kinds of cabinetry have been available for residential kitchens: stock cabinets that are mass-produced .by manufacturers and sold through dealerships; custom-made cabinets ordered from manufacturers by kitchen dealers; and custom-made cabinets designed and built by local craftspeople. Over the past several years, however, there has been a blurring of the line between custom cabinetry, which is produced to individual specifications, and stock cabinetry.

Because the quality of many stock cabinet lines has improved markedly over the past several years, *stock cabinetry* can be an excellent choice. Available in many different standard sizes and configurations, stock cabinets also offer a range of storage options, including pull-out drawers, swing-out shelves, and built-in spice racks and cutlery drawers.

The key reason for selecting stock cabinets, of course, is price. Using them can save up to 40 or 50 percent of the cost of comparable custom-made cabinets. Delivery time may also be shorter than it would be for made-to-order cabinets, an important consideration if you are operating under time constraints.

A wider choice of *"semicustom"* cabinetry is now available. These cabinets are also ordered from a manufacturer and mass-produced, but certain pieces can be made according to your individual specifications. The cost, of course, is greater than for stock cabinets.

Custom cabinetry is considerably more costly than the other two categories, but it can offer you more individualized design. You have two options: either to seek out high-quality crafts work or to choose the flexibility in design and wide range of special built-in devices available from a custom cabinet manufacturer. Be aware, however, that having cabinets custom-made isn't an automatic assurance of high-quality craftsmanship.

The chief advantage of working with a local craftsperson is that you can work together to create a look that is truly "one of a kind," and that he or she will field-measure the kitchen and build the cabinetry precisely to size. Craftspeople are also more knowledgeable about working with a wider range of woods than might be available through manufacturers.

The main advantage of working with a dealer representing a custom or semicustom manufacturer is the reliability factor: You can usually depend on them to match the quality of the sample cabinets shown you, to know the design options, and to provide follow-through service.

The Elements of Cost

Cabinetry should be assessed by judging costs in light of value received. The variables that affect the cost relate to quality, appearance, and functional effectiveness. These variables include overall construction quality, box materials and finishes, door styles (those with molding are more costly than the plain ones), hinges, joints, hardware, drawer glides, and storage options.

The cost of a basic box can easily double, in fact, with the addition of several built-in storage sections, an upgraded finish or raised-panel door style, and high-quality hinges and hardware. Frameless cabinets tend to be more expensive than face-frame cabinets (see "Types of Cabinetry," below), and they can be more time-consuming to install because they require professional craftsmanship.

Your choices, then, will depend on evaluating both your functional needs and your style preferences, weighing each, and possibly compromising to obtain the workability you need and the look you want at the price you can afford.

Cost-Saving Strategies

You can achieve substantial savings in several ways. First, shop around and visit dealers in several areas. A particular cabinet dealer 30 or 50 miles away from you may carry products that are comparable or superior to your local dealer's and may be able to offer a better price because of lower overhead or slower business conditions.

In ordering cabinetry, you'll have to accept the responsibility for accurately specifying and sizing the particular components to fit your plan. The measurements must be precise, especially if you're ordering frameless cabinetry. You can use the dealer's design staff or retain an independent kitchen designer to do this task for you.

Household retailers also sell stock cabinetry in a variety of sizes. If you are sure of your measurements and have a relatively simple plan, you can purchase these cabinets from stock in the stores and deliver them yourself. If you are an accomplished do-it-yourselfer, you can install them yourself. If not, have your contractor install them.

You can sometimes arrange with dealers to deliver the cabinetry without installing it. That becomes your contractor's responsibility, and the potential cost savings to you is 10 to 20 percent.

A variety of manufacturers offer stock cabinets unfinished. You can then finish them yourself with special stains or by antiquing, distressing, or pickling them. In this way, you will get the appearance of custom cabinetry at the price of stock.

Remember that several smaller cabinet components will cost significantly more than fewer but larger components in the same space, and that adjustable shelves cost more than fixed shelves.

The ultimate cost-saving strategy is to reface your existing cabinets rather than replace them. This will cost about half of what you would spend for comparable new cabinets. But such a strategy will work only if the basic room configuration and cabinet placement in your existing kitchen are to remain. Good cabinet suppliers can also fabricate new cabinets to match your existing ones. But refacing is not an appropriate solution if your cabinets have warped or sagged over time, or if their storage capacity is insufficient.

Refacing generally includes new door and drawer fronts as well as new end panels, rails, and stiles (the center support piece in a face-frame cabinet). You may also choose to reface the interiors, particularly if you are changing the look from dark to light. The delivery time for refacing work is usually shorter than it would be for new cabinets.

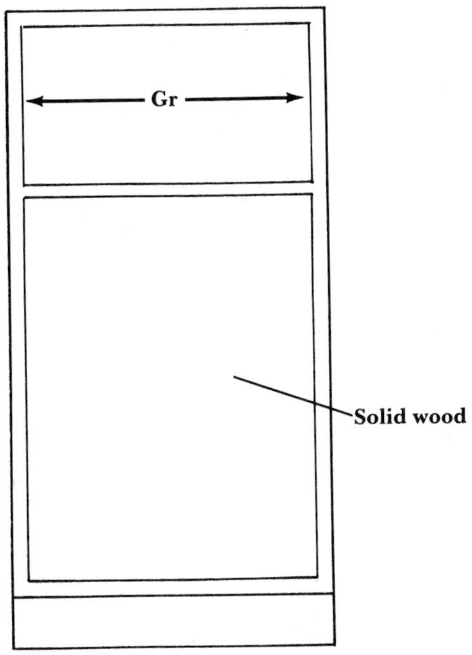

Maximum overlay

Gr

Solid wood

Routed-in wood pull
Maximum overlay

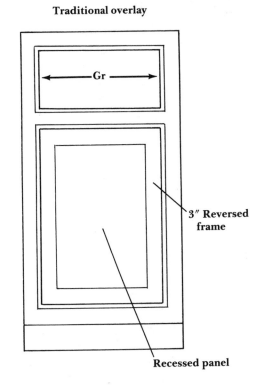

Figure 6.2   Doors

Maximum overlay

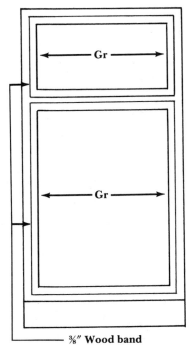

Gr

Gr

⅜" Wood band

Note: Vertical grain on door is available.

Figure 6.1   Doors

Traditional overlay

Gr

3" Reversed
frame

Recessed panel

Figure 6.3   Doors

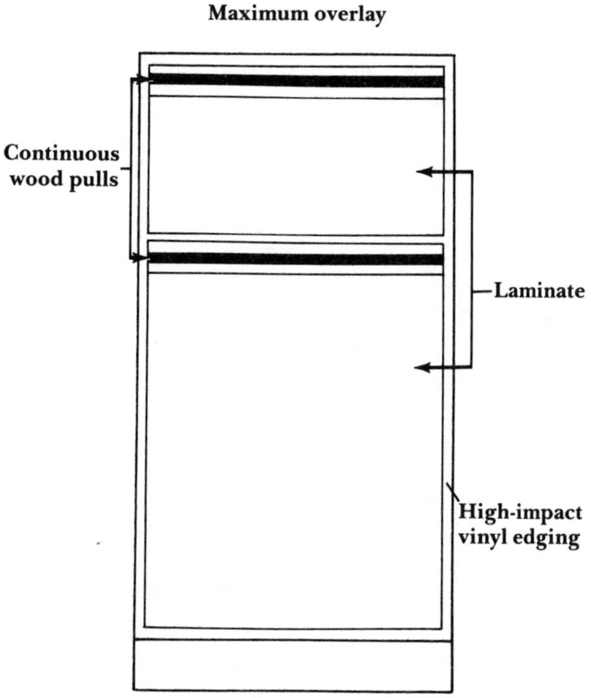

Maximum overlay

Continuous wood pulls

Laminate

High-impact vinyl edging

Figure 6.4 Doors

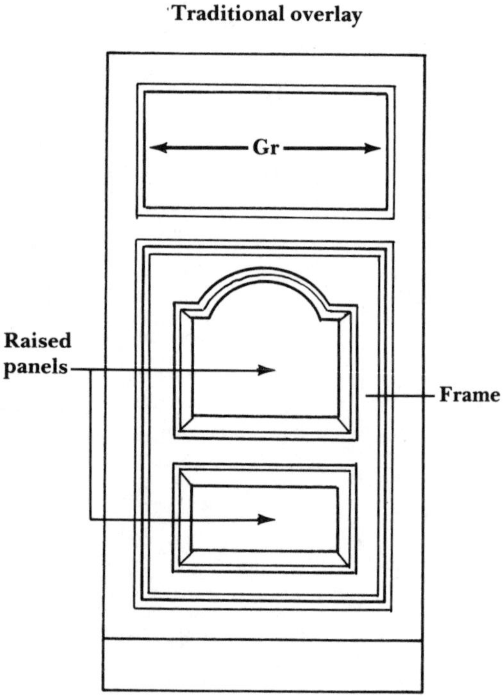

Traditional overlay

Gr

Raised panels

Frame

Figure 6.5 Doors

TYPES OF CABINETRY

Face-Frame Construction

There are two broad categories of cabinetry: face frame and frameless. Traditional cabinet styles are face-frame, in which a solid wood frame between cabinet doors is an integral part of the cabinet's support. Doors and drawers can fit these cabinet fronts flush, partially inset, or overlapping the frame.

The main advantage of face-frame cabinets, in addition to carrying a traditional design theme, is structural stability. The chief drawback is a slight loss of storage space and flexibility, because of the center frame and door openings that are smaller than they would be in frameless cabinets.

In face-frame cabinetry, exterior hinges expose the frame as edges around doors and drawers. This configuration is referred to as a "reveal." Some face-frame cabinets now have full "overlay" doors and concealed hinges, which makes them look more like European-style, frameless cabinets.

Frameless Construction

Sometimes referred to as "European style," frameless cabinets are associated with more contemporary design styles, and the better-quality products are in fact imported from Italy, France, and Germany. Laminate and wood cabinet companies in the United States also manufacture many frameless cabinet lines.

In frameless construction, doors hinge directly to the sides of the cabinet box and overlay the edges with little or no reveal. The hinges are concealed, inside the box. Sides are usually ⅝ to ¾ inches and connected to tops, bottoms, and backs that are either the same thickness or thinner. Some frameless doors can open as wide as 180 degrees.

Frameless cabinetry is often referred to as "32 millimeter" or "System 32" because holes, hinge fittings, cabinet joints, and mountings are set 32 millimeters apart, based on European manufacturing techniques.

The chief advantage of frameless cabinetry is the

ease of access it offers and its capacity for up to 10 percent more storage space than a comparably sized face-frame cabinet.

The major drawback, which can be overcome by trained and skilled workers, is that frameless cabinetry requires considerably more precision in installation than face-frame. Because there is so little room for error, installation can take longer than for face-frame cabinetry.

Cabinet Styles

Your choices don't end after you have decided whether you like face-frame or frameless construction. Both types are available with a dizzying array of door styles, finishes, colors, and door pulls that have a great impact on the cabinets' appearance. With different stains, hardware, and accessories, the same cabinets that create a contemporary, tailored version of a country style can also set a very traditional tone. Choices in materials and styles run the gamut from contemporary plastic laminates and wood veneers to traditional hardwood. Cabinet styling can be simple, carved, molded, or made with glass inserts.

Currently enjoying popularity are English Country–style cabinets, recognizable by the decorative use of carved wood, fretwork (cut-out patterns may be leaves, flowers, fish, or abstract), and open plate racks. Painted white, they can lend a touch of warmth yet still seem appropriate in an otherwise contemporary setting.

Newer to this country are Scandinavian cabinets, whose elegant simplicity recalls American Shaker style.

The late 1980s saw a return to the use of glass mullion doors, which give an old-world quality to the kitchen and allow you to display china, glass, and collectibles. Glass doors add charm and visual appeal by breaking up long runs of solid wood or laminate doors, and they work with any door style.

Cabinet manufacturers also offer a number of elements besides base, wall, pantry, and appliance cabinets that help set the tone of the kitchen. Among these are range hoods (often elaborately carved), matching panels for appliances, tambour-door appliance garages, open shelving, glass door fronts (with mullions or without, with beveled, frosted, leaded, or stained glass), vertical dish racks, wine racks, spice racks, valances used between cabinets over windows, moldings, and plate rails above wall cabinets.

In traditional kitchens, attention to detail and design continuity often leads to the use of moldings. Employed above wall cabinets (crown molding), on cabinet doors, chair rails, and base boards, molding is available natural, prepainted, or prestained, or in vinyl wrapped with a wood-grain finish.

If you have some woodworking skills, you can also create your own customized look by using standard doors. Order a simple wood overlay door, then apply a molding purchased from a lumberyard. If the cabinets are ordered unfinished, you can stain or paint the doors to match them.

JUDGING CABINET QUALITY AND MATERIAL

Whether you're selecting stock or custom cabinets, you should know how the cabinet is put together. Ask about core materials, veneers, the grade type of wood, plywood, or composition materials; the thickness of various components; how the box is glued and fastened; face materials; the type and location of drawer glides; the quality of hinges and hardware; and finishes.

Wood

Many dealers will tell you their cabinets are made of "wood," yet a single box can be made up of a wide range of products and veneers. Even in better-quality cabinetry, solid wood may be used only for doors and frames.

A cabinet made entirely of solid wood may not even be your best bet, particularly if you live in a high-humidity area. Wood reacts to humidity, or the lack of it, and to temperature changes in the environment, and therefore you can expect some shrinking or warping over time.

On the other hand, solid wood cabinetry looks, feels, and smells like "quality" and exudes a sense of warmth that cannot be matched by composite and synthetic materials. The best-quality cabinets match the wood grains of their faces and boxes.

Oak is the most common wood used for solid wood cabinets. Because of the strong "flower" grain in the wood, oak looks best in country settings. You can stain it almost any color, and since the graining is so strong, the grain will always come through the stain. To offset the reddish coloring, use either white oak, which is whiter in natural coloring, or, if you are using red oak, go "browner" in the stain selection. A cherry stain enriches the color of red oak.

Cherry, used primarily in formal cabinets with raised panels, either French or English style, is an elegant wood with a natural reddish coloring that is much deeper than oak.

Rift oak is a veneer much sought after by architects and designers. The oak flower is cut away, leaving the vertical grain. White oak is used for rift selection, so that when it is stained it becomes very light. This type of oak would generally be used in flush overlay construction, in which no frames would be visible.

Hickory, another wood used in country settings, is a strong brown wood with natural markings.

Birch has a very white, natural coloring. It takes a stain well and is often used in contemporary cabinets as well as in raised and recessed panel doors.

Ash is the whitest wood and often employed in cabinet interiors. It has very little graining or flower and takes a stain well in addition to easily accepting enamel or lacquer paint.

Pine, which has a yellowish cast, takes distressing and antiquing beautifully, one reason it is so often used in English, French, and American country settings. Its drawback is that it is a soft wood and can be nicked easily.

Maple is a hard wood that some manufacturers use primarily as a base for enamel or stains. It has little graining and tends to appear yellow.

More exotic woods, such as *wormy chestnut,* which is highly distressed, and *cypress,* which has a yellow cast, are primarily available regionally and are not offered by most cabinet manufacturers. Those who know best about how to work with these woods are specialty woodworkers.

In ordering wood cabinets, try to see a sample of currently produced work to check the colors. Samples can oxidize over time, so you'll want to see how the fresh stains appear.

Composite Materials

Composite materials have become widely used for the cores of all types of cabinetry. To understand the differences between composite materials, you need to know the differences between hardwood and softwood. Hardwood comes from deciduous trees (whose leaves fall off once a year), whereas softwood comes from evergreens.

Plywood is made of thin sheets of wood veneer that are laminated in alternating directions. It is strong and does not pose the warping/shrinking potential of solid wood. Both hardwood plywood and softwood plywood come in a variety of grades. A hardwood plywood panel for a cabinet should have one face graded A and the other graded 2 or better. Softwood plywood has a different system of ratings. It is rated according to its face veneer (the outermost plies) and should be rated B or better. Used as a core material, softwood plywood can be covered with a plastic laminate or wood-veneer face.

When you look at cabinetry, you cannot assume that a hardwood veneer is necessarily covering a hardwood core, so if you have doubts, ask your designer, dealer, or contractor to clarify the matter for you.

Hardwood plywood will generally be a better-quality core, although a *Medium Density Overlay (MDO)* softwood plywood, covered on one or both faces with a thin resin-fiber overlay, is suitable if you intend to paint the cabinets.

Grades of Hardwood Plywood

(Source: Hardwood Plywood Manufacturers Association and American National Standards Institute ANSI/HPMA HP-1983, Standard for Hardwood and Decorative Plywood)

SP Specialty Grade. Characteristics shall be as agreed upon between buyer and seller, and may include unusual decorative features.

A Grade. Face veneers are smooth, and the edges are tightly matched.

B Grade. Face veneers are smooth and tight. If more than one piece of veneer is used on the face, matching for uniform color and grain are not required but shall not contrast sharply at the joints.

2 Sound Grade. Face veneers are free from open defects, but discoloration and sound knots to ¾ inches in diameter and patches are permitted. The veneer on the face is not matched for grain or color.

3 Industrial Grade. May have knotholes to 1 inch in diameter, discoloration, and slight splits. Decay is not permitted.

4 Backing Grade. Open knotholes to 3 inches in diameter, open splits, and joints are permitted. Grain and color are not matched.

Grades of Softwood Plywood

(Source of ratings: American Plywood Association)

N Smooth surface, natural finish veneer. Select all heartwood, or all sapwood. Free of open defects. Allows not more than six repairs, wood only, per four-by-eight panel, made parallel to grain and well matched for grain and color. Available from some manufacturers on special order.

A Smooth, paintable. Not more than 18 neatly made repairs parallel to grain permitted per panel. May be used for natural finish in less-demanding applications.

B Solid surface. Shims, circular repair plugs, and tight knots to 1 inch across grain permitted. Some minor splits permitted.

C-Plugged Improved C veneer with splits limited to ⅛ inch wide, and knotholes and borer holes limited to ¼ inch by ½ inch. Admits some broken grain. Synthetic repairs are permitted.

C Tight knots to 1½ inches. Knotholes to 1 inch across grain and some to 1½ inches if total

width of knots and knotholes is within specified limits. Synthetic or wood repairs, discoloration, and sanding defects that do not impair strength permitted. Limited splits allowed. Stitching permitted.

D Knots and knotholes to 2½ inches wide across grain and ½ inch larger within specified limits. Limited splits allowed. Stitching permitted.

Two common varieties of composite materials are used as cabinet cores. *Medium-density fiberboard* is made of very fine wood fibers that are glued and compressed under great pressure. It has a very smooth surface and has greater screw-holding power than particleboard, the other composite material. It is less expensive than plywood but more expensive than particleboard.

Particleboard is a combination of wood chips, shavings, fibers, and adhesives. It differs from medium-density fiberboard in appearance, since its larger wood chips are in the core, and smaller, finer chips are on the surface. It is heavier than plywood, but not as strong.

If a plastic laminate is going to be applied to the core material, don't use any material of lesser quality than industrial-grade particleboard. Low-grade particleboard won't be able to support the weight of the laminate, and screws and staples won't hold over the long term, resulting in loose cabinets or doors.

One distinct disadvantage of choosing cabinetry constructed with pressed woods like particleboard, hardwood plywood, or medium-density fiberboard is the emission of a gas, formaldehyde, from the adhesives used in their construction. Of all the pressed woods, medium-density fiberboard emits the greatest amount of formaldehyde gas.

According to the U.S. Environmental Protection Agency, formaldehyde gas can cause respiratory and other physical ailments in some people exposed to elevated levels of it (above 0.1 parts per million). Although the EPA estimates that most older homes have significantly less concentration than that, the levels can be greater than 0.3 parts per million in

Appearance Grades of Softwood Plywood

N Special-order "natural finish" veneer. Select all heartwood or all sapwood. Free of open defects. Allows some repairs.

A Smooth and paintable. Neatly made repairs permissible. Also used for natural finish in less demanding applications.

B Solid-surface veneer. Circular repair plugs and tight knots permitted.

C Knotholes to 1″ (2.54 cm). Occasional knotholes ½″ (1.27 cm) larger permitted providing total width of all knots and knotholes within a specified section does not exceed certain limits. Limited splits permitted. Minimum veneer permitted in exterior-type plywood.

C Improved C veneer with splits limited to ⅛″ (0.32 cm) in width and knotholes and borer holes limited to ¼″ x ½″ (0.64 x 1.27 cm).

D Permits knots and knotholes to 2½″ (6.35 cm) in width and ½″ (1.27 cm) larger under certain specified limits. Limited splits permitted.

Plywood Fabrication

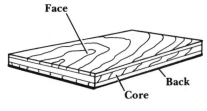

Three-ply veneer core

Multiple veneer core

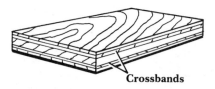

Five-ply veneer core

Five-ply particleboard core

Figure 6.6   Wood and Plywood

Unsanded Grade Marking

Grade of veneer on panel back ──────────
Grade of veneer on panel face ────────── **A-C** GROUP 2
Species group number ──────────
Exposure durability classification ────────── EXTERIOR

Mill number ────────── 000
Product standard governing manufacture ────────── PS 1-83

Typical Interior Plywood Marking

Grade of veneer on panel back ──────────
Grade of veneer on panel face ────────── **A-D** GROUP 1
Species group number ──────────
Exposure durability classification ────────── EXPOSURE 1

Mill number ────────── 000
Product standard governing manufacture ────────── PS 1-83

Grade of veneer on panel face
Grade of veneer on panel back
Exposure durability classification
Product standard governing manufacture

A•B • G-1 • EXT-APA • 000 • PS1-83

Species group number (1-5)   Mill number

Classification of Softwood Species

Group 1	Group 2		Group 3	Group 4	Group 5
Apitong[ab]	Cedar, Port Orford	Maple, Black	Alder, Red	Aspen	Basswood
Beech, American	Cypress	Mengkulang[a]	Birch, Paper	Bigtooth	Poplar, Balsam
Birch	Douglas Fir 2[c]	Meranti, Red[ad]	Cedar, Alaska	Quaking	
Sweet	Fir	Mersawa[a]	Fir, Subalpine	Cativo	
Yellow	Balsam	Pine	Hemlock, Eastern	Cedar	
Douglas Fir 1[c]	California Red	Pond	Maple, Bigleaf	Incense	
Kapur[a]	Grand	Red	Pine	Western Red	
Keruing[ab]	Noble	Virginia	Jack	Cottonwood	
Larch, Western	Pacific Silver	Western White	Lodgepole	Eastern	
Maple, Sugar	White	Spruce	Ponderosa	Black (Western Poplar)	
Pine	Hemlock, Western	Black	Spruce	Pine	
Caribbean	Lauan	Red	Redwood	Eastern White	
Ocote	Almon	Sitka	Spruce	Sugar	
Pine, Southern	Bagtikan	Sweetgum	Engelmann		
Loblolly	Mayapis	Tamarack	White		
Longleaf	Red	Yellow Poplar			
Shortleaf	Tangile				
Slash	White				
Tan Oak					

[a]Each of these names represents a trade group of woods consisting of a number of closely related species.
[b]Species from the genus *Dipterocarpus* are marketed collectively: Apitong if originating in the Philippines, Keruing if originating in Malaysia or Indonesia.

[c]Douglas Fir from trees grown in the states of Washington, Oregon, California, Idaho, Montana, Wyoming, and the Canadian Provinces of Alberta and British Columbia shall be classed as Douglas Fir no. 1. Douglas Fir from trees grown in the states of Nevada, Utah, Colorado, Arizona, and New Mexico shall be classed as Douglas Fir no. 2.
[d]Red Meranti shall be limited to species having a specific gravity of 0.41 or more based on green volume and oven dry weight.

homes with considerable amounts of new pressed wood products. Moreover, emissions increase with increasing humidity and temperature.

If your cabinetry is made of particleboard, plywood, or medium-density fiberboard, determine whether urea formaldehyde or phenol formaldehyde was used in its manufacture. The latter is less of a health hazard. Another strategy is to make sure that your kitchen is well ventilated and that you can prevent the temperature from fluctuating dramatically.

One comforting thought is that, over time, these emissions diminish. Stock cabinets may already have emitted a good deal of gas if they had been built and were in stock for about three months before arriving at your home.

Laminates

A number of varieties of laminates are available, and they vary in performance, cost, durability, and appearance. Generally, laminates are durable and easy to clean. You can get a laminate in many solid colors or in any number of patterns and finishes, including wood grains, metallics, and faux stone.

Plastic laminate consists of paper saturated with phenolic resin, layered and bonded under high pressure. The core is covered with a sheet of paper for color and pattern. Then it is covered with a protective shield.

Low-pressure laminates, also known as melamine, tend to chip and crack with lesser-quality core materials. High-pressure laminates perform better but are proportionately more expensive. Continuous high-performance laminates are newer and less expensive than the high-pressure variety.

Resin-impregnated foil is less costly than low-pressure laminate and is also more durable, although prices can vary greatly since its suppliers are outside the United States.

Vinyl films are inexpensive, too, but patterns may not have the quality of high-pressure or continuous high-performance laminates. Hot-stamped transfer foils are less expensive than high-pressure and continuous high-performance laminates and are available in a wide range of colors and patterns. They cannot be used on particleboard, and their thinness makes them less resistant to stains and wear.

Types of Joints in Cabinetry

How frames and doors with frames are put together can reveal a lot about the quality of a cabinet. There are four possible ways. The most accepted—and best—method is the *dowel joint,* in which two pieces of wood are joined by glue and two dowels, which protrude about ¾ inch into the wood.

A *mortise-and-tenon joint* connects the wood with one piece of wood carved out and extended into the other piece of wood. Variations are the *tongue-and-groove joint, dovetailed joint,* and *rabbetted joint.* Dowel joints and mortise-and-tenon joints are generally found in expensive wood cabinets.

Less desirable is a *butt joint,* which consists of two pieces of wood placed side-by-side and glued, nailed, or screwed together, so the quality of the bonding is a key issue.

In a *lap joint,* the sections of wood are machined to overlap each other, glued, and then pinned in place. This type of joint, which is least desirable, is generally found in low-end, stock cabinets. Plate (or biscuit) joinery is increasingly common for framing as well as cabinet construction.

No matter which method is used, there should be no signs of separation at the joints.

The box will most likely be nailed or stapled together as well as glued at the joints. Nails are more effective in the long run than staples. The quality of the core material is an issue, too; you cannot use a nail twice in the same place if it pops in a particleboard core.

Drawer Glides

No matter how attractive the cabinetry in a showroom appears, its appeal will quickly diminish in your home if its hardware is of poor quality. Just as you would test-drive a car before you buy it, test the cabinetry for yourself. Do the drawers open easily and quietly? Or do they rumble, stick, or tilt down when you open them? Are they "full extension"—that is, do they come all the way out of the box? Or do they make access more difficult by opening only part of the way?

The best-quality drawer glides operate on nylon wheels or ball bearings made of polymer or steel. They also have built-in bumpers to cushion the impact of the drawer front closing against the cabinet. The top-of-the-line glides allow for full extension, although three-quarter extension glides can be a practical alternative. Higher-quality drawers are self-closing when they are pulled out approximately an inch. Load ratings are also important—not all slides can support the same weight.

Drawer glides are side-, bottom-, or corner-mounted. The bottom-mounted glides can be used only on face-frame cabinets. They should include a pair of rollers mounted to the face-frame, so that the drawer won't tip when it's opened.

Hardware: Hinges, Shelf Supports, and Pulls

Cabinet hardware is not the place to stint on quality.

In a frame cabinet, a better-quality hinge wraps around the frame. It will prevent the door from swinging open too widely and will be self-closing so that the door won't stay open.

One drawback of the traditional "leaf" or "butt" hinge is that during installation, if doors "droop" or otherwise don't seem to line up correctly, the installer has to remove the entire hinge before adjustments can be made. New holes may have to be drilled and old holes filled, all of which takes time.

In frameless cabinets, concealed hinges move on a series of pivots. They can allow a door to open as little as 90 degrees (suitable for a corner cabinet), 100 degrees (for a glass-door cabinet), to nearly 180 degrees, in which the cabinet door swings clear of the sides of the box almost flat against the cabinet.

The hinge is made up of a base plate, an arm, and a cup, and is adjusted by turning one or two screws that secure the arm on the base plate.

These adjustable hinges, which operate like a step-in ski binding, can make up for the problems posed by uneven floors and walls. Some can be adjusted up, down, or sideways in three or six ways so that doors will line up and the cabinets will be square.

Standard European hinges used on frameless cabinets will hold 20 pounds per hinge. This means that for a standard cabinet door, ⅞ inch thick and up to 24 inches wide by 25 inches high, two hinges will suffice. For larger cabinet doors, such as pantry doors, three or more hinges may be necessary.

Concealed hinges are also available for face-frame cabinets. The same mounting plate can be used for all frame thicknesses. Alternatively, you can select a decorative fully exposed hinge or a semiconcealed hinge for face-frame cabinets.

Adjustability is a desirable quality in cabinet shelving. Metal pilasters, or metal channels (two of them are mounted vertically on each side of the cabinet wall), are the most common way of providing it. Shelves are supported on metal clips that snap into slots in the pilasters. The clips can be moved from slot to slot, so that you can adjust the shelves to the heights you prefer. The pilasters must be aligned so that the shelves won't rock when they're set in place.

The pilasters can be surface-mounted or, better still, routed (carved) into the inside of the box. They are available in a limited number of colors.

An alternative to using metal pilasters is to attach support clips directly into holes drilled at regular intervals in the cabinet wall. Plastic clips with steel pins inside them are stronger than plain plastic clips. A hardwood plywood box will be more stable than composition materials for this type of shelf support.

The tremendous array of choices available in kitchen design extends to the smallest elements. Door and drawer pulls are now available in so many styles and materials that they must be carefully selected so as to avoid making a jarring or contradictory design statement.

Today pulls are made of combinations of solid surface materials mixed with traditional materials as well as the tried and true plastics, wood, brass, metal, porcelain, and chrome. They can be simple U shapes, circular "button" pulls, or elaborately carved or painted pulls that complement traditional-style wood cabinetry.

Simple wire pulls are more appropriate for contemporary, frameless cabinetry. The better-quality pulls have threaded inserts cast into the body of the pull for added strength and durability, and are made of high-quality cast resin.

Wood or solid surface U-shaped pulls can work well with frameless cabinets as well. With a complementary countertop edge treatment (see chapter 10), door and drawer hardware can add a sense of warmth and can break what might be the monotonous appearance of a run of cabinets.

Pulls can also be flush, which means that they don't protrude from the door. They can be molded into the underside of the door, or built into the door front.

A variation is the continuous pull, or "edge pull," which is recessed into the width of a cabinet door or drawer. In a contrasting material or color, it serves as a decorative element as well as a functional one. You open these doors or drawers with a bent finger instead of with a fingertip.

For an ultracontemporary look, many designers prefer to eliminate pulls completely. Doors can be opened and closed using catches attached to the underside of the upper box and to the inside of the cabinet door.

Whichever style or material you select, the pulls should be easy for you to reach, grip, and use; appropriate for the size and weight of the door or drawer; and harmonious with the cabinet style.

Finishes

Cabinets take a lot of abuse over the years: spills, stains, grease, moisture, door slamming, and nicks and scratches. How they stand up to that abuse depends in part on how they are finished and sealed.

Currently enjoying popularity are pickled finishes, which consist of white pigment rubbed into the wood. It lightens the appearance of the cabinetry and can make a traditional-style cabinet look equally at home in a contemporary or country setting.

Polyurethane finishes form a coating on the cabinet surface and can be applied over the wood, the stain, or a paint wash. Brown paste waxes are also acceptable finishes, applied over a sealer coat of shellac, varnish, or oil. One advantage of a polyurethane finish is that it can seal in formaldehyde gases, cutting

down on emissions in your home. But to be effective, it must cover *all* surfaces and edges, and remain intact.

Among the newer choices are polyester and lacquer finishes, which give a high-gloss appearance. Polyester is harder and more durable than lacquer and therefore more damage-resistant, but it is more difficult to repair. The polyester coating is either clear or pigmented. Polyester is solvent-resistant, but lacquer can be washed off with a solvent as well as recoated and retouched.

These high-gloss surfaces are not recommended if you have active young children in your household; toy automobiles, tricycles, and other mobile items can easily chip the cabinetry. Breaks are less visible on a grained, softer-gloss finish.

For a custom look, you can order cabinets unfinished and have them finished on the job site.

Industry Standards

The presence of a certification seal from the Kitchen Cabinet Manufacturers Association (KCMA) is one quick way of assessing cabinet quality. The association formerly was known as the National Kitchen Cabinet Association. Its standards for strength, construction, and finish quality have been adopted by the American National Standards Institute (ANSI) and represent a baseline of quality to help you compare different manufacturers' products. (The only drawback to using the seal as a guideline is that not all cabinet manufacturers are KCMA members, and the products of those who are not, which may exceed the standards, are not tested.)

Still, the seal is a useful guide. Cabinets are tested by independent laboratories—tests measure more than 60 performance requirements—before certification is granted. Once a year, products are retested after an unannounced visit to the manufacturer's assembly plant. If the cabinets do not pass the tests again, the manufacturer is given some time to correct deficiencies. Certification is removed if the deficiencies are not corrected within that time.

The tests simulate the wear and tear that the cabinet structure would need to withstand over a 10-year period, and that the finish would need to withstand over a five-year period. They measure the cabinets' ability to withstand heavy loads and impact, and finish tests measure resistance to heat and humidity, extreme temperature changes, water and detergent and food and beverage stains.

Among the KCMA's general requirements for certification are the following:

- All cabinets must be fully enclosed with backs, bottoms, sides, and tops on wall cabinets; and backs, bottoms, and sides on base cabinets, except for kitchen sink fronts, sink bases, and oven and refrigerator cabinets.
- All cabinets that rest on the floor must have a toe space at least 2 inches deep and 3 inches high.
- Utility cabinets must meet the same requirements as base and wall cabinets.
- Doors must be properly aligned and must close without excessive binding or looseness.
- All materials must ensure rigidity. Face-frames must provide rigid construction, whereas the ends, tops, bottoms, and backs of frameless cabinets must be thick enough to provide rigid construction.
- Corner or lineal bracing must be provided where necessary to ensure rigidity and the proper joining of components.
- All wood parts must be dried to a moisture content of 10 percent or less at the time of fabrication.
- All exposed plywood and composition board edges must be filed and sanded, edge-banded, or otherwise finished.
- All exposed parts of cabinets must have nails and staples set and holes filled.
- All exposed construction joints must be fitted in a workmanlike manner.
- There should be no sign of looseness in connections between cabinets and hinges or doors and hinges.

In addition, cabinet finish should be free of ridges and other imperfections, scratches, and residue. Door finish should show no discoloration, blistering, whitening, or swelling. And all interior exposed surfaces in the cabinet and drawers should have at least one coat of clear finish.

MEASUREMENTS AND DIMENSIONS

Once you've selected the types of cabinets you want, the next step is to determine how they will be configured to fit your floor plan.

The number and the measurements of the cabinets you will need in your kitchen depend on a variety of factors. The most important will be the location of and the relationship between key work centers in the kitchen. Placing the sink, refrigerator, cooktop, ovens, and microwave oven comes first; their placement will determine where the cabinetry can be situated.

All measurements should be double-checked against the manufacturers' specifications for the appliances you select. Otherwise, there is a danger that they won't fit properly without major adjustments during installation, or won't fit at all without ordering a new cabinet component.

Second in importance is the degree of singularity of your plan and your individual needs. Unless your plan is highly unusual, you probably will be able to use various configurations of stock and semicustom cabinets to provide storage that is efficient and attractive. Custom-made cabinetry, using other-than-standard widths, heights, and depths, is required only for an installation that is unique or in which standard-height countertops and wall cabinets cannot accommodate the needs of the very tall or very short cook or household member with physical limitations.

Third, you must know your own taste. Do you like open shelving at the end of cabinet runs? Do you like the visual interest of a run of cabinets with varying depths? Do you prefer a sleeker look with built-in appliances? Do you prefer drawers for pot storage under the cooktop? Do you want shelves or pull-out drawers behind cabinet doors?

Stock cabinets are planned on the assumption that they will be accommodating standard-height work surfaces and appliances. The standard countertop is 36 inches high, which is comfortable for the "average" person and accommodates standard dishwasher, oven/cooktop, and trash compactor installations. Of course, plans can be drawn and fixtures installed for those who prefer higher or lower work-surface heights.

In addition to the extra cost that goes with customization, its major drawback is the potentially negative

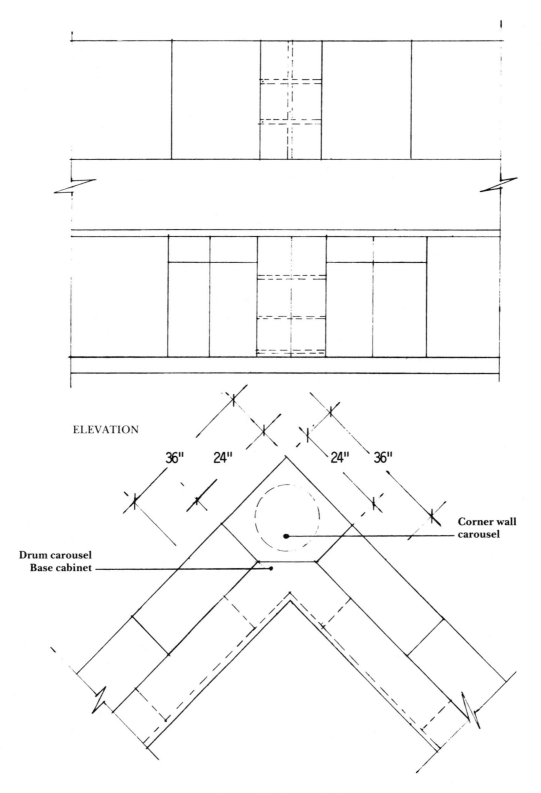

ELEVATION

36"   24"   24"   36"

Corner wall
carousel

Drum carousel
Base cabinet

Figure 6.7   Corner Cabinets

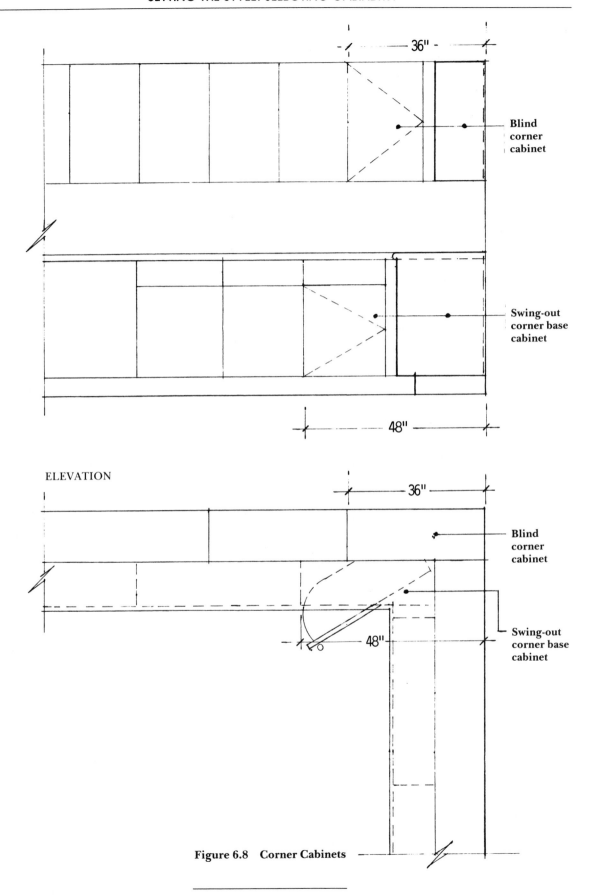

ELEVATION

Blind
corner
cabinet

Swing-out
corner base
cabinet

Blind
corner
cabinet

Swing-out
corner base
cabinet

Figure 6.8   Corner Cabinets

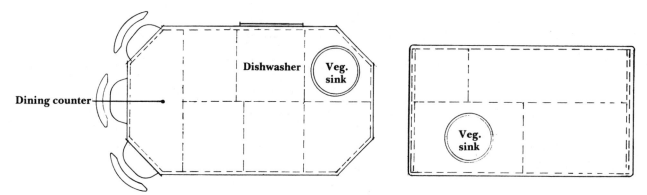

Figure 6.9   Island Configurations

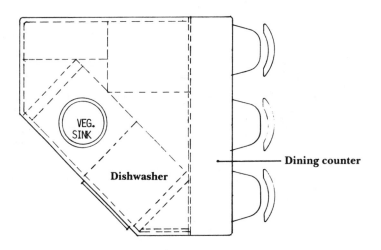

Figure 6.10   Island Configurations

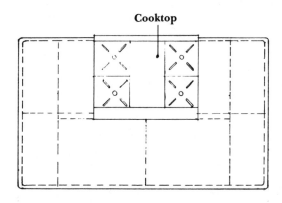

Figure 6.11   Island Configurations

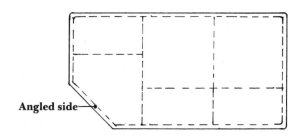

Figure 6.12

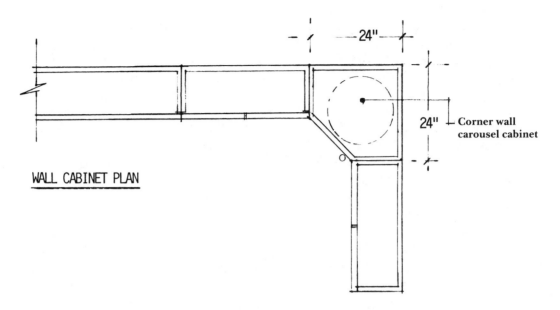

24"

24" — Corner wall
carousel cabinet

WALL CABINET PLAN

Figure 6.13   Corner Cabinets, Wall Cabinet Plan

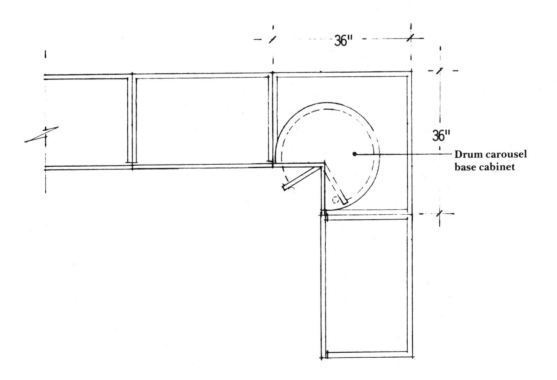

36"

36"

Drum carousel
base cabinet

Figure 6.14   Base Cabinet Plan

effect it will have on your ability to sell your home in the future. Like the presence of a swimming pool, a highly individualized kitchen that clearly suits one person's specialized needs tends to limit the number of available prospective buyers, no matter what the price category of the home.

Stock cabinets are available in widths that begin at 12 inches and range in 3-inch increments up to 48 inches. Base cabinets are typically 24 inches, and wall-hung cabinets are 12 to 15 inches deep. Pantry cabinets are available in 12- to 36-inch widths, and 12-, 15-, 18-, and 24-inch depths. Standard height for tall cabinets is 84 inches, although some manufacturers offer 96-inch heights as well.

Wall cabinets are typically placed 15 to 18 inches above the countertop and are 12 to 33 inches high. Base cabinets are 34½ inches high, which allow for a 1½-inch countertop. Toe space at the bottom of the base cabinet is typically 3 inches deep and 4 inches high.

A run of cabinets can be designed in a variety of configurations. The designer's challenge is to break up a run into individual components that maximize access and storage ability as well as establish a harmonious, aesthetically appealing look.

The plan should minimize "dead" corner space or provide adequate solutions for corner storage. Many designers and contractors don't like to use lazy Susans because they waste up to 50 percent of the available space inside the box. Much will depend on your taste, too, of course. If you are willing to give up a certain amount of space in return for the convenience of revolving shelves, a lazy Susan can work for you.

Other corner solutions that enhance access, though they too waste some available space, are "pie cut" shelves that can be fixed in place or revolve; and swing-out shelves. Hinged corner cabinet doors can ease access to corners, as can wall cabinets angled at the corner.

Your cabinet configuration may require the use of "fillers"—so called because they literally fill irregular spaces. Generally they are employed to fill space in corners, so that drawers and doors have enough clearance to open and close. Fillers can run from ¾ to 6 inches and are available in 3-inch increments. They are particularly useful in older homes whose walls may be irregular. A filler can also have a panel

attached to it, to house a refrigerator, dishwasher, range, or microwave.

If you have an angled plan, make sure that your designer has included fillers adjacent to corner cabinets so that adequate clearance will be ensured. If the plan calls for cabinet doors with rounded edges, make certain that the hinges are on the correct side (so they don't conflict with appliances) and have adequate clearance. The plan should not depend on an excessive number of fillers to accommodate stock cabinetry, however, since they add up to a good deal of wasted space.

In custom cabinetry, either wood or laminate, the filler can be made an extension of the cabinet where it meets a wall rather than inserted as a separate piece. Have it made slightly larger than measurements require so that it can be cut to fit when it's installed. Do the same thing at the end return, where the side of the cabinet is visible. This strategy not only is economical but adds greatly to the cabinetry's visual appeal.

Similarly, if you plan a range hood or a microwave oven in a wall cabinet, it will look better if the wall cabinet is made so the bottom is flush with the rest of the wall cabinetry, rather than recessing it. Otherwise, you will have to have a separate panel installed on site.

Remember that while larger cabinets are less expensive than a grouping of smaller cabinets, they can also pose problems. A large door is heavier than a smaller one, and over a period of time it can sag. Maneuvering around a large open door is also awkward. And, unless the larger box is designed with shelves, trays, or vertical storage racks, much of its space will be wasted.

INSTALLATION TECHNIQUES

After the shipment of cabinets has arrived and been checked to make sure that it matches your order, the cabinet installers should mark all cabinet locations on the walls as well as marking the studs to which the cabinets will be attached.

Measurements come first. The installer should find the "high spot" on the floor where the cabinets will be installed. Most floors in older homes are not level, and cabinet installation must work with the reality of

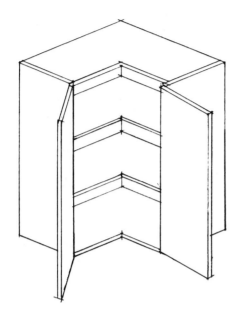

Figure 6.15   Corner Wall Cabinet

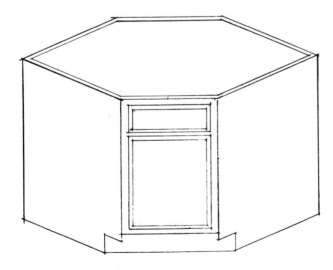

Figure 6.16   Corner Base Cabinet

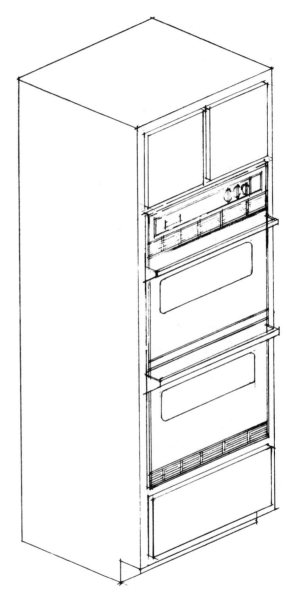

Figure 6.17   Double-oven Cabinet

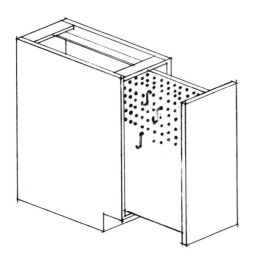

**Figure 6.18   Base Cabinets,
    Base Pullout Utility Cabinet**

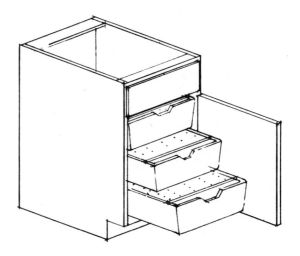

**Figure 6.20   Base Cabinets,
    Fruit and Vegetable Cabinet**

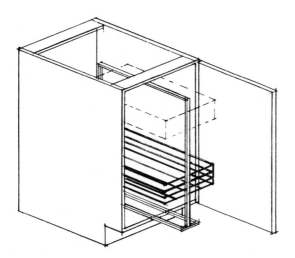

Figure 6.19   Canned-food Cabinet

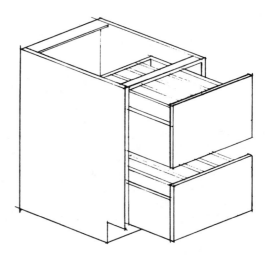

Figure 6.21   Cookie Sheet Cabinet

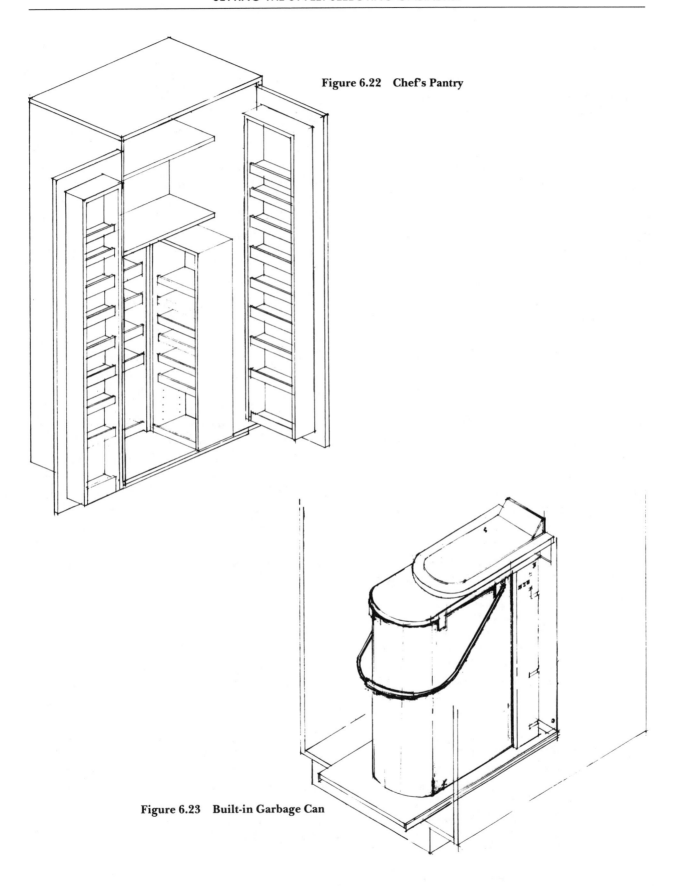

Figure 6.22 Chef's Pantry

Figure 6.23 Built-in Garbage Can

your home's condition. Similarly, walls may not be plumb or square, even in relatively new construction, and the installer must check them first before any cabinets can be installed. Doors to wall cabinets should be removed before installation.

The base cabinets set the standard for the rest of the installation. Before installation, they should be lined up and connected to one another. First they should be clamped together for perfect alignment and then connected through the sides by screws. This method is far more precise than attaching components to the wall separately, one after another.

Once the base cabinets are lined up and connected, your contractor will be able to tell what kind of "shimming" may be needed on the walls and floor. A shim is a narrow wedge of wood that works much like a matchbook placed under the leg of a wobbly table in a restaurant. If your floors or walls are at all "wavy," as is the case in many older homes, shimming will be necessary.

Most frameless cabinets are screwed directly to a wall. If hanging rails are to be used, however, they should be cut and screwed to the studs, usually about 2½ inches below the soffit. This will allow the installer to lift the cabinet up above the rail and then to lower the cabinet onto it.

Wall cabinets should be installed starting in a corner, and working outward. In a U-shaped kitchen, the two corner cabinets should be installed first. As each cabinet is hung, it should be fastened to the preceding one so that they are perfectly aligned. When all of the wall cabinets have been installed, they should be checked to make sure that they are level, plumb, and square.

Most base cabinets require leveling legs which should be attached to their bottom corners. In standard installations, the installer makes a mark 34½ inches above the high point of the floor, along the walls that the base cabinet will be placed. This assumes that the height of your countertop is going to be the standard 36 inches.

Toe-kick moldings are an aesthetic feature that screens the leg levelers from view and provides a floating look to the base cabinets. Some can be snapped into place.

Finally, doors and drawer fronts are attached, using adjustable hardware to align them and make the opening between the doors even from top to bottom. Doors should not have more than ¼ inch of space between them.

Face-frame cabinet installation does not differ greatly from that of frameless cabinetry, except that face-frame cabinets usually are screwed to the wall through a mounting strip. Because they have more inner construction, face-frame cabinets do not rack as easily as frameless. Because the door can be adjusted on the frame, face-frame cabinets also offer some flexibility in door placement, provided that the doors haven't been predrilled.

PROBLEM SOLVING

If you've ordered your cabinetry through your contractor, he or she should provide some kind of warranty for it. The Home Owners Warranty Remodeler Program, for example, calls for replacing or repairing doors or drawer fronts if warpage exceeds ¼ inch, and eliminating gaps of more than ¼ inch between cabinets and ceilings or walls.

Most floors in older homes are not level, and their walls are neither straight nor plumb. Unless the installer knows how to compensate for less-than-ideal conditions, the cabinetry won't be installed correctly.

But what happens in cases where there is a problem with the cabinetry, and your contractor isn't at fault? If you have selected KCMA-certified products, you have additional recourse with the cabinet dealer or manufacturer. If you contact the dealer and receive no satisfaction, the KCMA will contact the manufacturer's service representatives for you, and generally an appropriate settlement can be reached.

In some cases, a dispute may arise as to whether or not a problem actually exists. For example, although you may think that your cabinet doors are not uniform in color, it's possible that the wood may have natural variations, and the dealer may then have a legitimate argument against replacing them. Still, if you believe you cannot live with the extent of the variations, contact the KCMA. Its representatives may be able to convince the manufacturer to replace the doors as a show of good faith.

7
Choosing Major Appliances

Appliances are the true workhorses of the kitchen. They are the focal point of each work station in the room. How functional the kitchen will prove to be over time depends largely on the placement and the quality of the appliances you select.

Aesthetic considerations play an important role in appliance selection, just as they do for cabinetry, flooring, countertops, and other major design elements of the kitchen. Fortunately, appliance styles have evolved over the years to suit a variety of tastes, although in rural areas especially you may have to research the availability of appliance styles that are not considered standard by contractors or dealers in the region.

If you like the "nonkitchen" look, in which the appliances seem to disappear into the cabinetry, built-in appliances with trim that matches the cabinetry will be an appropriate choice. If you like the pristine "laboratory kitchen" look, all-white appliances, including glass cooktops, would be appropriate. Or, if you prefer the look of a restaurant kitchen and plan to do considerable specialty cooking and entertaining, the "neoprofessional" style, in which the appliances themselves are the highly visible focal points of the kitchen, might be the one you choose.

Aesthetic considerations aside, your biggest choices in appliances will probably center on the issue of cost versus value—that is, how much are you willing to spend for the latest computerized "bells and whistles," and are those extra functional benefits ultimately worth the expense?

In general, appliances can be divided into three categories: food storage (refrigerators and freezers); cooking (cooktops and ovens); and cleanup (dishwashers, trash compactors, garbage disposers).

(You'll find *Consumer Reports* product Ratings and guides to product features in appendix C. They give Consumer's Union's evaluations of refrigerators, ranges, microwave ovens, microwave/convection ovens, and dishwashers.)

FOOD STORAGE: REFRIGERATORS AND FREEZERS

Basic Design Elements

Refrigerator design has evolved dramatically over the years to include better energy efficiency, more convenience features, better-organized storage and

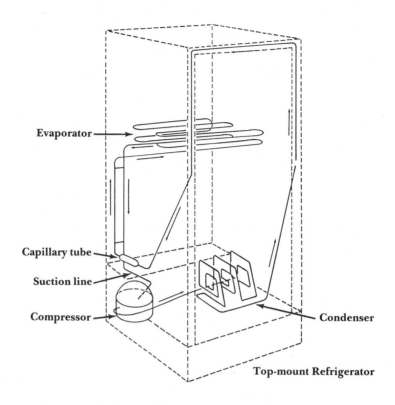

Evaporator

Capillary tube

Suction line

Compressor

Condenser

Top-mount Refrigerator

Figure 7.1 Components of the Refrigeration System

ever-increasing capacity. Nevertheless, the refrigerator is still basically a big box with several major components.

The major components of a refrigerator are the following:

The compressor consists of a motor and pump sealed inside a steel case; it is concealed within the refrigerator structure. The pump compresses refrigerant vapor and sends it to the condenser.

The condenser is a long folded tube that receives hot, high-pressure refrigerant vapor pumped by the compressor. As the heat leaves, the vapor inside it cools and condenses back to a liquid. Condensers in many built-in refrigerators are located at the top of the appliance.

The capillary tube connects the condenser to the evaporator, metering the flow of liquid refrigerant to the evaporator.

The evaporator, also a long tube, receives liquid refrigerant from the condenser. The liquid boils and vaporizes as it picks up heat from inside the cabinet. In a side-by-side refrigerator, it may be found behind the rear wall of the freezer, whereas in a top-mount

(see Figure 7.2), it is usually found between the refrigerator and freezer.

Except for the horizontally shaped residential appliances manufactured by Penguin Products, today's refrigerators and refrigerator/freezers are still designed as vertical boxes. Their three basic configurations are referred to as top-mount, bottom-mount, and side-by-side.

In a *top-mount* refrigerator, the freezer compartment is above the refrigerator compartment, usually accessible by a separate door. This, the most popular configuration, is particularly efficient in terms of usable cubic footage. Top-mount refrigerators that use a single door for access to freezer and refrigerator lose energy efficiency because the refrigerator door must be kept open every time you need access to the freezer compartment. On the other hand, most such refrigerators have manual defrost, a process which, though time-consuming, consumes less energy than an automatic defrost system. Very few manual defrost models are manufactured now, and they are available only in smaller sizes of 15 cubic feet or less.

The drawing below gives an outline of the conveniences to look for, and the Ratings in Appendix C note how given models measured up. But a few individual niceties are worth noting here: A partial shelf in the tested *Amana* can be used to catch meat drippings or as a beverage-can dispenser. Part of a *Gibson* shelf can be used as a wine-bottle holder or a can dispenser. The lower doors of the *Amana* and *Caloric* are sculpted to hold beverage cans, a clever use of space that might otherwise go to waste.

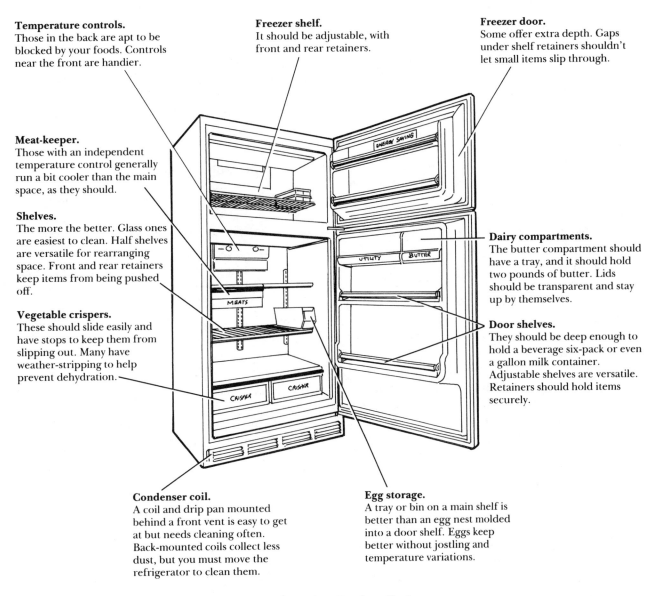

Temperature controls.
Those in the back are apt to be blocked by your foods. Controls near the front are handier.

Meat-keeper.
Those with an independent temperature control generally run a bit cooler than the main space, as they should.

Shelves.
The more the better. Glass ones are easiest to clean. Half shelves are versatile for rearranging space. Front and rear retainers keep items from being pushed off.

Vegetable crispers.
These should slide easily and have stops to keep them from slipping out. Many have weather-stripping to help prevent dehydration.

Freezer shelf.
It should be adjustable, with front and rear retainers.

Freezer door.
Some offer extra depth. Gaps under shelf retainers shouldn't let small items slip through.

Dairy compartments.
The butter compartment should have a tray, and it should hold two pounds of butter. Lids should be transparent and stay up by themselves.

Door shelves.
They should be deep enough to hold a beverage six-pack or even a gallon milk container. Adjustable shelves are versatile. Retainers should hold items securely.

Condenser coil.
A coil and drip pan mounted behind a front vent is easy to get at but needs cleaning often. Back-mounted coils collect less dust, but you must move the refrigerator to clean them.

Egg storage.
A tray or bin on a main shelf is better than an egg nest molded into a door shelf. Eggs keep better without jostling and temperature variations.

Figure 7.2   How Handy to Use?

In a *bottom-mount* refrigerator, the freezer compartment is below the refrigerator compartment. This configuration's chief benefit is that, particularly with the freezer's pull-out container, it is convenient for a seated cook. It also places cold food at eye level, so that a minimum of bending and stooping is required to retrieve it.

Like top-mount and side-by-side refrigerators, bottom-mount refrigerators are available as free-standing or built-in. The built-ins are usually 24 inches deep, and their motors are easily accessible on top of the appliance, although no periodic maintenance is required. The built-in can be faced with the same materials as the cabinetry or with stainless steel, plexiglass, or mirror as accents. It can also be ordered with an appliance finish.

In a *side-by-side* refrigerator, the freezer and refrigerator compartments run vertically, to the full height of the refrigerator, and are accessible by separate exterior doors. These refrigerators, and bottom-mounts, are generally available in larger capacities, 18 cubic feet and greater.

The chief drawback of the side-by-side refrigerators is that the freezer compartment may be too narrow to store the occasional 20-pound turkey. An advantage to the two doors is that they are narrower and thus need less space in front for doors to be opened, which is useful in a galley-shaped or small kitchen.

Whichever configuration suits you, be particularly aware of how your refrigerator's doors will open. Some models have reversible doors, so they can be fitted for either left-sided or right-sided opening.

Other important design elements to consider are cabinet material, hinges, shelving, interior insulation, and drawer material, as well as relative ease of moving.

For the refrigerator's interior, a material such as high-impact polystyrene or ABS plastic is used to prevent cracking and staining.

Polyurethane foam is currently a popular insulation material for the cabinet and doors because it takes up less space than fiberglass, which was used previously, and thus allows greater storage space within the same outside dimensions.

Hinges should be made of heavy plate steel or die-cast for proper door alignment. If the doors are not aligned, cold air can escape, cutting down on energy efficiency.

Those refrigerators at the top of their manufacturer's price lines tend to have glass shelves, which are easy to clean and don't interfere with air flow inside the refrigerator. Wire shelving can be as serviceable as glass, as long as the wiring is heavy and spaced close together for added strength and to keep small items from falling through. A white epoxy coating is easy to clean and resists corrosion.

Top-of-the-line refrigerators also tend to have see-through drawers and bins, made of polycarbonate. Rollers will help the drawers slide in and out more easily than plastic glides.

Because the refrigerator has to be moved from time to time to allow you to clean behind it, wide wheels make this task a bit easier. They should have locks to keep the refrigerator in place when it's in its ordinary setting and should also be adjustable, for leveling purposes.

Sizing the Refrigerator

To determine what size refrigerator you need, consider such variables as the size of your household, your cooking and entertaining habits, and whether you must store large quantities of fresh produce. The old rule of thumb was that two people needed a minimum of 12 cubic feet, plus an additional 2 cubic feet for every additional household member. That would mean a 16-cubic-foot refrigerator for a family of four.

But total cubic footage, like total square footage in a home, can be deceptive. Even the most efficient refrigerators have some unusable space, for which you must compensate in your calculations. The fact is, the American consumer shows no signs of giving up the notion that "bigger is better," which is why refrigerators of 25 to 27 cubic feet have grown popular.

On the other end of the spectrum, secondary, below-counter refrigerators and wine coolers that have a capacity of up to 6 cubic feet can provide some functional flexibility and additional food storage.

Width, depth, and height measurements vary widely, too. The size of the refrigerator will depend not only on your food storage needs but also on practical realities. The refrigerator has to fit through your entry door as well as through the entry to the kitchen. It cannot be so wide that it engulfs much of the available wall space in a modest-size kitchen. It cannot be so deep that it protrudes awkwardly (if not danger-ously) into the path of traffic.

Refrigerators generally range from 28 to 36 inches in width. Custom and built-in models can be as wide as 48 inches. Built-in refrigerators are generally 24 inches deep (except for door handles) so that they will be flush with cabinetry. More conventional refriger-ators can be as deep as 30 inches.

Energy Considerations

The initial cost or the appearance of a refrigerator should not be the sole determining factor in deciding which size, configuration, and model suits you best. The costs of yearly energy consumption, and of pos-sible repairs, are key factors as well. Refrigerators consume more energy than any other appliance in the kitchen. A more expensive refrigerator that con-sumes less energy over time than a comparably sized, lower-priced model should invite your consideration.

You should also be aware that opting for greater conveniences—such as larger size—sometimes translates into higher energy consumption. As tested by Consumers Union, built-in refrigerators used more energy than conventional refrigerators: almost 50 percent more, cubic foot for cubic foot.

The Federal Trade Commission administers the EnergyGuide labeling program, a useful tool in com-paring energy use of comparably sized refrigerators, refrigerator/freezers, and freezers. The yellow label, displayed on the front of the models in an appliance store, gives the *estimated annual operating cost* of that particular model. It also gives the estimated annual operating cost for the model in this size range that costs *least* to operate, as well as the model that costs the *most* to operate.

The calculations also are based on federal test pro-cedures, which call for a 38-degree refrigerator and a 5-degree freezer. CU's estimates, however, are based on a 37-degree refrigerator and a 0-degree freezer.

For another detailed energy cost comparison, you can contact the Association of Home Appliance Man-ufacturers, which annually publishes a "Consumer Selection Guide for Refrigerators and Freezers." It's available for $1.50. The guide lists all models by brand name, model number, total volume in cubic feet, and FTC energy cost. The energy cost is broken down into two components: one estimate is based on

the rate of 8.04 cents per kilowatt-hour; the second, on a more recent representative average of 7.7 cents per kWh established by the Department of Energy.

Freezers

You may want to consider supplementing the refrigerator with a separate freezer if you live far from the supermarket and other suppliers, or if you buy food in large quantities and have room in your basement, between the kitchen and the garage (assuming it is not an unhealthful area)—or even in the kitchen itself.

Freezers come in two configurations: as upright (vertical) units or as horizontal chests. Both have strengths and drawbacks. The upright freezer takes up less floor space but requires more aisle space to open its door. A chest takes up more floor space but requires no aisle space since the door opens on top.

Generally, chest freezer capacity ranges from 5 to 28 cubic feet, whereas the capacity for upright freez-ers ranges from 2.6 to 31.1 cubic feet. All chest freez-ers have manual defrost; some upright freezers feature automatic defrost systems. Chest freezers are less expensive to purchase and operate, and require less frequent defrosting than manual defrost uprights, but they are less convenient for some peo-ple to use. They require more bending and stooping to retrieve food than the vertical freezers do. And for the forgetful, food stored on the bottom is likely to be forgotten.

NOW YOU'RE COOKING: RANGES, COOKTOPS, AND OVENS

Flexibility in Cooking

Until a few years ago, our major cooking choices were fairly simple: whether to employ gas or electric-ity as a heat source; whether to choose a conventional oven or a combination oven-broiler; and whether to use a microwave. But in recent years, a virtual revo-lution has taken place in cooking appliances, surpass-ing the visions of the home economists—and the futurists—of our childhood. Self-cleaning ovens have been the major innovation during the past 20 years. At the same time, pricing has undergone sig-nificant changes, so that appliances tend to fall into the "basic" or "top-of-the-line" category, with the middle range gradually disappearing.

Major changes have taken place in surface cooking. Influenced by European design and technology, even American manufacturers have introduced a variety of sleek-looking cooktops. Serious cooks may have opted solely for gas heat in the past because its responsiveness gave a sense of control over the cooking element, but now electricity offers similar advantages in a number of ways.

Induction Cooking. The chief benefit of induction cooking is that while the food heats up, the cooking surface doesn't; it turns on and off instantly, and its flat glass-ceramic surface is easy to clean up. It's also energy efficient, because its consumption is based on the size of the pan, not the burner.

How does inductive cooking work? An electromagnetic field reacts with a magnetic pan, which heats the food. The catch is that, for the system to work, the pan must be ferromagnetic—iron, steel, or porcelain enameled-steel. If your pots won't attract a magnet, they won't work on an induction cooktop.

Halogen Cooking. The halogen cooking system also offers fine temperature control, has a smooth glass surface, and heats up and cools down quickly. It can accommodate any type of cookware.

Most elements contain a filament and two quartz-glass tubes filled with halogen gas. The cooktop surface sends heat from the bulbs to the pan. Largely because halogen is expensive, most halogen cooktops offer a combination of conventional concealed coils and a single halogen element.

Radiant Heat. Like induction and halogen cooktops, a radiant-heat cooktop has a smooth glass surface. Underneath it are electric resistance coils that transmit heat. The heating areas, which are delineated with decorative circular designs, glow red when they are turned on. This type of cooktop is not really new; its forerunners were introduced more than 20 years ago. But the technology has improved considerably: the new cooktops heat up faster, use less energy, and are easier to keep clean.

Solid Disk Burners. Also called "hobs," solid disk burners are flat surfaces made of cast iron or ceramic glass with the heating element underneath the surface. Although they heat up more slowly than halogen or induction cooktops, they retain their heat so that food can simmer even after you've turned the power off. Solid disk burners have sensors that protect against overheating or boilovers. The drawbacks of solid disk burners are that they don't work as well with very small or very large pots and pans. Some designers report that they fail to produce enough high-intensity heat for quick cooking, such as sautéing.

Conventional Exposed Electric Coils. Conventional exposed electric coils are the most inexpensive electric heating system. They conduct heat from the coils to the pots and pans. Although heating speed is good, the biggest drawback is that the drip bowls below the coils are not as easy to clean as the smooth-cooktop surfaces.

Gas Cooktops. The technology for gas cooking has not stood still while these advances in electric technology have taken place. Glass surfaces have been introduced, as has the pilotless ignition, which saves up to one-third of the energy used by an older cooktop with a pilot light. Sealed drip pans now keep food spills away from gas jets, also eliminating the need to lift the top of the cooktop to clean beneath it. Some manufacturers also have introduced an "automatic restart" feature that starts the burner again if the flame goes out during cooking.

Contemporary cooking flexibility involves more than the various types of heating systems. The trend is toward *modular* cooking elements that mix various types of systems in one appliance. Some cooktops, such as Frigidaire's Euroflair, can incorporate both gas and electric elements. Jenn-Air has developed a downdraft grill-range with a gas cooktop and an electric oven that offers conventional and convection heat. Modern Maid has pioneered a gas downdraft system.

Other manufacturers, including Gaggenau, Miele, and AEG/Andico, offer interchangeable elements such as grills, griddles, and deep fryers to enable you to cook in a variety of ways with a single appliance.

Downdraft ventilation is available for both electric and gas cooktops. At the high-cost end of the spectrum, cooktops may contain five or six burners instead of the conventional four.

The oven may have toppled from its earlier position as the most-used kitchen appliance and moved out of the primary "work path" of today's cooks, but its technology also has evolved over the past several years. Whether you opt for a single, double, or combination unit, you'll find increasing flexibility in oven cooking technology.

There are four basic categories in oven cooking:

The *conventional,* or *radiant,* mode, fueled by either gas or electricity, is the least expensive category. Heat radiates from a gas flame or an electrically heated element to the oven's sides and top.

The *convection* oven uses a fan to circulate heat evenly throughout the oven cavity. It cooks more rapidly than a conventional or radiant oven because the hot air is moved around much faster than the convectionally circulated air in a conventional oven. Besides saving time and energy consumption, convection ovens are claimed to brown meat and poultry while sealing in juices and require no special baking dishes. Food must be cooked uncovered, however, and it may take some time for you to "translate" conventional cooking times to suit the convection mode.

The *microwave* oven does not brown meat and poultry as well as conventional and convection ovens, but it offers several distinct cooking benefits. Microwaves cook quickly, generate very little heat, and are very easy to keep clean. In a microwave, high-frequency radio waves bombard food, activating the water molecules in it and creating the friction that heats and cooks it. The waves come from a magnetron, which is the "broadcasting station" within the oven.

The *CMT (convection microthermal)* oven is a standard-size, built-in unit that combines microwave functions with convection bake and broil functions. This flexibility allows you to combine cooking methods simultaneously or in sequence to prepare foods quickly. Although they are not as costly as commercial equipment, these ovens are far more expensive than conventional, conventional, or microwave ovens.

Armed with this basic explanation of the cooking technology choices available, you can now choose the appliances that are most suitable to your kitchen plan.

Gas and Electric Ranges

The free-standing all-in-one range consists of a cooktop, an oven, and a broiler. Its biggest advantage is that it's a space saver, a particular boon to apartment and townhouse dwellers because it frees counter and wall space. A range organizes the cooking center into a compact area, which can be very efficient as long as there is sufficient work space around it. It's also efficient for people who don't use ovens or broilers often.

A range's second major advantage is price. One of these units will cost less than purchasing a cooktop, a conventional oven, and/or a microwave and broiler separately. You'll save not only on the equipment but also on any gas or electric connections that might have to be installed to accommodate these separate components.

A range's very compactness can also be its biggest drawback, however. It would be awkward, for example, for one person to be sautéing vegetables while another is trying to use the oven to bake cookies. And for people who do use their ovens often, a range requires more bending and stooping than a wall oven does, which can be particularly difficult if you are handling a very heavy casserole dish or a roast.

Another disadvantage is that many electric range models place the controls along a back panel, which can be awkward if you have to reach over or between large pots and pans that already are cooking. Controls mounted along the front or side of the cooktop are preferable, although they may be safety hazards in homes with young children.

There are four types of ranges: freestanding, drop-in, slide-in, and high/low. The freestanding range, as the name implies, is finished on both sides. Although its appearance seems to imply that it can be situated at the end of a cabinet run, it shouldn't be, for this placement poses a serious safety hazard—you could easily knock over a hot pot as you pass by it in the aisle. Placing it between cabinets is safer.

Slide-in and drop-in ranges have unfinished sides and also fit between cabinets. The main difference between them is that the drop-in is set atop a low base, whereas the slide-in is set on the floor. A high/low is a 30-inch-wide range that incorporates a cooktop, a below-cooktop oven, and an eye-level oven.

Cooktops

If your kitchen is spacious enough and cooking is often a joint effort in your household, having a cooktop surface separate from other cooking appliances enables you to create separate cooking "stations."

Most cooktops are 30 to 36 inches wide, although smaller apartment-size versions and wider models are also available. Depths may be 18 to 22 inches, and most measure 2⅛ to 6 inches high, though most are less than 6 inches. The typical cooktop has four burners with controls in the center or side of the appliance. The larger and more costly cooktops have five or six burners.

The burners in some cooktops are staggered, while others have their burners lined up parallel to one another. A case can be made for either configuration. Staggered burners allow you to see what's cooking and work with back-burner pots and pans without having to reach over utensils on the front burners. On the other hand, a parallel configuration allows you to slide pots and pans easily from front to back without having to lift them. The choice, then, is a matter of personal preference.

Other cooktops have burners on either side, with a work space in the middle. Or a fifth burner—a griddle or a grill—can take up the space, with a removable work surface that can be set on top of it. Modular cooktops have interchangeable plug-in units such as grills, woks, and rotisseries.

Burners are generally 6, 8, or 9 inches in diameter, and many cooktops contain both larger and smaller-size burners.

Controls also are an important feature to consider. Electronic controls not only give a sleek appearance but are also easy to clean.

Gas appliances use either natural gas or liquefied petroleum (LP) gas. It's important to know which type your selected appliance will use, since equipment designed to use one kind of gas may not be convertible to the other. A gas line has to be professionally installed and must meet local codes. If you want a pilotless ignition, you will also need a 120-volt electric line.

Most electric cooktops need a special 208- or 240-volt line. Double ovens take a 50-amp circuit.

Whether you choose a gas or electric (or combination) appliance need not depend on energy considerations. Despite the fact that electric appliances cost more to operate than gas, the difference between the two over the life of the appliances is not great.

According to the most recent figures from the Department of Energy, an efficient gas range (pilot-less) will save $26 a year over an electric range, that is, $28 versus $54 for electric. Over an average product life of 19 years, that amounts to less than $500.

Cooktops are typically finished in porcelain enamel because it resists heat, acid, stains, scratches, yellowing, and fading. Side panels may be of baked enamel or electrostatically applied polyester, which resist chipping better than porcelain enamel. Porcelain drip bowls are easier to clean than metal. The sides of the cooktop may be trimmed in chrome, which protects the edges but is a dirt-catcher.

These surfaces are available in a variety of colors. Both black and white glass cooktops are gaining in popularity, however, as is stainless steel, which resists corrosion, dents, and stains.

Microwave Ovens

The "zapper" has found its way into about three-quarters of all U.S. households. That means more people own microwave ovens than own VCRs or food processors. Increasingly, people are purchasing their second microwave.

This ubiquitous appliance is not the answer for all cooking needs, of course. Its most glaring deficiency is that meats and poultry do not brown, a fact that some combination microwave/convection ovens address. Nor do pasta or cakes (other than mixes made expressly for microwaves) do well in the microwave. Simultaneously cooking an entire meal composed of several courses also presents difficulties.

Still, even for those who purchase the appliance on the assumption that they will use it primarily to defrost food quickly, to heat up leftovers, and to make single cups of coffee, the microwave can prove to be a versatile and invaluable tool. With midsize models now priced between $200 and $300, microwaves also represent good value vis-à-vis the frequency and variety of their use.

Like dishwashers, the newer top-of-the-line microwaves have many "bells and whistles" whose absolute necessity is questionable. For example, because food should be turned while it's cooking in the microwave, some ovens include a turntable for this purpose. Some ovens have a moisture sensor that determines when the food is cooked by gauging the moisture level in the oven as the food releases steam. Many ovens have auto-reheat and auto-defrost cycles.

How you use the microwave, or anticipate using it,

will determine where you place it and what size, configuration, and features will suit you best.

Microwave ovens come in compact, midsize, and full-size models. Be sure to check the insides of the oven before you choose one; usable space can differ even in comparably sized appliances. You can bring a plate, casserole dish, or container along with you to test for yourself the oven's size suitability.

The compact ovens generally contain .5 cubic feet of oven capacity and have 400 to 500 wattage. This version is suitable for a small household or one in which microwaving is limited to defrosting or reheating meals. Midsize ovens range up to 1 cubic foot in size and from 600 to 700 watts. Full-size models can range up to 1.5 cubic feet in size and up to 750 watts. The greater the wattage, the more powerful the oven, and therefore the quicker the cooking. Most microwave recipes are written with a midsize 600–700-watt appliance in mind.

Microwave ovens are available as countertop appliances, built-ins, and under-wall-cabinet models, incorporating a light and vent hood. They can also be installed in a custom-designed wall cabinet.

Safety. All the microwave ovens tested by *Consumer Reports* were well within the U.S. Bureau of Radiological Health's standard for microwave-radiation leakage. To keep leakage to a safe level, it's important to follow the manufacturer's instructions for maintenance of the oven's door seal.

Although a microwave is easy to operate and clean, it is not without inherent dangers. A microwave oven that's been dropped or that has suffered a fire or other serious overheating incident should not be used. It may have a warped or misaligned door and thus pose a hazard. The sensitive interlock on the oven door should keep an oven with a damaged door from operating, but the interlock may not always do the job. If any doubt exists about the safety status of the oven, have it checked by a qualified professional.

Other hazards should also be noted. Just because there is no "flame" doesn't mean that burns are not possible. And, considering that the microwave is used by so many children—it seems to be a "badge of honor" for children to operate these appliances at younger and younger ages—special safety precautions should be taught to help them avoid injuries.

Ideally, children should not operate these appliances without supervision. If that's not possible, however, here are some guidelines for safe operation:

- The Food and Drug Administration advises people to stand "an arm's length away" from the oven while it is operating; CU recommends 4 feet.
- Most containers should have an opening or a slit to allow steam to escape. When removing a lid, open it away from you so that steam is not aimed at you.
- Always use a potholder when removing containers from the oven. Even if the container isn't hot enough to burn you, the liquid or sauce in it can be.
- Don't assume that food is cooked to an even temperature throughout. It may be lukewarm in one spot but scalding in another.
- Don't warm baby bottles in the microwave oven. When they are shaken, their liners can explode over you and the baby. The contents also can be easily overheated.
- Don't turn the oven on if there's nothing in it.
- Don't place anything but food in the oven, even in jest. (That includes paper, clothing, a toy, or the proverbial household cat.) Nor should you use metal utensils or aluminum foil in the oven.
- To avoid food poisoning, make sure that poultry is cooked to an internal temperature of 180 degrees; pork should be cooked to 160 to 170 degrees.

Wall Ovens

Wall ovens may be placed outside the cook's primary work pattern, unless the oven(s) is to include a microwave or combination appliance that will be used relatively often. If you are an ardent baker, the oven(s) may be the focal point of a separate baking center, with sufficient storage and counter space located around it.

Whether you need one oven or two, or a conventional, convectional, microwave, or combination, depends largely on your household's needs. For example, unless you do a lot of cooking for a lot of people, a double oven plus an additional microwave may be excessive. On the other hand, it may be less costly to purchase a double oven and a microwave than it would be to purchase a double oven that combines microwave/radiant/convection modes, which can cost between $2,000 and $3,000.

Single ovens are generally 25 to 39 inches high, 23 to 27 inches wide, and 23 to 28½ inches deep. Double ovens are generally 44 to 56 inches high, 24 to 27 inches wide, and 23 to 28 inches deep.

Ovens are fueled by gas or electricity. If the gas oven has a pilotless ignition, a clock, or electronic controls, it will require a 120-volt electric line in addition to a separate gas line.

Basic (no-frills) ovens require manual cleaning. Many wall ovens on the market now, however, are "continuous-cleaning" or self-cleaning. In a continuous-clean oven, ingredients in the interior surface oxidize food stains when the oven is operating. Some cooks and designers dislike the continuous-cleaning feature because they find it doesn't clean effectively and also makes for difficulty in cleaning the oven manually.

Self-cleaning ovens have a special high-heat cycle that reduces food bits to a white ash that can be wiped away. The newer self-cleaning ovens have improved insulation and an air flow system, so they are more efficient than their earlier counterparts. The self-cleaning feature was limited to wall and gas and electric freestanding ovens until Modern Maid introduced its gas self-cleaning wall oven in 1988.

Self-cleaning, as might be expected, adds to the cost of the oven, as do such special features as programmable controls, automatic temperature probes, door windows, digital clocks, removable doors, and rotisseries. White glass doors and controls are more expensive than black.

THE CLEANUP CENTER: DISHWASHERS, GARBAGE DISPOSERS, AND TRASH COMPACTORS

Dishwashers

The dishwasher represents a good opportunity to limit your expenses without compromising function and quality because, as Consumers Union found, you can get very good washing, comparable to top-rated, without buying top-of-the-line. CU thinks you need only two or three cycles—Normal, Heavy, and perhaps Light—to handle all the loads you can reasonably expect a machine to wash.

Design elements. The functional heart of the dishwasher is the wash system. It consists of arms that rotate like lawn sprinklers to shower the dishes, a pump to circulate water through the arms and eventually down the drain, and often filters to snag floating bits of food. Basic dishwashers have one wash arm, whereas higher-priced models have two, three, or four.

Dishwashers can be built-in or portable. Both are powered by electricity. A built-in is 24 inches wide and fits under a countertop. (If you have back problems or use a wheelchair, the dishwasher can be set on a platform so that it will be above counter level.) It is wired into a 120-volt electric line and attached to a hot-water supply pipe and a drain.

The portable dishwasher is usually 24 inches wide, although 18-inch models are available, and is not attached to the hot-water pipe and drain. Instead, its power cord is plugged into an electric outlet, with hoses linking the dishwasher to the sink's hot-water faucet and sink drain.

All dishwashers contain two pull-out racks of plastic-coated wire and a flatware basket or two. The higher-priced dishwashers have especially handy racks—sometimes an adjustable upper rack that can be set higher to provide extra clearance for oversize dishes below or set lower so that tall glasses can be fitted in.

The dishwasher should be constructed to resist internal scratches and chips that expose underlying metal to corrosion. (Stainless steel can be dented but is judged most durable of all materials. Porcelain-coated steel resists abrasion better than solid plastic but can be chipped. Plastic can withstand substantial impact without damage.) All the plastic-tub models tested by CU, as well as many with porcelain tubs, feature a plastic panel for the door's inner surface. That's a good material for an area otherwise likely to be damaged by dropped items.

Since the din of an operating appliance can make the kitchen an unpleasant environment, noise control is a big factor in choosing a dishwasher. Most machines are wrapped with a layer of fiberglass or felt insulation to muffle the sound.

Controls and Cycles: The "Bells and Whistles." Like many other major appliances, dishwashers are beginning to sport snazzy electronic control panels. Some provide a digital countdown and present an illuminated message to show the cycle you've selected and the phase of operation that the machine is in. This feature may or may not be an advantage. In some models, it provides little in the way of amenities that can't be matched by mechanical controls. Further, electronic controls can lose their memories if the dishwasher is running when a power outage occurs. Some "systems monitors" are useful, however.

Some machines can be set for an automatic start several hours later. This feature can come in handy if your household is chronically short of hot water or if your utility company offers lower rates during off-peak hours. You shouldn't use this feature to run the washer while you're away from your home, however.

Dishwasher cycles are basically a combination of washes and rinses. Although names like Pot Scrubber, Sani-cycle, and China/Crystal may lead you to think the machine can handle practically anything, that isn't quite true.

A typical Normal cycle includes two washes and two or three rinses. Then the heating element in the bottom of the cabinet dries the dishes, unless you switch it off to save energy. Other cycles are all created from these basics.

To make a Heavy or Pots and Pans cycle, a manufacturer might extend the wash periods, add a third wash, make the water hotter, or combine those factors. A Light cycle typically has only one wash. Water in a China/Crystal cycle may be pumped through the wash arms with reduced force. A Sani-cycle may use extra-hot water for the final rinse. But "sanitized" doesn't mean "sterilized, " and even if dishes actually were sterile when they came out of the dishwasher, they'd quickly pick up household microbes again when they're stored.

To increase the number of cycles, a manufacturer may include a couple of optional phases or count each cycle more than once. Or a part of an existing cycle can be renamed as a separate cycle. If a machine runs through its first wash cycle and then drains and stops, you have a Rinse-and-Hold cycle.

Except for Rinse and Hold, a cycle that might have some use for small families that accumulate dishes slowly, CU doesn't think that most other extra cycles add much to a washer's utility. Pots and pans are not apt to emerge cleaner from a Heavy cycle than they would from a Normal cycle, and you may not want to risk good crystal and china, especially pieces with gold trim, in a cycle that might subject them to jostling and harsh detergents.

Energy Considerations. Dishwashers consume energy in two ways. The biggest cost is incurred by the water heater. The higher the water heater's temperature setting, the more it costs to heat a tankful of water and keep it hot. Even so, conservation does not necessarily translate into major monetary savings. At national average utility rates, a change from 140 to 120 degrees can save you about $32 a year with an electric water heater and about $11 with gas.

Dishwashers need 140-degree water to liquefy some fatty soil and dissolve detergent fully. If the water isn't hot enough, the machine boosts the water temperature and often runs longer, at least for one wash period. On many models, you set a control to provide that boost. Others provide the boost as part of the regular cycle. The most sophisticated models are controlled with a thermostat and heat the water only when needed.

The secondary energy cost is electricity. Running the machines CU tested takes roughly 0.6 to 1.1 kilowatt-hours of electricity per cycle—about 5 to 9 cents at an electricity rate of 8 cents per kilowatt-hour, or less than $32 per year. Letting the dishes air-dry won't save much—about a penny or two a load, or less than $8 a year.

Like all refrigerators, refrigerator/freezers, and freezers, dishwashers are required to carry an EnergyGuide label that shows their estimated annual operating costs, as well as the lowest- and highest-operating costs for similar models in their size range.

Garbage Disposers

Knowing that recycling and conservation have become buzzwords of the 90s, manufacturers are promoting garbage disposers as a new-age method of being kinder to planet Earth. In fact, these appliances have been available for quite some time. Precisely how much they can help the cause of environmental protection is still arguable. Consumers Union has not studied this issue. Garbage disposers pulverize and liquefy food waste and then discharge it through the home's drain lines to the sewage system or to the home's private septic system.

Manufacturers claim that this process drastically

cuts down the amount of food waste that winds up in our nation's landfills; hence the environmental benefit claimed. On the other hand, food waste can be composted at home, and even if it isn't, it will biodegrade once it reaches landfill.

Whether or not to purchase a garbage disposer, then, may depend more on habit and taste than on environmental benefit. If you are accustomed to using a garbage disposer and have come to rely on it for waste management, you'll probably find it a necessary feature in your kitchen. On the other hand, if you have lived happily without one, you can certainly continue to do so.

If you are considering a garbage disposer, find out if your local building code includes any specifications that might affect your decision. Some communities have banned disposers; others allow them; and still others mandate them. If you live in an apartment, you'll want to determine whether the building's drains are sufficient to withstand disposer use or whether there might be back-up problems.

Of the two types of disposers, the most popular for residential use is the *continuous feed,* which is operated by a wall switch. You can load the continuous feed disposer as it runs.

The second type is the *batch feed,* which must be loaded in advance and only then turned on by rotating the skin stopper. The batch feed can handle approximately 1 quart of waste at a time. Both types operate on standard household current, powered by an electric motor. They are wired into a 120-volt grounded outlet. For safety reasons, batch feed disposers are recommended for families with small children.

Considering what a relatively small appliance a garbage disposer is, the models vary greatly in price and features. Prices may range from less than $75 to more than $300 (not including installation), and strength from ⅓-horsepower to 1-horsepower. The more powerful (and not coincidentally, more expensive) disposers grind up food more quickly, pose less of a chance of jamming, and tend to be better insulated, resulting in quieter operation. The disposal's interior grind chamber may be made of plastic or stainless steel.

No matter how powerful the appliance is, however, there are several items that it won't handle, and others that it won't handle well, such as clam and oyster shells and corn husks or other fibrous material—celery, for example.

Nonfood items, such as aluminum foil, bottle caps, or tin can covers, should never be put through disposers.

Manufacturers advise homeowners with their own septic systems that a home equipped with a disposer, an automatic washer, or a dishwasher should have a tank that is 40 percent larger than a home without these appliances—that is, a 700-gallon tank as opposed to a 500-gallon tank. The field should be larger, too.

Most disposers fit the standard 3½- or 4-inch drain outlets of kitchen sinks, although the sink trap will have to be altered to fit the appliance. The dishwasher drain hose should be attached to the disposer drain fitting on the disposer's side. Your contractor or plumber should be certain to check local code requirements before installation.

Trash Compactors

Environmental protection is also one of the rallying cries of trash compactor manufacturers. After all, they say, when you can compress garbage to approximately one-quarter its original volume, it's a boon to our garbage-laden landfills.

Trash compacting can be a convenient way to handle the prodigious amount of nonfood garbage generated by a busy and active household. Since some municipalities may charge by the number of cans emptied, having fewer bags of garbage to be picked up could save you money. Compactors range in price from $400 to $600.

Certain caveats should be kept in mind, however. First, you must trade off the convenience of fewer trips to the outdoor garbage cans (or the trash chute in an apartment building) for the burden of hauling heavyweight bags. A standard 15-inch-wide compactor produces a 25-pound bag, and an 18-inch-compactor produces a 40- to 50-pound bag. If you have a bad back or other physical limitations, the prospect of hauling these bags even a short distance is not a happy one.

Second, unless you are seriously committed to using the equipment properly, problems can arise. To work well, trash compactors must be used frequently. Even though some compactors have an automatic spray-deodorant dispenser, material that is left sitting for several days can begin to smell and attract bugs. Be aware, too, that some communities now mandate recycling of these items.

Like disposers, compactors plug into a standard household current. Their ½- to ¾-horsepower motors drive the ram that compacts the trash. You load the trash from the top of the appliance into a special plastic-lined bag. Compactors usually pull out from beneath the counter, but doors can also be hinged on the left or right side of the appliance.

Handy features to look for include a foot-pedal opener, which frees your hands for other tasks; a key lock to prevent children from playing with the appliance; a safety switch to prevent accidental use when the door is open or the container is out; and a light signal that indicates whether the appliance is working or may be jammed.

BASICS OF APPLIANCE INSTALLATION

Appliances are hooked up either by direct feed (a cable that is wired directly into the appliance) or by plugging a power cord into an outlet. Many European appliances are the direct-feed type, the drawback of which is that the appliance is much more difficult to disconnect than a plug-in. If this is an issue, discuss with your electrician the possibility of converting the direct feed of an electric range into a plug-in.

Dishwashers and ranges must be level. Many come with their own leveling legs to compensate for less-than-level floors. The front of refrigerators should be raised so that the door closes automatically if the door is opened about halfway.

Electric ranges must be powered by an individual 120-/240-volt, 50-amp circuit. If it is not directly wired, the appliances' power cord must have 50-amp plugs and attach to 50-amp outlets.

Make sure your electrical system can accommodate the new appliances. Whereas most homes average 100 to 150 amps, some older apartments may have as few as 20 to 60 amps and some areas, such as New York City, have 208-volt lines. (This applies to electric appliances only.) The difference in appliance performance won't be great; if a dish must be baked for an

hour at 350 degrees in a conventional oven, it may need to be baked about 5 minutes more if you have a 208-volt line. If your area has a 208-volt line, check with your electrician regarding the use of adaptable transformers from manufacturers.

Gas ranges can generally be relocated up to 6 feet from the old gas connection. If you need a new gas line, it should be installed by a licensed plumber, one who is familiar with your local building codes.

Drop-in cooktops are installed in the same way as a sink, anchored with the manufacturer's hardware from below. The power connection may be to one side of the unit or in the cabinet below the cooktop.

Wall ovens slide into place, resting atop support shelves and attached to the wall cabinet through the sides or on the front.

Microwave ovens are relatively simple to install. They operate on 120 volts and should have their own electric circuit, since they can use as much as half of a circuit's amperage.

Installing a garbage compactor is also relatively simple. After carefully positioning it in place, it should be leveled by shimming or adjusting any built-in legs. Then it can be plugged into a 120-volt, 20-amp grounded outlet.

If you are considering installing a compactor or disposer in the future, you should have the rough electrical work done now. You cannot rewire for them after the kitchen is finished. These appliances also should be on their own circuits, if possible.

PROBLEM SOLVING

What happens if, after installation, the oven doesn't work, ice cream melts in the refrigerator's freezer compartment, or the dishwasher leaks? If the appliance is under warranty, the manufacturer must send a service person to check it. You should also apprise your dealer or distributor of the problem. If these steps do not resolve the problem, contact the manufacturer directly. If the manufacturer then claims that the product is not at fault, your next line of defense is the Major Appliance Consumer Action Panel of the Association of Home Appliance Manufacturers.

Disputes can be resolved in one of two ways. First, armed with the documentation you provide, staff members will try to get the manufacturer to reconsider the issue. If no resolution is achieved, the association's next step is to present your complaint to an impartial panel of unpaid outside experts, who are not affiliated with the appliance industry. If this panel decides the matter in your favor, they'll make that recommendation to the manufacturer. The recommendation is nonbinding, however.

THE PROFESSIONAL KITCHEN

Some people are drawn to commercial kitchen equipment the way others are drawn to exotic automobiles. It may be an equally irrational impulse; you generally have no more serious *need* for a mega-BTU, $8,000 range than you need a car that can speed up to 180 miles per hour.

Without question, commercial or commercial-type equipment can be a boon for people who do a lot of high-volume cooking: those who do extensive entertaining, or who must feed a large family, for example. These ranges are larger, heavier, more powerful, and burn hotter than residential appliances. For the serious cook, that translates into the ability to sauté, flambé, boil, or otherwise manage surface cooking more quickly than with a conventional appliance. Commercial ovens heat by convection, which is also quicker than a conventional oven.

Using this type of equipment also presents drawbacks, however, and the necessity for extra safety precautions. If you're adamant about wanting a professional-style kitchen, here are the important issues to consider:

Be aware of the differences between commercial ranges and modified commercial ranges. In the past few years, such manufacturers as Garland, Viking, Wolf, and Thermador have introduced a number of ranges that have the size, output, and appearance of a commercial range, but with adaptations that make them more suitable for residential use. Other European manufacturers such as La Cornue and AGA specialize in commercial-style equipment that can be installed in a home kitchen.

The key differences between commercial and modified commercial appliances center on the issue of safety. For example, the American Gas Association, which certifies natural gas appliances for compliance with national safety standards, certifies professional-type ranges for residential use but does not do so for strictly commercial ranges.

Modified ranges are insulated; commercial ranges are not. Modified ranges have "child-proof" knobs that have to be pushed in and turned in order to be activated, whereas commercial ranges do not. Modified ranges have "zero clearance," which means that they can be placed next to walls and cabinets without the 6-inch clearance or the fireproof materials required for commercial ranges. Modified ranges require vent hoods, but not the sprinkler systems that owners of commercial ranges must install for fire safety. Some modified ranges also have pilotless ignition and built-in broilers, which commercial ranges do not.

A commercial range may also require fireproofing, such as stainless steel, tile, stone, or brick, on the walls and surfaces that surround it. Before considering any installation, you must learn what your local codes allow. A commercial range may be governed by commercial building regulations, which can be prohibitively costly to comply with. If no code applies, your contractor should follow the manufacturer's recommendations. Consider putting fiberglass insulation between the range and the adjacent cabinets for additional protection.

Warranties also vary between commercial and modified or commercial-type equipment. Be aware that the warranty on a commercial range *will not apply* for residential use.

Design Features of Professional Ranges

Despite their differences, commercial and modified commercial ranges do have more in common with each other than they have with strictly residential appliances.

Size. Professional equipment takes up considerable space in your kitchen. Ranges can vary in size from 2½ to 5 feet wide, 3 to 5 feet high, and 2½ to 3 feet deep.

Cooking Elements. Professional ranges have four to 12 burners, plus a single or double oven (possibly with built-in broiler); options may include a griddle (also used for warming) and a grill. Some models, such as the Garland commercial-style ranges, have their own built-in stainless steel backsplash.

Construction. Made of extremely durable materials, professional equipment is generally composed of cast iron or steel. Their construction makes these appliances extremely heavy, however; a standard residential range may weigh 200 pounds, but a professional range can weigh 800 pounds or more. Your flooring may need to be reinforced to accommodate it, and if you live in an apartment, the weight may be such that you may not be able to install it at all. Be sure to check with your building management.

Energy Considerations. The fuel requirements for a professional-style range are far greater than they are for a standard residential appliance. (The four-oven AGA, for example, which is never turned off, requires 17 hundred cubic feet [CCF] of natural gas or 18 gallons of LP gas per week.) It's important, then, to check with your utility company to estimate the cost of operating one of these ranges. You may also need to install a larger gas supply line than the one you have now.

Ventilation Requirements. Commercial and commercial-style equipment needs far more ventilation to remove heat, odors, grease, and moisture than do residential models. Codes vary from community to community, but the National Kitchen and Bath Association recommends these basics:

- The hood should be 6 inches wider than the stove, while its bottom edge should be 66 to 69 inches from the floor. Minimum depth of the hood should be 27 inches plus the distance from the wall to the back of the stove.
- 900 cubic feet per minute (CFMs) should be planned for every four burners. Griddles and barbecues require the same amounts. If they are combined in the same stove, two sets of blowers are needed: one over each unit, or for each 30 inches of hood length, use 900 CFMs of free air.

As mentioned, ventilation for a commercial range should have a sprinkler system built in. Commercial-style equipment does not need it.

BTU Output. A top-of-the-line residential cooktop may produce 10,000 to 12,000 BTUs per burner, but a professional range produces 15,000 to 22,000 BTUs per burner, and 18,000 to 30,000 BTUs per oven. The high heat is excellent for certain types of cooking, such as frying and sautéing, but the cook may find it difficult to control the flame to a low simmer, or to heat up small portions. (The AGA cooker addresses this issue by including two surface cooking disks: one set for simmering, the other for boiling. Each cooking disk can accommodate as many as three pots and pans at a time.)

Special Considerations. Because of the high heat output of a professional range, you'll find it best to use professional-style pots and pans, which are heavier and better equipped to stand the heat than conventional utensils. Maintenance is an issue, too. Some ranges include self-cleaning ovens; most don't. Professional cooktops generally can't be lifted up for cleaning, although the Garland has removable modular rangetop sections and slide-out drip and crumb trays.

Cost. At the lower end of the cost spectrum, you can find a relatively small range for approximately $3,000. Prices vary widely at the upper end—from $5,500 to $8,000, and more for the customized, imported models.

You also should anticipate the cost of having the range cleaned. Because of grease buildup, you'll need to have the assistance of a commercial servicing company. Cleaning should be done at least once every few years, unless your cooking habits require it more often.

Commercial Refrigerators

If you want to continue the professional look in your kitchen, you can also opt for commercial-style refrigerators (as well as freezers and wine coolers). Such refrigerators are made of stainless steel, and many feature glass panels so that you can see the food stored inside without opening the door. Aside from the cost, the key issue is aesthetic. Will such a refrigerator fit into the style of your kitchen?

Unlike commercial ranges, these refrigerators are not as deep as their standard residential counterparts. Measuring 24 inches deep, the same depth as standard base cabinets, they impart a built-in appearance to the kitchen as a whole.

The primary differences between commercial refrigerators and standard models is that their compressors are more powerful, as are their temperature and humidity controls. They are also much noisier, but you can have the motor placed in a remote location, such as a basement, to avoid the noise in the kitchen. This is a more expensive type of installation, but it makes the refrigerator easier to service.

Traulsen, which manufactures both commercial and the Ultra line of modified commercial refrigerators, recommends the latter for residential use. If you plan to buy one of the commercial or modified commercial models, be sure that the refrigerator has enough clearance to enter your home or apartment, and, if necessary, to fit into an elevator. These appliances cannot be dismantled. They have no special power requirements but should be on their own circuit. Prices are steep, ranging from about $5,500 to close to $9,000.

CFCs in Refrigeration:
On Their Way Out

Two types of of chlorofluorocarbons (CFCs) are used in a refrigerator: CFC-11 is used in making foam insulation, and CFC-12 is used in the coolant. CFCs eat away at the Earth's protective ozone shield, and for that reason the Clean Air Act of 1990 calls for production of CFCs to cease by the end of the century. Appliance manufacturers and chemical companies are currently working on developing replacements for CFCs.

Short of waiting until the turn of the century to buy a new refrigerator, what can you do to strike a small blow for the environment? Choose an energy-efficient model, and keep it working well by cleaning the coils regularly and checking the door seals. Dirty coils and leaky seals force the unit's cooling system to work harder. Keep the freezer compartment reasonably well filled to reduce the amount of warm air brought in each time the door is opened.

8

The Water Works:
Sinks, Faucets, and
Water Purification Systems

Starting with the basic plumbing system, your kitchen's water plan must be designed so that you'll have water available for food preparation, cleanup, and drinking at the most useful temperature and water pressure level. The design must also ensure that in addition to *delivering* water to you for various uses, it can *remove* water and waste quickly and safely.

Because of our growing national concern about water quality and conservation issues, the design may also include a system for removing chemicals and other contaminants, toxic and otherwise, as well as conserving the amount of water used in the course of the average day. And of course the visible aspects of these systems must fit into the rest of your design.

PLUMBING SYSTEM BASICS

Think of the plumbing system as your home's circulatory system, with the piping for supplying and removing water and waste as the system's veins and arteries. Your water source may be a public water main or a well on your own property.

The most common plumbing problems that may need to be addressed when you remodel your kitchen include the following:

- It takes too long for hot water to reach the tap at your kitchen sink. The problem may be due to long and/or inefficient piping runs, low water pressure, or poorly insulated pipe. Solutions can include installing a separate hot-water heater, adding a recirculating line between the sink in question and the hot-water tank, or installing an in-line water heater.
- The hot-water tank is too small. The proper size depends on the size of your household, your water-use habits, and the requirements of different appliances (the dishwasher, ice maker, washing machine, and so forth). Recovery time is important if your have periods of high demand.
- The water pressure is too low. Recommended water pressure ranges from 45 to

60 pounds per square inch. Problems arise from residue buildup in the pipes, which cuts down the flow in the home's "circulatory system"; from the excessive length, angles, and turns of piping runs; and from the inappropriate sizing of the diameter of a supply pipe. (Generally, a 1-inch-diameter pipe is sufficient to supply three fixtures.)

The *supply* system consists of a water service entrance, where the main supply line divides into two, with one line for cold water and the other for hot, to be heated by the water heater. The pipes rise vertically through the floor or wall to reach the sink(s), dishwasher, hot-water dispenser, and ice maker (if any). If the water is to be softened or filtered, it will pass through these additional systems before reaching the water heater or the faucets.

If you're adding new fixtures, rearranging the layout of your existing fixtures, or seeking to correct problems you may have had with insufficient pressure, or improper temperatures, then new plumbing will have to be installed.

How efficient the water-supply system is depends largely on the piping system. If the pipes have a long, circuitous route from the water source to your faucet, efficiency will suffer; the water flow will lack force, and it may seem to take an inordinately long time to heat up. Efficiency also requires that the fixtures and appliances that use water should be grouped as closely as possible.

Your local building code, of course, will dictate the general size and materials of the supply piping that can be installed. If yours is an older home, the current piping is likely to be of cast iron or steel connected by threaded fittings, or copper joined with soldered fittings. Adapter fittings are available so that you can use plastic piping as a replacement to existing piping, assuming that it is permitted in your area.

The *removal* system is more complicated than the supply system. Known as the drain, waste, and vent (DWV) system, it consists of piping that takes waste water and solid wastes to the sewer line or, if you have a septic tank, to a leaching field.

Your home has a main "soil stack" that is the pri-

mary drainpipe. This stack also vents gases through its upper end, which extends through the roof. All your home's plumbing fixtures have drainpipes that lead to the soil stack, either directly or through "branch" drains. If the branch drains for your fixtures and appliances are distant from the main stack, you may need a secondary vent stack.

The DWV system is governed by extensive code requirements. Your local code will determine where and how a new drainpipe or branch drain can tie into the main stack, for example. It will also spell out the size of the piping, and the distance allowable from the traps to the main or secondary stack.

Like supply pipes, many DWV systems in older homes are made of cast iron. Although plastic piping is not allowed in certain areas, its chief advantage is that it is a lighter material and therefore easier to install. Another advantage is that no lead, rust, or corrosion will build up with plastic piping.

If you live in an apartment building, where there may be multiple main lines, you can still move plumbing lines around. Main sink drains are usually located 14 inches above the floor. It's safer to install piping close to the drain line as opposed to across the room because the building itself may have water backup problems. The piping *can* be installed across the room, however, as long as it is pitched to the drain. If you are planning to move piping across the room, be sure there is enough room under the finish floor to bury the piping and maintain the proper pitch; if there isn't, the floor will have to be raised.

WATER QUALITY ISSUES

Remodeling a kitchen is a good time to think about the quality of your water. Reports of toxic waste leaching into a community's water system are by now a staple of the evening news. What makes the water pollution problem especially insidious is that health-threatening contaminants are often colorless, tasteless, and odorless, and therefore almost impossible to detect; as a result, their damaging effects accumulate over a long period.

The U.S. Environmental Protection Agency has identified maximum acceptable contaminant levels (MCL) for many different kinds of contaminants, starting with its Safe Drinking Water Act (SDWA) of

1974, since revised. But even if the water in your community meets these standards, there are several important issues to consider:

- The EPA standards apply to water at its point of origin—that is, the pumping station of your water company. Water can pick up such contaminants—especially asbestos, mercury, and lead (which might come from your own pipes or from solder)—between the time it leaves the station and it runs out of your tap.
- The EPA does not monitor water from private, underground wells, which provide water for an estimated 20 million people in the United States.
- The standards are deemed acceptable for most people. If your household contains young children or pregnant women, the minimum lead standards, for example, may not suffice.

Some Primary Water Contaminants

Virtually hundreds of contaminants have been identified in the drinking water in the United States. The Environmental Protection Agency has not developed standards for all of them. Nor can it easily monitor our water supply, which includes not only 60,000 public water systems but also millions of private wells for which the EPA has no responsibility.

Whatever your concerns, finding out about the safety of your own water can be done by you. If you are having your water tested, these are among the common contaminants to be aware of:

NITRATES

Coliform bacteria. These are present in human and animal feces. If your well water has coliform, it may require disinfection.

Nitrates, nitrites. These substances, which leach into the ground water, are found particularly where agricultural or waste disposal takes place. Nitrates may be converted to nitrite in the gut and thence to carcinogenic nitrosamines.

Excess fluoride. According to the EPA, the maximum acceptable amount in drinking water is 4.0 milligrams per liter. Since fluoride is helpful for preventing tooth decay, it is often added at the level of 1.0 milligrams/liter to public water supplies.

TRACE METALS

Arsenic. This metal, which occurs naturally in some water, has been used in herbicides and pesticides.

Barium. No more than 1 milligram per liter is acceptable, according to the EPA.

Lead. This is a most dangerous contaminant, and its cumulative effects are particularly hazardous to health. If the level of lead in your water is greater than 20 micrograms/liter, you should takes steps to lower it. Old pipes and solder may contain lead; new pipes and solder must be lead-free, at least since 1986. Some brass fixtures contain up to 8 percent lead.

Mercury. Industrial and agricultural waste have contributed to the problem of mercury in our drinking water.

ORGANIC CHEMICALS

Pesticides, herbicides. These toxic agents are found in agricultural runoff into rivers. If you have a well, use this rule of thumb: Don't put persistent chemicals into your own garden that you wouldn't want to find some day in your drinking water.

Radon gas. This substance occurs naturally. Dissolved radon gas is a by-product of radium decay. Radon-contaminated water is found in ground water, such as in water wells of small homes. Drinking radon-contaminated water is not considered to be a health hazard by the EPA, but the radon that escapes from water used in showers and washing machines is a respiratory hazard.

Volatile organic chemicals (VOCs). These include compounds that are carbon-based, and may contain chlorine- or bromine-based elements (among others). Benzene, for example, is a VOC. Trihalomethanes are another type of VOC; this group includes chloroform, created when chlorine mixes with vegetable matter in the water disinfection process.

WATER PURIFICATION SYSTEMS

Fortunately, you can exercise some control over your home's water quality. There is a plethora of water filtration systems on the market, designed to treat a variety of problems. The available equipment ranges in price from under $100 to more than $2,000.

Home water purification systems are divided into

two categories: *point of entry (POE),* which treats water when it enters the house and is often referred to as a "whole house" system; and *point of use (POU),* which treats water for only one or two faucets. The point-of-use systems are the less expensive and are generally smaller, but they may remove just as many contaminants as the point-of-entry systems, depending on the design. No individual system is fully efficient or removes all contaminants under all conditions; all the systems have potential drawbacks, as outlined in what follows.

Which system is appropriate for your home? The first step is to have your water tested. Contact your local health department or water company to see whether they can provide you with basic information on water quality, such as local municipal test results for coliform bacteria. The size of the water utility determines how many tests the EPA requires. If they cannot or if you have your own well water, find an independent laboratory to test the water. You can get a list of qualified labs from your state's health department or from the Water Quality Association.

The basic components which domestic water is usually tested for are coliform bacteria, nitrates, organic contaminants, iron, pH, and water hardness (a condition which is found in 85 percent of all homes in the United States, according to the U.S. Geological Survey). *Hardness* refers to the amount of calcium and magnesium in the water and is measured in grains per gallon (gpg) or in parts per million (1 gpg equals 17.1 ppm). Moderately hard water has 3.5 to 7 grains per gallon, whereas hard water has 7 to 10.5 grains per gallon, and very hard water has more than 10.5 grains per gallon.

Hard water causes all kinds of mischief in your home. Mineral deposits can form in your appliances and build up in your pipes and plumbing equipment. They can also form an insulation barrier on the heating elements in your water heater and thus require you to spend more on heating the same amount of water.

Aesthetically, hard water can be a problem as well. The residue formed by soap and hard water leaves a "film" on tubs, tiles, backsplashes, and dishes.

The EPA has set maximum contaminant levels for organic and inorganic water pollutants. Some of the tests are for secondary contaminants, which may not pose the hazards to your health that the primary contaminants do but nonetheless can make your water aesthetically unappealing. If your water smells bad, looks cloudy, tastes awful, and/or discolors fixtures, secondary contaminants may be at fault.

Choosing an Appropriate System

Once you have the laboratory test results (which may or may not include recommendations for treating your water), the next step is to determine what types of equipment you need. The solution may include a combination of filtering equipment.

Clouding the water purification issue are unscrupulous individuals in the business who use scare tactics, make unsubstantiated claims, and oversell the need for their equipment. The best way to avoid being taken is to seek help from reputable companies. Check their qualifications in the same way as you would for a general contractor. You can also contact the National Sanitation Foundation, which certifies products by test and provides a list of the types of contaminants removable by different types of equipment.

The National Sanitation Foundation's membership consists of scientists, engineers, technicians, and public health/environmental analysts. Its mark on a piece of equipment indicates that it has been evaluated, the manufacturer's claims have been verified, and the product meets the foundation's standards. Although products are rated for capacity, they are not ranked in order of overall quality.

Water purification systems can be installed by a dealer who represents a manufacturer or by your contractor. If you are handy, you can install a point-of-use system yourself. (In addition to testing equipment, the Water Quality Association certifies installers and provides lists of them on request. This association's membership consists of manufacturers, dealers, and installers.) A whole-house system can be a more complex job than a point-of-use system and may have to be installed by a professional. Unless the equipment is specifically designed to disinfect water (chlorine, ozone), home water treatment devices are intended for use only on microbiologically safe water.

Here are the most common types of equipment:

Activated Carbon Filtration. This process uses an adsorbent material, usually in granular or solid block form, and capable of entrapping gases.

Liquids and/or suspended matter adhere on its surface and in its exposed pores. Carbon filters are good for removing organic materials, including those that cause poor taste and odors. Their drawback is that they can harbor bacterial growth on the filter if you don't change it regularly.

Cation Exchange Softening. This system softens hard water by removing calcium and magnesium ions, as they pass through a resin bed, in exchange for sodium ions. It is also good for removing iron, manganese, barium, and naturally occurring radium. Its potential drawback is that because it adds sodium to the water, the water may be inadvisable for some hypertensive people to drink.

Distillation. In this process, water is converted into vapor by heating, then cooled and condensed to liquid, and finally collected in a sequence that removes nearly all suspended and dissolved matter from the water. Distillation is good for removing inorganic materials: arsenic, barium, fluoride, lead, mercury, nitrates, and metallic and salty tastes. It costs about 25 cents worth of electricity to distill a gallon of water, on average.

Reverse Osmosis. In this process, pressure is used to force water through a semipermeable membrane, which permits the passage of the water but rejects most things dissolved in it. The system can be used alone or in combination with other purification elements. Reverse osmosis will remove most inorganics and some organics: arsenic, barium, fluoride, lead, mercury, nitrates, radium, pesticides, and metallic and salty tastes. Although the reverse osmosis process itself does not remove chloroform well, most commercial units add carbon filtration, which reduces organics, including chloroform.

Ultraviolet Disinfection. The rays that are bad for your skin are good for destroying waterborne bacteria by radiation. In order for the process to work properly, water must remain for a specified time in a radiation chamber. The units need to be kept clean so that the light can penetrate the water being treated.

Installing Filtration Systems

Point-of-use systems can be installed in three ways:

1. installing the filter on the cold-water line leading to the faucet;

2. mounting the filter on the faucet itself; and

3. mounting the filter on a line that diverts cold water to a third faucet.

All systems will require filter changes, but the last two may require fewer because both allow you to filter only drinking and cooking water. Most faucet-mounted filters have diverters, so you filter water on demand; this prolongs the life of the filter.

All activated carbon filters need to be maintained as recommended by manufacturers in order to remain effective. Cartridges will need to be replaced periodically (how often depends on the size of the filter, the amount of water to be filtered, and the extent of contamination of your water). You can replace the cartridges yourself or sign a maintenance agreement with your supplier.

Other systems must be maintained faithfully, too. The membrane and filters in a reverse osmosis filtration system must be replaced regularly, for example, as they become saturated by contaminants. An ultraviolet disinfection system must be cleaned regularly to prevent buildup of sediment and algae.

In apartment buildings, branch lines supply water from risers, and each apartment has its own supply line. Installing a filter can be a simple matter of connecting it at the sink.

TIPS FOR WATER CONSERVATION

In the past, not only did we take the quality of our water for granted; we also assumed that the quantity of our water supply was inexhaustible. Today water is in short supply in many communities, especially in the West, and thus the issue of conservation affects everyone.

The first line of defense in the battle against water scarcity is to cut down on water waste. A slow-dripping faucet can waste 15 gallons per day, whereas a continuously running toilet can waste several hundred gallons in 24 hours. An inefficient shower head can waste two to three gallons per minute, compared with a water-saving model.

By installing an aerator on a faucet, you will experience what seems to be an increase in water flow but in reality is not. Aerators create this effect by adding bubbles to the water and thus increasing the sense of volume. As a result, water usage may be decreased.

In addition, you can conserve water by changing some of your own habits.

- Instead of running the tap water until it's cold every time you want a glass to drink, use a bottle of water kept in the refrigerator for this purpose.
- Scrape leftover food from plates with a sponge or cloth rather than using the force of water to rinse them off.
- Don't use the dishwasher until it's full.

SINKS AND FAUCETS

Once you may have settled for a rudimentary, rectangular, single-bowl stainless steel or enameled steel sink and a chrome faucet without even thinking about how it would add or detract from the decor of the kitchen. Over the past few years, however, with a new profusion of colors, shapes, and configurations available, sinks and faucets have become fashion items.

True to the nature of all fashion items, some of the sinks with pricier designs and colors can cost up to $1,000. And since some of the top-of-the-line faucets can also cost more than $500, high-style design in the sink area can translate quickly into a major expense.

Before you decide about sinks and faucets, you must first determine

- whether you want one sink area for both food preparation and cleanup
- where the sink(s) will be located, given your home's plumbing realities, and the estimated costs of rerouting piping and installing new piping
- whether you want a garbage disposer (see chapter 7), and if so, at which sink
- what sink configuration, width, and depth suit your needs. Although sinks are available in a variety of shapes (circular, square, rectangular, and elliptical among them) and sizes, they fall into four basic categories.

Self-rimming sinks have a ridge that fits over the countertop. When caulking is applied between the sink and the countertop, the ridge forms a tight seal, preventing water from splashing over onto the countertop.

Flush-mounted sinks are recessed in a countertop, affixed with tight-fitting metal rims. They are not as effective as self-rimming sinks in preventing splashing.

Recessed sinks, as the name implies, are recessed under the countertop, and complement solid-surface countertops particularly well. These undermounted sinks are not recommended with laminate countertops, because of potential water seepage.

Integral sinks are one-piece sink-and-countertop units, which may be made of a solid-surface material or stainless steel. The advantages include their ease of maintenance—grime, grease, and grit cannot get caught at the rims—and the opportunity they offer for designing in a functional drainboard.

Sinks come in a variety of configurations: single-bowl, double-bowl, and triple-bowl, as well as double units whose sinks are angled for corner installations. Single-bowl sinks generally measure 12 to 33 inches wide and 15 to 22 inches deep, whereas multiple-bowl sinks are 33 inches wide or more and typically 21 to 22 inches deep.

Multiple-bowl sinks can prove functional in kitchens with only one sink area, because they allow food preparation and cleanup to be separated. But no one has yet made a definitive determination as to whether a single-bowl sink is superior or inferior to a multiple-bowl sink and probably no one ever will.

Note that if a 33-inch-wide sink has two equal-size bowls, each basin measures 13 inches. One bowl can easily accommodate most everyday plates and smaller pans and pots, but even with a "goosenecked" faucet it is awkward for larger equipment, such as woks, stock pots, and fish poachers. An alternate configuration, with an 18- to 24-inch basin and the remainder as a garbage disposer basin, is more efficient.

If you choose to install two sinks, a small (18-inch) sink can be used for preparing food, whereas a larger sink can be used for cleanup. A garbage disposer, should you decide to install one, can serve well in either sink, depending on your cooking and cleanup habits. (If it will be used in the smaller sink, be sure that the drain opening is larger than the standard 3½ inches in order to accommodate it.)

An important factor in sink selection is the *depth* of the basin. Assuming that the sink is to be installed at the standard counter height of 36 inches, the sink depth should allow you to work comfortably without bending over or raising your shoulders. Typical sink

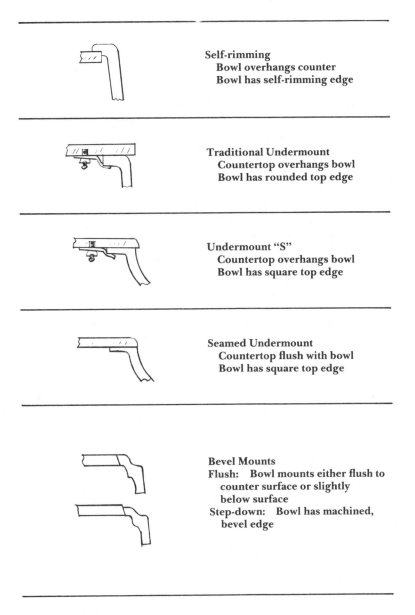

Self-rimming
    Bowl overhangs counter
    Bowl has self-rimming edge

Traditional Undermount
    Countertop overhangs bowl
    Bowl has rounded top edge

Undermount "S"
    Countertop overhangs bowl
    Bowl has square top edge

Seamed Undermount
    Countertop flush with bowl
    Bowl has square top edge

Bevel Mounts
Flush: Bowl mounts either flush to
    counter surface or slightly
    below surface
Step-down: Bowl has machined,
    bevel edge

Figure 8.1   Optional Sink Installations

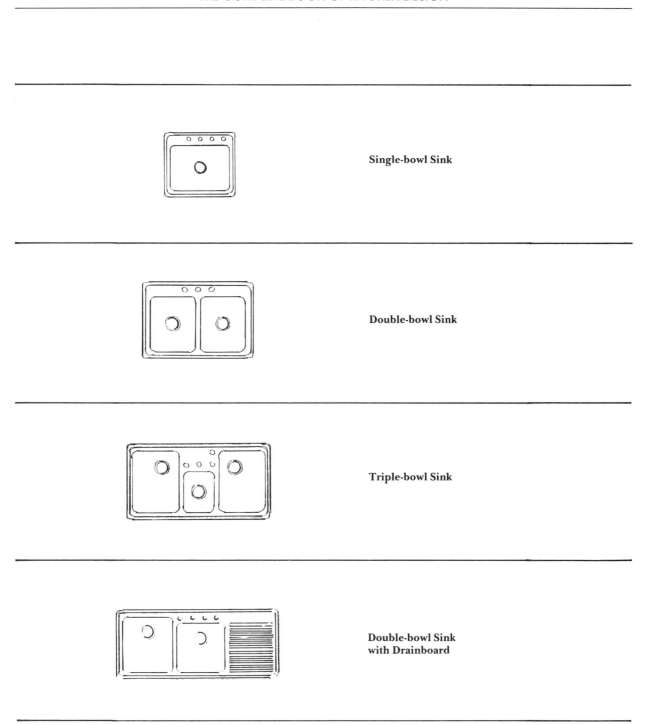

Single-bowl Sink

Double-bowl Sink

Triple-bowl Sink

Double-bowl Sink
with Drainboard

Figure 8.2   European-style Sinks

depths are 5 to 8 inches. The deeper sinks can better accommodate larger pots and pans, but if you are shorter than average, such a sink may be difficult for you to work in.

You may also be surprised by how many sink accessories are available. They include cutting boards that fit over the sink for conveniently preparing fresh produce, meat, fish, and poultry, and drain bowls, both plastic-covered wire and stainless steel, for use in washing and peeling fresh fruits and vegetables, for example. Colanders, and plate racks that fit inside the sink or stand freely adjacent to the sink, are also available.

Some sink installations have their own built-in drain boards, but generally these are too small to handle anything but a few small items.

Sink Materials

Homeowners as well as designers and contractors like stainless steel sinks because they are light, relatively durable, and easy to clean. They also complement the look of a professional kitchen, which may include a commercial-style stainless steel range and countertop.

Stainless steel comes in varying weights and finishes. A 22-gauge, mirror-finish stainless steel sink is more likely to show scratches and water spotting and is less resistant to dents than a 20-gauge brushed-finish nickel–and–stainless steel sink, for example.

An *enameled stainless steel* sink runs the risk of chipping and staining. An enameled cast iron sink, however, is more resistant to chipping. Its big drawback is that it is heavy and therefore more difficult to install than other materials.

Even more durable is an 18-gauge brushed-finish nickel–and–stainless steel sink with an optional coating on the underside, which cuts down on the noise of a food waste disposer. But better quality is costly. An 18-gauge stainless steel sink can cost twice as much as a 20-gauge, and nearly four times as much as a 22-gauge stainless steel sink.

Vitreous china is easy to clean and retains its glossy surface, but it can be chipped.

One of the newer sink materials is *Asterite®*. A man-made material of acrylic and quartz, it is nonporous, which means it is scratch-, stain-, and chip-resistant. It can be molded into a variety of shapes and is available in more than 100 colors, in a high gloss or matte appearance. In one of its forms, it mimics the look of granite, which makes it an interesting complement to a natural stone countertop. Its performance over the long term has yet to be determined, so while some designers are very optimistic about the material's prospects, they are also adopting a "wait-and-see" attitude.

Faucets

The simplest faucets are single-handle chrome faucets that contain either plastic internal parts or a washer. You can purchase these for $100 or less.

For $100 more, you can find single-handle chrome faucets with replaceable cartridge valves. These are more durable than the least expensive faucets and less likely to leak.

For up to to $350, single-handle faucets are available with ceramic disk valves instead of replaceable cartridge valves. These may have some of the characteristics of higher-priced faucets; the key difference is the material. Polished chrome, for example, is significantly less expensive than colored porcelain.

For $350 and up, you will find high-quality finishes, colors, and design. The better-quality faucets have hot-water temperature adjustment settings to prevent scalds as well as settings to control the intensity of the water flow.

In the $700-and-up range are "automatic" faucets that turn on when their infrared sensor detects an object (such as your hand) below and turn off automatically when the object is removed. Temperature is adjusted by using a single rotating temperature control knob. Made of brass, these faucets are available in white, chrome, matte black, and a variety of other colors.

Beyond their "bells and whistles" appeal, the automatic faucets have two key advantages: They are especially convenient for the handicapped, and because water flows only when it is actually needed, they serve the cause of water conservation.

Goosenecked faucets have been popular because of their contemporary styling and their practicality. Deep pots can easily be placed underneath them for cleaning. They are generally available in a variety of moderate and medium prices.

Chromed faucets are usually brass inside; some

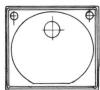

Single-bowl Sink

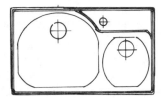

Double-bowl Sink

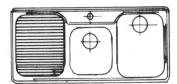

Double-bowl Sink with Drainboard

Figure 8.3 Sinks

4-hole Faucet
Gooseneck Spout
Lever Handles with Spray

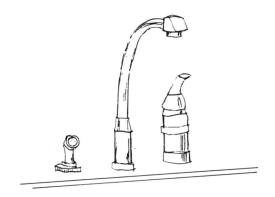

3-Hole Faucet
Single Lever with Spray

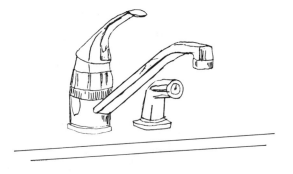

2-Hole Faucet
Single Lever with Spray

Figure 8.4   Faucets

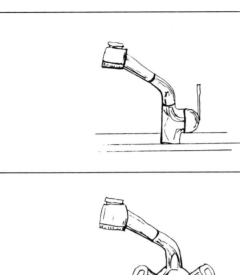

Single Lever with Spray

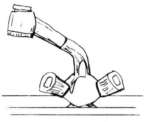

Dual Control with Spray

Single Lever, Gooseneck

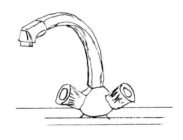

Dual Control, Gooseneck

Figure 8.5   Faucets

brasses contain lead. If your water is particularly soft or corrosive, those faucets can add lead to your water, especially when they are new.

Sprays and Other Accessories

Most American and some European sinks come with predrilled holes for faucets, sprays, and soap- or hot-water dispensers, which provide boiling water on tap. (The holes are capped with fillers if you don't buy the accessories.) These accessories add a touch of convenience and function to the sink center.

Some faucets have a built-in, pull-out spray wand so that you need not add a separate spray installation. But be aware that certain problems may arise with their use. If the spray wand doesn't have an airgap, or a diverter valve that can be switched to an airgap, and is immersed in dirty water, it can create a dangerous backflow condition that can lead directly to some types of diseases and even to toxic poisoning.

There are ways of preventing backflow, however. The Building Officials and Code Administrators International suggests three alternatives. In ascending order of cost, they are the following:

1. Install pressure vacuum breakers on the faucet, one on the hot-water line and the other on the cold.
2. Install two backflow preventers with intermediate atmospheric vents.
3. Install a reduced-pressure principle backflow preventer on each line. Be aware that these units can easily double the original cost of the spray wand itself.

Hot-water dispensers are relatively simple to install. They consist of a faucet connected to a storage tank mounted under the countertop. The tank is also connected to a cold-water pipe and has an electric heating coil to heat the water to a temperature suitable for your morning coffee. The dispenser may plug into a 120-volt grounded outlet or be wired directly into a grounded junction box.

Installing Sinks and Faucets

Assuming that the sink cutout has already been made in the countertop, preferably using a template from the sink manufacturer, the faucet and strainer assembly can be hooked up first.

The strainer assembly consists of the strainer, the body into which it fits, and a series of gaskets, washers, couplings, a trap, and a cleanout plug. The strainer body is pressed in place first, into the sink opening.

Both self-rimming and frame-rimmed sinks need to be sealed with putty or a silicone sealant along the edge of the countertop cutout. The sink is pressed down into the cutout, and excess putty is removed. It is then anchored from below at 6- to 8-inch intervals, usually with clamps or lugs provided by the manufacturer. Then the drain trap and supply pipes can be hooked up.

The faucet is set in position on the sink surface, with flexible tubing being threaded through the sink hole on the surface. Then the faucet is pressed to the surface, secured by a rubber gasket on the bottom, or by sealing it with putty. The flexible tubing is attached to the shutoff valves.

In an undermounted sink, the faucet comes up through the counter, and, for the sake of stability, it's important to use the clips provided by the manufacturer. To give this type of sink a finished look, it should be beveled or polished around the rim. If it is to be installed in a granite countertop, the bowl should be sent to the countertop fabricator so it can be fitted perfectly to the counter.

Hot-water dispensers are installed by first attaching the dispenser to the surface from below. The tank-mounting bracket will be screwed to the wall or back of the cabinet, with the tank mounted on the bracket. Next, it will be tapped into the cold-water supply pipe. One supply tube is hooked up to the storage tank from the dispenser, while the other is hooked up to the supply pipe from the storage tank. After the water supply has been turned on again and the installer has checked to make sure there are no leaks, the power to the unit can be turned on.

9

Flooring: Combining Style with Ease of Maintenance

There is no perfect kitchen floor surface. Some materials will feel more comfortable and easier to maintain than others. This is a matter of personal preference. Floors have to withstand heavy traffic, spills, scuff marks, scratches, and other abuse. In general, you will find that either vinyl, wood, or tile will prove to be serviceable. How well any material holds up over time, however, is largely dependent on how well you maintain it.

No flooring material is indestructible. Spike heels and furniture without casters are enemies of all flooring. Nor can flooring material long survive being soaked with water; moisture has a way of seeping into even the most seemingly impervious surfaces, causing warping, buckling, or lifting. *Light mopping* is appropriate for all floors. Beyond that, you should follow the guidelines for care and cleaning that manufacturers provide with their flooring products.

The three broadest categories of kitchen flooring are vinyl, wood, and ceramic tile. Carpet and rubber are also sometimes used in the kitchen, but they are not recommended as they are either impractical (spills and food bits quickly make kitchen carpet look old) or difficult to maintain.

COMPARING FLOORING COSTS

It is virtually impossible to determine exact "apples-to-apples" comparisons of vinyl, wood, and ceramic tile flooring. The costs of the materials themselves are not the sole factor. Particularly in an older home, at least some work will have to be done to prepare the subfloor, and the cost of installation (labor) must be accounted for as well.

Wood floors are more complicated to install in the kitchen, which contains relatively more detail and trim work, than they are in such wider and less detailed expanses as the living room. As a result, you'll pay more for the craftsmanship it takes to create the patterns required and to cut the material.

Staining, bleaching, finishing, and sealing wood floors also adds considerably to the basic per-square-foot cost of the wood, which may be $4 to $9 per square foot.

The cost of ceramic tile varies dramatically, too, from a low of $1 per square foot up to $10 per square foot or more. Special tiles, such as patterned antiques, can cost as much as $75 per tile. Labor and additional materials (underlayment, adhesive, and grout) can double the basic material cost. Using a mortar bed is a more expensive way of attaching tile to a glass-mesh cement board or to plywood than using an adhesive, for example.

Unquestionably, vinyl is the least expensive and least time-consuming in terms of installation, ranging from $6 to approximately $30 per square yard or more for the material, depending on geographic area, quality, and design.

VINYL

Because of its modest cost, vinyl is the most popular kitchen flooring material. One of the key benefits of using it is that, like laminates that mimic the appearance of high-cost natural materials, vinyl flooring can copy the look of higher-priced alternatives, such as stone, brick, wood, and ceramic tile.

Most people find vinyl comfortable to stand on and to walk on, and relatively quiet as well. This may be a particularly important concern if you have young children or if your kitchen plan is to open to a dining nook and family room.

Vinyl is available in sheet form or in tile. The sheets come in 6- and 12-foot widths, and before your designer or contractor orders it, ask if any seaming will be required on your floor, where the seams will be, and how they will be joined. Seams may be necessary, but they should be relegated to the least obtrusive places in the kitchen. Poorly joined seams attract dirt and grease and create a potential for eventual moisture damage.

Vinyl flooring is available in as many different colors and patterns as ceramic tile. Some manufacturers offer "textured" or "sculptured" vinyl, which reveals its pattern as light strikes it from different angles.

Currently enjoying popularity are vinyl floors that simply look like high-style vinyl floors: randomly flecked or designed with geometric patterns. Some manufacturers also have brought back the look of 50s-style linoleum in vinyl patterns.

Patterns are either rotogravure printed with vinyl inks rendered onto a mineral-coated backing, or built up from vinyl granules and inlaid, fused by intense heat and pressure. These inlaid floors, though more expensive than the rotogravure printed, are more durable. The pattern extends through the thickness of the floor down to the backing.

A third manufacturing process places colored vinyl particles onto a printed pattern and fuses them.

With the advent of the computer, improved ink systems and engraving, and the introduction of synthetic polymers, vinyl flooring has taken a major leap forward in both design and production. Simply put, anything a video camera or scanner can scan can be exactly reproduced as a flooring design.

Judging by what is being produced, there is no single design trend in vinyl flooring today. That is, virtually anything goes. Demand is great for classic black-and-white checkerboard patterns and imitation wood, tile, and stone styles, as well as for abstract patterns. White is an important color in the kitchen, as are various shades of blue and blue-green. While matte finishes are available, high-gloss finishes have become increasingly popular.

Vinyl floors' durability and resistance to scuffing and staining are much greater than they were as recently as five years ago. Recognizing that you do not want to spend your leisure time on your knees cleaning your floor, most manufacturers have improved finishing materials to make maintenance considerably easier than it used to be. The key drawback of vinyl flooring is that even the so-called no-wax vinyls, which have a clear, urethane surface, lose their sheen over time. And scuff marks, stains, and spills are still more difficult to remove from vinyl than they are from ceramic tile or wood. The higher the quality of the surface finish, the higher the price of the floor.

Problems that arise with vinyl floors, however, usually have more to do with poor subfloor conditions or the use of inappropriate adhesives than they do with the material itself. Manufacturers say that the average vinyl floor lasts from seven to 11 years and is replaced not because it wears out but because people want a new look.

Most manufacturers offer warranties on their vinyl flooring, but the terms vary. Typically, the more expensive products have longer warranties. But the warranties may cover labor only if the flooring is installed by a professional and may not cover damage from burns, stains, scuffs, or prolonged exposure to sunlight. Neither may the loss of gloss be covered, if it can be attributed to improper maintenance.

Both vinyl sheet and tile can serve as an excellent basis for achieving a custom look. On an all-vinyl floor, you can use one color for the kitchen's border and another pattern or color for the center of the room, repeating the outer border in the center if you like. Or you can use wood strips as a border around the kitchen perimeter and then install the vinyl for an inlay effect.

Patterns can be created with vinyl tile just as easily as they can with ceramic. Vinyl tiles are available in self-sticking 12-inch squares and are easier to install yourself than sheet vinyl. If you haven't installed them before, try your hand at a closet installation to improve your technique. Some manufacturers offer accents and borders to complement their sheet flooring and provide recommendations regarding which accents and borders mix particularly well with different patterns.

If the floor is being installed professionally, sheet vinyl will take less time to install than individual vinyl tiles. Before you commit to a particular supplier, however, make sure that you have compared bids that cover the same items and type of work. Some suppliers quote flooring prices inclusive of installation charges, but others charge extra for installation. Don't assume that having itemized installation charges will save you money. If the supplier charges for tasks such as removing molding and moving appliances, for example, the costs can add up quickly and surpass a "package" cost quoted by another supplier.

Installing Vinyl Flooring

A subfloor or underlayment in proper condition is truly the "foundation" for a well-installed, long-lasting vinyl floor.

Most floors in older homes and apartments are far from perfect, so it's best to remove the existing finish floor before you install a new vinyl floor. Installing a vinyl floor over an uneven surface eventually will result in nail pops or in sections that separate and lift up. If the subfloor is uneven—if it contains valleys, crevices, or "hills"—it should be adjusted to be level with the high point of the space.

Vinyl flooring is usually installed over a ¼-inch-plywood underlayment. If this underlayment is not installed properly, or if it has suffered moisture damage or cracking, the vinyl floor will suffer, too. If you

live in a particularly humid climate, or if you have had a problem with moisture penetration, a moisture barrier of plastic sheeting may be added between the subfloor and the new underlayment.

The new vinyl can be installed directly over an existing vinyl floor as long as it is level, imperfection-free, and has not been waxed. (The adhesive won't work if it has.) If you do install new vinyl on top of old, be aware that you may need to shave the bottoms of doors in the room because of the extra height of the floor.

Your contractor or designer probably will order slightly more material than is absolutely necessary for your job. This "waste" will allow for more flexibility in laying out the floor, and leftover material will come in handy for repair jobs later on. You may need to make a trade-off: using more material in order to have the floor seamed in an unobtrusive place, for example.

The flooring should be stored in the kitchen for at least a day or so before it is installed, to let it "adjust" to the temperature and humidity of the room. The temperature should be at least 65°.

Baseboards and molding must be removed from the floor, and any doors (with any saddles) leading into the kitchen should be removed before the new floor can be installed.

Vinyl sheets are installed in position, leaving about 3 inches that extend up each wall; the edges are then cut to fit. If a second section of sheeting is being used, it should be positioned overlapping the first, but the pattern should align perfectly. Both layers should be cut simultaneously for a double-cut seam. The seam edges are then lifted, and adhesive is applied to the underlayment. The two seam edges can then be pressed accurately into place.

Corners are trimmed next. Edges are attached all around the room; a staple gun can be used where the edges will be covered by molding. The rest of the floor is then secured by adhesive. A metal edging strip can be placed at doorways and passageways, unless there is a sill or threshold to replace.

Unlike sheet flooring, which is installed by starting at one edge of the room, individual *vinyl tiles* are installed from the center of the room out. After you have determined the exact center of the room, the most efficient way to install the tiles is to cover, consecutively, each of the four "quarters" of the room,

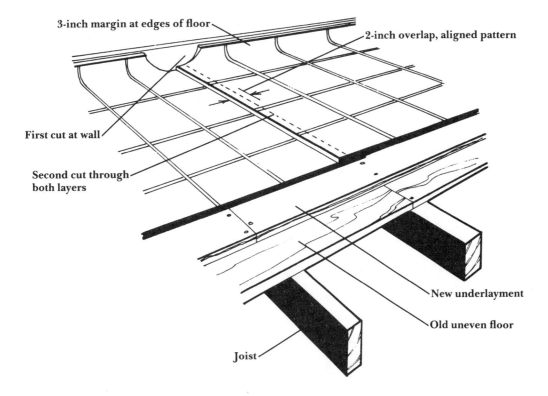

3-inch margin at edges of floor

2-inch overlap, aligned pattern

First cut at wall

Second cut through both layers

New underlayment

Old uneven floor

Joist

Figure 9.1　Laying Sheet Flooring

in a pyramid sequence. If you are doing the installation yourself, apply only as much adhesive as you can tile over before the adhesive sets. (This does not apply, of course, to self-sticking individual tiles.)

While we've described in a general way the installation process for both vinyl sheets and tiles, you should get complete step-by-step instructions from the supplier if you plan to do the job yourself.

WOOD

Until perhaps five years ago, wood was considered too impractical to install in the kitchen because of the perceived risk of water damage. But with the advent of improved finishing techniques, coupled with a growing popular preference for traditional style throughout the home, wood flooring has become increasingly popular.

According to the National Oak Manufacturers Association, which publishes specifications and manufacturing and grading rules for hardwood flooring, all grades of hardwood are equally strong and serviceable. What determines differences in grading is appearance.

Oak, for example, is divided into four basic grades. *Clear* refers to flooring that is practically free of defects and made up mostly of heartwood. *Select* is almost clear but has knots and color variations. *Common* oak contains more markings than clear and select. The grades are sometimes combined; short oak pieces are generally graded "#1 Common and Better Shorts" or "#2 Common Shorts."

Prefinished oak flooring is graded *prime, standard,* and *tavern.* Unfinished hard maple and unfinished pecan are graded *first, second, second and better, third,* and *third and better.*

The final color of a wood floor depends not only on the grade of the wood but on how it is sanded and stained. Although complete uniformity is unattainable and may not be a design goal, color is more likely to be uniform in clear and select grades.

Generally, the smoother a floor is sanded, the less color will be accepted by the wood, because whereas the soft open grain will accept stain, the hard grain will remain almost natural. A more uniform color can

 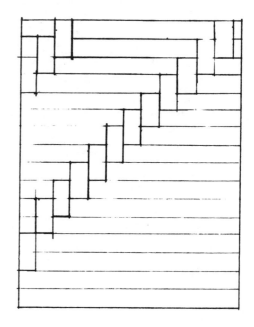

Herringbone

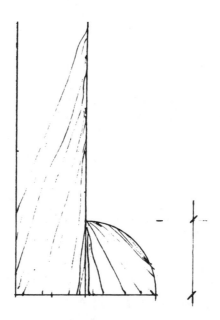

Quarter round molding

Figure 9.2   Wood Flooring

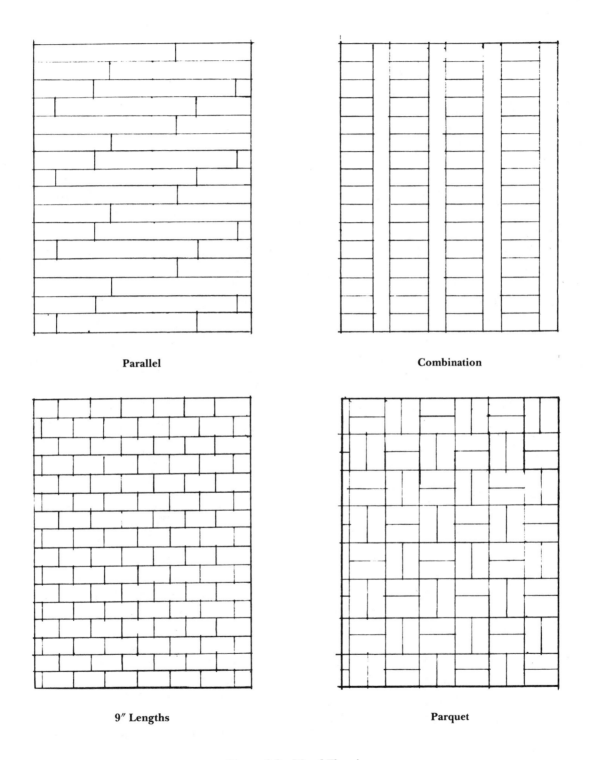

Figure 9.3   Wood Flooring

be achieved by wiping the floor *lightly* with water and allowing it to dry before staining.

Sanding should be done after all other interior work is completed and immediately before applying stain or finish. The body of the floor is sanded first, followed by the edges. The floor should be sanded several times, using progressively finer sandpaper. Generally, a large machine will be used for most of the floor, whereas a smaller one will be needed for corners. (Sanding is not easy to do well, unless you're very experienced. If you are unskilled, you can damage the floor.) Once the dust is entirely removed, staining can begin.

Unlike paint, stain is applied and then wiped off. Whether they use pigments or dyes, and whether they are based in water, oil, lacquer, or alcohol, stains simply don't work on floors the way paint does on walls. While the color is determined by how much stain penetrates the wood fibers, applying too much stain, or not wiping enough off, can result in peeling or chipping.

Light Wood: Avoiding the Pitfalls

Light woods have become particularly popular for kitchen floors. Bleached and pastel- or white-stained, they add a sense of spaciousness to the kitchen and are suitable for a variety of styles.

Having a floor bleached will lengthen the construction process, because it takes a great deal of time to dry—as long as ten days. Remember, too, that since wood is a natural material its basic grain and texture will not be totally uniform; therefore the floor may not accept stain uniformly either.

If you want a white floor, make sure that you and your contractor are talking about the same appearance, because there are several ways to achieve the same look, and they employ different woods and different techniques. White floors can be produced from red oak, white oak, ash, and first-grade maple. The oak should be select or clear grade. (As we've noted, higher grades of wood allow higher degrees of uniform coloration, which isn't possible with wood that is studded with knots, minerals, or other marks.)

Mineral streaks in white oak, when bleached, tend to turn greenish, so although it takes more time to bleach out the pink or reddish color in red oak, it will ultimately yield a more uniform appearance.

Approximating uniform color also requires proper sanding techniques.

If you want a whiter color, wiping ash or white oak with a damp towel or sponge mop will raise the grain so it will accept more white stain.

A white floor will be more costly than a traditional wood floor because it requires more time and labor and better materials. If you want to achieve the light look while avoiding great expense, consider these possibilities:

- Use maple, ash, pine, or another light brown tone of wood instead of white or red oak. This way, you can avoid the white staining process and achieve a frosted look with bleaching and finishing with a nonambering waterborne finish. It will save a couple of days' drying time, too.
- No matter what wood you choose, it should be well-enough finished to withstand the considerable wear it will take in the kitchen. At least three coats of top coat are needed to protect bleached white-stained floors.
- Be prepared to recoat the floor periodically, perhaps as often as every two years.

Light or bleached floors show wear and dirt more easily than dark floors, and they require more maintenance. They also show the small cracks between flooring boards that occur during periods of high heat and dryness, though the cracks will diminish and become less noticeable when the flooring expands again in higher humidity. Light-colored finishes will also change over a period of years to a grayish or light amber tone.

If you become tired of the bleached look, you can change it. To do so, the floor must be sanded down to the bare wood and a new finish applied.

Types of Finishes

The key to long-lived wood flooring is the way it is finished and subsequently maintained. The floor should not be finished until a week to three weeks after installation. All dust on windows, doors, frames, sills, baseboards, and floor should be wiped, using a painter's tack rag.

Shellac, varnish, waxes, and penetrating sealers

were the most commonly used finishes prior to the early 50s, but manufacturers have developed several finishes since then that pose less of a problem in flammability, environmental damage, application, and cost. Although no general consensus exists about the best way to make wood water- and damage-resistant in the kitchen, certain finishes are considered acceptable:

Oil-modified Polyurethanes. The most common finishing products, these can produce a high-gloss, semigloss, or matte finish; scratches will be less apparent in the matte finishes. They are easy to apply but dry slowly. Because they tend to yellow, they are not recommended for white floors. For an effective finish, two to three coats are required. Damaged areas are difficult to repair. Prices are moderate.

Moisture-cured Urethane. Because it dries very quickly, this type of finish is best handled by a professional. It provides a highly durable, clear finish with low flammability but emits a strong odor during application. Two to three coats are recommended. Like the finish provided by oil-modified polyurethanes, damage is difficult to repair. Prices are moderate to expensive.

Water-based Acrylics. These quick-drying finishes produce a low-gloss appearance. Easy to apply, they are not flammable and emit only mild odors during application. They are fairly durable and easy to repair. Three coats are required. Prices are moderate to expensive.

Water-based Urethanes. Although they are more expensive and more difficult to apply than their acrylic cousins, the water-based urethanes are highly durable and relatively easy to repair. Also quick-drying, they require four coats, which produce a satin to low-gloss appearance.

Swedish Finishes. These are not as durable as moisture-cured urethane, but they are more durable than oil-modified urethane. They are available in two basic categories: a two-component alkyd-type, in which an acid hardener is added to the base before application, and a "conversion varnish," in which an alkyd-type material is used as a base coat, topped off with an 80-percent-alcohol precatalyzed finish coat. Two to three coats are required, producing a clear to slightly yellow color. Swedish finishes are difficult to apply and repair, and application by a professional is recommended. Flammability is higher than for oil-

modified urethanes, but not as high as for lacquers. Prices are moderate to expensive.

Your local building code will specify if any of these finishes are prohibited in your area. Solvent-based coatings, for example, are prohibited in many areas on the East and West coasts, as well as in Phoenix and Fort Worth.

One manufacturer, Tibbals Flooring, offers Hartco prefinished oak flooring that has been impregnated with acrylic at the factory. It is very practical and attractive for the kitchen. Some contractors, working from the theory "better to be safe than sorry," also add a surface coating of wax for added protection of the prefinished flooring.

The one big drawback of acrylic-impregnated prefinished flooring is that it cannot be sanded down and refinished.

Preventing Moisture Damage

Most problems that arise with wood flooring have to do with moisture. Either the humidity in your kitchen turns out to be significantly different from the moisture content of the flooring when it was delivered, or there is a problem with your basement, subfloor, or foundation. Many designers and contractors put down vapor barriers beneath the new floor to prevent moisture from coming up from below. This is particularly important if your home is built on slab—that is, if it has no basement or crawl space.

Because of changes in humidity levels, "normal" cracking in wood flooring will close up in summer months and won't require repairs. If abnormal cracks develop, they can be repaired by troweling a filler that matches the finish into the cracks. A new coat of polyurethane can be applied when the floor is dry. If the finish you used has been waxed, however, a new coat of finish will not adhere. In this case, use a fine steel wool on the crack, clean the surface, and wax it.

To prevent water damage that might arise as a result of some problem with the dishwasher, consider creating a "tray" underneath it. The tray, a shallow construct coated with a urethane finish, creates a border around the dishwasher space, preventing leakage. If your kitchen has a crawl space beneath it, small holes can be drilled in the tray, and any overflow can drain into the crawl space. This technique, of course, is not possible in an apartment, in a home built on slab, or in one that has a full basement.

Patterns and Varieties

There are three categories of hardwood flooring:

- wide-board flooring (which can be made of soft wood as well as hard), also known as random width, which must be cut so that both ends will finish over a joist unless it is tongue-and-groove end-matched
- narrow-strip flooring, typically oak, maple, or pecan, 2 to 4 inches wide, made with a tongue-and-groove joint along the sides and the ends. The ends of these strips need not be positioned over a joist
- block or parquet flooring, made of squares or strips of a variety of woods. "Tiles" of 12-by-12-inch squares, glued together, are common.

Flooring patterns can vary widely, from the relatively simple look of random plank flooring, which is especially suitable for an American colonial or country style, to the more complex and formal, including herringbone, diagonal, hexagonal, basket weave, and diamond patterns.

Installing Wood Flooring

Since wood is sensitive to the environment and can shrink or expand with significant changes in temperature and humidity, your contractor should plan on having flooring delivered at least several days before it is to be installed, if it is prefinished, so that it can adjust to your home's "climate." Avoid having it delivered in the rain. If the flooring is not prefinished, however, it should be delivered several weeks in advance—and not at all in extreme weather.

As with any flooring material, the condition of the subfloor is crucial; it has to be level, smooth, clean, and, above all, dry. If the subfloor is plywood, it should be ½ inch or thicker. The underlayment should be securely nailed down to the subfloor so that squeaks will not be a problem later on.

In apartments, the subfloor may be composed of concrete (slab) or of old existing wood flooring. In these cases, you can use plywood to level the floor.

Instead of nailing, you can use "liquid nails," an adhesive that bonds the new wood flooring to the plywood. Check with the manufacturer for recommended types of adhesives. This method is actually good for any type of wood flooring that is to be finished after installation, because the wood adheres evenly. The adhesive is troweled on, and the floor is installed immediately.

Like vinyl tiles, a properly installed wood floor depends on starting from the center of the kitchen. The first plank, strips, or squares must be laid parallel to the center. Of course, in many kitchens locating a precise center will be impossible; they may be irregularly shaped or may open to other rooms. In these instances, the center can be judged visually.

If your room is small and you want to expand the space visually, consider installing the flooring in a diagonal pattern. (This strategy applies to vinyl tile and ceramic tile installations as well.)

Narrow tongue-and-groove strip flooring is attached by blind-nailing, which means that the nails are attached at an angle through the tongues (the ridge that extends along the length of the strip) so that the nailheads won't show.

Long flooring strips should be used at entrances and doorways. Short pieces should not be grouped in one area but dispersed throughout the floor.

If you have an island or peninsula plan, one optional flooring pattern would be to "frame" the island or peninsula, using mitered joints at the corners. For added visual drama, the wood strip "frame" may be stained in a contrasting color from the rest of the floor.

If you're replacing a floor in an existing kitchen, all moldings and grilles should be removed before the new floor is installed. After installation, the floor should be finished with a wood baseboard or "shoe" molding, which allows for expansion and contraction.

In an apartment building, you can reduce noise transmission from your kitchen to your downstairs neighbor's by covering your subfloor with ½ inch or thicker cork or insulation board laid in glue, and covering that with another ¾-inch-plywood subfloor also laid in mastic. The finish strip or plank flooring is nailed to the plywood. Block or parquet floors are laid in mastic on the plywood, which should be at least ½ inch thick.

CERAMIC TILE

Tile is made from a mixture of clay that is shaped or pressed, then dried and fired in a kiln at high temperatures. Some tile is fired more than once. The higher the temperature and the more times the tile is fired, the stronger and less porous the tile will be.

Once the firing is completed, the tile can be left unglazed, or it can be glazed and/or decorated. Glazing is done by applying a thin coating of minerals and pigments and then returning the tile to the kiln. The glaze can be matte, high gloss, smooth, or textured.

The hardened, glazed surface determines the color and texture of the tile, whereas unglazed tile relies on the natural clay bisque (the flat-shaped bodies of the clay before firing).

Some tile is made by hand, but a great deal of it is machine-made. Machine-made tile lends itself to more precise and uniform installation.

Some people won't consider the use of ceramic tile for kitchen floors because they believe that it is colder and noisier to walk on, and ultimately harder on the feet and the back than other materials. Another complaint is that because tile is harder, plates or glasses are more likely to break when dropped.

These objections matter less to others, however. Tile aficionados prefer it for the kitchen because of its durability and ease of maintenance, as well as its beauty and design appeal. One of tile's biggest advantages, in fact, is the almost limitless creative design possibilities it offers. Used as a finishing material, it adds character and helps set the style of the room.

Here are just a few of tile's design possibilities:

- Use terra-cotta to lend a rustic, country feeling to the room. Terra-cotta with miniature tile inserts gives the kitchen a French Country quality.
- Employ a sleek manufactured glazed or "paver" tile to enhance Italian, or Euro-style, design in the kitchen.
- Art Deco design can be carried out by using a border of three rows of 2-by-2-inch tiles, followed by 8-by-8-inch or 10-by-10-inch tiles for the center part of the floor. The design can be picked up on the backsplash by using a 2-by-2-inch or 4-by-4-inch tile there.

One of the growing trends in tile design has been the shift toward using large-size tiles—12 by 12 inches and larger—for the kitchen. It is no longer true, manufacturers contend, that small rooms require small tiles whereas larger rooms need larger ones. Nor are you limited to using one size tile throughout; you can create patterns for floors and walls with a variety of different-size tiles.

Another continuing trend is the neo–Art Deco look of black-and-white "checkerboard" flooring. In re-creating a vintage 30s apartment, you can use a horizontal brick pattern on the walls and a large checkerboard on the floor.

If you prefer a more rustic look for a country-style kitchen, you can choose the larger, often irregularly shaped tiles and allow for greater-than-standard spacing between them. The grout spaces can be as wide as ½ to ¾ inch; standard spacing for conventionally styled floors is ⅛ to ¼ inch. The flooring design can be tied in with a tiled backsplash. In a country setting you can achieve a rustic feeling by using antique-looking, irregular tiles with fruit, vegetable, herb, or animal patterns.

Just as some types of tile are appropriate for countertops but others are not (see chapter 10), certain types are more suitable for floors than others.

The Nature and Quality of Tile

Generally, the less water-absorbent the tile is, the harder and more resistant to stains it will be. The American National Standards Institute (ANSI) specifies four categories of tile, divided in terms of their relative water absorption:

impervious tile, which absorbs less than 0.5 percent water

vitreous tile, which absorbs between 0.5 and 3 percent

semivitreous tile, which absorbs between 3 and 7 percent

nonvitreous tile, which absorbs more than 7 percent

Nonvitreous tile is not recommended for kitchens, but semivitreous tile—such as some quarry tile, which absorbs 4 to 5 percent—can be suitable, particularly if a waterproof membrane is installed beneath the tile.

Another classification system comes from the Italian Tile Council, which rates Italian-made tiles for abrasion resistance and recommended usage. Group I and Group II are suitable for light traffic and general traffic areas in the home, except for the kitchen. Group III is suitable for maximum traffic areas in the home, including the kitchen, and Group IV is strong enough for commercial (that is, restaurant, office, and hotel) installations.

Manufactured tiles are preferable to handmade for flooring because they tend to be less permeable and more uniform in shape. The types of tile most appropriate for kitchen use are:

Paver Tile. Though such tile is available glazed or unglazed, the unglazed version is a better choice for the kitchen because a glaze offers less traction and may wear out over time. Pavers are made of clay or porcelain and usually have a textured face and rounded or irregular edges. Tiles come in 6-, 8-, and 10-inch sizes. Dense and hard, they are easy to maintain and will not lose their color over time, though some lighter-colored porcelain pavers tend to stain more visibly than darker colors.

Quarry Tile. This type of tile, which has a deep red, tan, or dark/neutral hue, has a slightly textured surface—a benefit, since you'll be less likely to slip on it. It may be vitreous or semivitreous; make sure you check with the supplier to determine which it is. Usually left unglazed, quarry tile can be finished with a sealer for added stain resistance.

Ceramic Mosaics. Available in squares, hexagons, and rectangles, this type of tile resembles paver tile but is smaller. Mosaics can be made of clay or porcelain, glazed or unglazed. Again, unglazed is preferable; good traction means fewer slips and falls in the kitchen. The small size of the mosaics (the squares can be as small as 1 inch) gives them great design potential. Geometric and bordered patterns are relatively simple to achieve. Some manufacturers also offer stock patterns, which give you a customized look at a decidedly noncustomized cost.

Glazed wall tile, and decorative thin wall tile, as the names imply, are not suitable for floors because they are not strong enough. Marble tile has a rich appearance, but it is not recommended for floors because of its porosity.

Before You Begin

Selecting tile is a process that can be confusing precisely because there is so much choice, from both domestic and foreign manufacturers, with so little uniformity of quality. Your first task is to determine whether or not your home will be able to support the weight of the installed tile. Some strengthening of the subfloor may be necessary to prevent sagging.

Prewar apartments in urban centers like New York, Chicago, Philadelphia, and Boston usually have a concrete base floor, but some older structures have wood-base flooring. In that case, the wood should be removed, a subfloor of cement poured, and the floor leveled before a new floor can be installed, usually ⅜ inch thick.

If you live in a co-op, you will probably not need board approval to install tile, granite, or marble in a kitchen or bath. But you should confirm this before installation begins. Approval *is* likely to be required if you are planning to extend a tile installation along greater spans, such as into a hallway, living room, or dining room.

Once you have determined that your home is structurally able to accept a tile floor, the next step is to visit showrooms to see the different colors, textures, and types of tile for yourself. Fortunately, most larger showrooms group different types of tile according to their most appropriate use.

When you've found a tile you like, buy several pieces, bring them home, and lay them on your existing floor. This will give you some perspective of how the new floor will look and feel.

Installing Ceramic Tile

Like vinyl or wood, tile requires a level, firm, smooth, and dry subfloor. Although it can be installed directly over existing flooring, the tiling cannot correct deficiencies in the subfloor. As discussed above, subflooring problems must be attended to first.

The tiles should be laid out in a "dry run" before they are installed. This entails finding the focal point of the floor—such as a center island—and starting the tile layout from there rather than along a wall. An alternative, from an aesthetic point of view, is to start the tile layout from the entry to the room, which is particularly visible. The object of any of these methods is to minimize the number of cuts that need to be made in the tiles and to avoid cutting that results in less than half a tile.

The goal, too, is for interruptions in the pattern to appear only in the least visible places. If the laid-out tiles don't make a complete row, for example, the row should be adjusted so that extra space is left at the end of the room, where cut tiles can be placed most unobtrusively.

Some tile comes with "spacers," which make it easier for the installer to create uniform group spaces between tiles. The spacers should be removed before the adhesive sets, and before grouting takes place.

There are two basic methods for installing tile: using *thick-set mortar* or *thin-set mortar or adhesive*. In both techniques, the tile is laid in the mortar or the adhesive bed. Then grout is applied over the entire surface. The grout "haze" is wiped away with a clean, soft rag, and the grout is tamped down with a striking tool to make sure there are no air pockets in it.

In the *thin-set* method, the tile is laid over an adhesive or mortar applied with a trowel. The bed will be approximately ⅜ inch thick, depending on how irregular the floor is.

In the *thick-set* method, the bed is deeper. There are two varieties of thick-set installations. In one, the tile is set in the bed when the bed is still wet; in the other, the mortar bed is already dry—a glass-mesh concrete underlayment board, for example. The advantages of using the dry-bed method are that the boards weigh less than a conventional mortar bed and are less likely to expand or be otherwise affected by moisture.

Although more expensive, the thick-set mortar (also called mud) technique is usually recommended for flooring because it will yield a more uniform look and will provide better cushioning. Doors leading to the kitchen may need to be shaved to accommodate a new thick-set floor, because the mortar bed required is 1 to 1½ inches deep. The greater floor height will also affect how the "transition" area—that is, the lower-height flooring in an adjacent area—is handled. The installation of a wood, tile, or marble

threshold can be installed as a "bridge" to these areas.

The new flooring height may also affect the toe-kick space under base cabinets, so be sure that your flooring and cabinet installers are coordinating information with one another and using the same measurements in your kitchen.

Ideally, tile should be set after the existing surface has been removed. Otherwise, you run the risk of having an uneven floor, or having the old surface rise underneath the new. Some practitioners maintain that tile can be set directly over old tile, vinyl, and wood floors *as long as subfloor conditions are clean, dry, solid, well-bonded, and level.* If the tile is to be set over vinyl or wood, the existing floor must be sanded first. The tile will adhere better to the resultant "grittier" surface.

Tile also can be applied over a concrete floor, but if you have a moisture problem, it's advisable to install a waterproof membrane over the mortar (before it dries) and set the tile into a second mortar bed over the membrane.

Grouts and Grouting. The appearance and long-term performance of a tile floor depend on the type of grout you select. Types of grouts include *unsanded,* used for tight joints on walls and floors; *sanded,* used on wide joints of ⅛ inch or larger, usually on floors; and *epoxy,* used on wall and floor tiles, for both tight and wide joints. An epoxy is a three-part mixture of cement and liquid.

Grout can stain an unglazed tile, but a *grout release* can prevent staining by sealing the tile. Grout releases can be cleaned with ammonia and water.

Unless you need a colored grout in a matching or contrasting color as part of the design motif of your floor, a better choice would be a neutral, gray, or charcoal gray. These oxidize easily and won't show as much dirt as some of the colored grouts. Epoxy grouts, the most water-resistant, are also the most expensive and come in a variety of colors. They are tricky to work with because they dry very quickly, so application is best left to a professional.

The grout must completely fill all seams and contain no hidden air pockets. When one section is finished, the excess is wiped off with a damp sponge. By the time the floor is finished, the first sections will be dry, with a thin "haze" on the surface.

While the grout is curing (hardening completely),

avoid walking on the floor. In hot, dry climates (or during the summer elsewhere), cement-type grouts may require "damp curing"—that is, the floor must be covered with plastic until the grout hardens. This process may take several days.

It's a good idea for the installer to gently hammer a small piece of wood or plywood over the tiles as they are being set into place, to make sure that the flooring is all level. If there is any space under a tile, you could have a cracking problem later on.

10

The Counter Revolution

Countertops are the second biggest visual element in the kitchen, after cabinetry, and arguably they take more abuse. Consequently, they not only must appeal to the eye but must also be able to resist stains, heat damage, warping, fading, cuts, and scratches. They must also be relatively easy to maintain.

A wide variety of countertop materials available today meet these conditions. They come in an almost endless array of colors and patterns, and there seems to be virtually no end to the creativity possible in designing inlays and edge treatments. Remember, materials can be mixed for aesthetic reasons as well as for functional ones.

You can use a material like marble in a baking center, because it's a good surface on which to knead dough. You can also inset a butcher-block cutting board into a countertop, so that you don't have to dig out a portable chopping board every time you prepare a meal. Creating a built-in trivet by insetting ceramic tile set into a countertop is functional, too, because hot pots won't scorch, blister, or burn the tile.

Be aware, however, that there is a surprising cost differential in countertop materials, and this must be taken into consideration as you compare the advantages and disadvantages of each. If a laminate countertop were to cost $1,000, for example, the same size countertop made of a solid surface material could cost $3,000 or more. Natural stone and stainless steel would cost even more. The complexity of the fabrication could change that equation.

Any special inlays or edge treatments add significantly to the cost. Although prices will vary markedly depending on areas of the country, in the most expensive urban centers a solid-surface countertop with a special edge treatment can cost $110 to $180 per lineal foot, installed, versus $40 to $80 for a standard-edge laminate.

Moreover, whereas skilled do-it-yourselfers can install a laminate or tile countertop themselves, solid-surface and natural stone countertops must be custom fabricated and installed by skilled craftspeople, which adds substantially to the total cost.

PLASTIC LAMINATES

The most common countertops, plastic laminates, are also the least expensive. The biggest drawback of using laminates is that they offer a *resting* surface, not a *working* surface. In other words, you cannot cut, chop, or otherwise prepare foods directly on these countertops. Nor can you place hot pots and dishes directly on them. Chopping boards, trivets, or hot pads must be close at hand.

The second drawback of laminate countertops is the thin black line visible where sections of the material are joined. These lines seem unobtrusive to many people, and you may be one of them. If they trouble you, however, other design solutions will be appropriate, such as the so-called *solid-color laminates,* which are more costly than basic laminates but cost less than solid-surface materials.

Another drawback is that despite their durability and ease of maintenance, laminates are not impervious to certain stains (such as shoe polish and berry juice). Nor are they completely waterproof; standing water should not be left in areas where the top has been joined, for example, because it can damage the base material.

In addition to cost, the chief advantage of laminates is the great variety of colors, patterns, and styles from which you can choose. Virtually any natural material has a laminate look-alike; these include wood grains, and *faux* stone, as well as metallics, suede, and leather look-alikes. Laminates also offer numerous exuberant abstract, geometric, flecked, and dotted patterns that are wonderful for a retro-50s look or an ultracontemporary kitchen.

Laminates are actually "sandwiches" of kraft (filler) paper impregnated with phenolic resin, with a color or pattern sheet and a melamine overlay added to the top. The "sandwich" is pressed at between 800 and 1,200 pounds per square inch for about an hour, at 280 degrees or more. The resulting sheet is 1/16-inch thick, usually applied to a 3/4-inch particleboard or plywood base. Because only the top layer of the "sandwich" contains the color or decorative surface, if a chip occurs, it cannot be repaired, and scratches or cuts are particularly noticeable.

Dimensional laminates—for example, those that are textured like slate or copper—are not appropriate for kitchen installations because their surfaces tend to collect remains of food and liquid and are therefore not as easy to maintain as a smooth surface. The laminates used most frequently for countertops are of the smooth-surfaced, high-pressure variety because they offer more resistance to stains and abrasions than low-pressure laminates and metallics.

If damage does occur, it's less noticeable with *solid color* laminates. Also called *color-through,* these use melamine color sheets throughout the material. As a result, when you cut through it, you see solid color instead of a black line.

A laminate can be *postformed*—that is, rounded or otherwise shaped so that you can have a single countertop/backsplash, for example, or a countertop contoured at the front edge so that spills on the countertop cannot run onto the floor.

Generally, a countertop is constructed to have a built-up 1½-inch front edge, faced with the laminate, but the base under the rest of the laminate is likely to be ¾-inch particleboard or plywood. Assuming that measurements have been done properly, installing a laminate countertop should not be a complicated matter. First the countertops are fitted (carpenters call it "scribing") in place. Then cutouts for sinks and appliances are made, and, if you need an L- or U-shaped top, joints are fitted.

To avoid moisture problems, the backsplash laminate should be installed before the countertop. This will prevent water from running down or penetrating the underside of the laminate backsplash. The counter must be notched so that it can be scribed to the backsplash. A metal or vinyl strip can be installed where backsplash and counter are joined. The reason some contractors prefer to install the backsplash after the countertop is to make future repair or replacement of electrical outlets easier. Some countertops have integral backsplashes. However, it is very difficult to fit such an installation with more than a 4-inch backsplash—if the wall is not straight, there will be a gap between it and the backsplash.

SYNTHETIC SOLID-SURFACE MATERIALS

Synthetic solid-surface materials made their debut some 20 years ago, and the technology has improved in recent years, resulting in harder, more scratch-resistant products. Originally, some of these materials developed problems with expansion due to heat and sunlight, including fading and cracking. But the technical advances have resolved such difficulties. The biggest advantage of these synthetic solids is that they can be easily repaired.

The most widely known solid-surface materials are Avonite (Avonite, Inc.), Corian (DuPont Company),

Fountainhead (Nevamar), Solidex (Guardsman Products, Inc.), and Surell (Formica Corporation). All but Solidex offer 10-year warranties on their material, provided that proper fabrication, installation, and maintenance have been followed. (Solidex has a 12-year warranty.)

Made of cast plastic—acrylic or polyester with mineral filler—these materials have many of the advantages of marble and granite and none of the disadvantages. Available in solid colors or patterns that simulate natural stone, the materials have an opaque appearance. They usually are available in a matte finish and can also be polished for a glossier appearance. As resistant to stains as granite, but lighter in weight and therefore easier for craftspeople to manage, they are also more resistant to acids and chemicals than marble and granite.

Unlike laminates, synthetic solids can be repaired if they get burned, scratched, or gouged. The burns can be rubbed out, the scratches sanded out, and the gouges can be filled. Seams are virtually invisible.

Moreover, synthetic solids can be cut, shaped, drilled, and otherwise worked as easily as wood, so they lend themselves to creative design in edge treatments and inlays. Because the material is solid all the way through, you see no "sandwich" of layers and veneers when you cut it.

The disadvantages of solid-surface materials include their high cost and the limited variety of colors available in comparison with laminates and tile. As with other countertop materials, darker colors and glossy surfaces show abuse more readily than lighter colors and matte surfaces. Manufacturers recommend that you use trivets or hot pads to protect the surfaces from hot pots, and warn against cutting directly on these surfaces.

Solid-surface countertops are made in ½- and ¾-inch thicknesses, and sheets are made in 30- and 36-inch widths, in lengths up to 12 feet. Vertical surfaces, such as backsplashes, are made in ¼- and ⅜-inch thicknesses. DuPont also manufactures Corian self-rimming and integral kitchen sinks and drainboards, and Formica manufactures Surell bar sinks. Nevamar manufactures separate double-bowl and bar sinks. Corian and Surell also offer integral backsplashes.

Although the different brands of solid-surface materials have more in common than they have differences, certain distinctions exist between them.

Avonite is made of polyester alloys and mineral filler. It is made by curing a liquid polymer into a solid and then pulverizing it into particles, which are then used as suspended particulates during final casting. It comes in a relatively extensive variety of colors, and custom colors can be designed. Seams are joined not by an adhesive but by a resin. The material can only be sold to certified fabricators, who can do the installation, although the countertop is generally installed by the contractor.

Corian, which is acrylic-based with a mineral filler, is available in solid colors as well as veined and stonelike patterns. The color selection has broadened considerably from the original basic white offered nearly 20 years ago. The manufacturer recommends that only certified fabricators should be selected to make and install the countertop.

Fountainhead is a homogeneous, thermoset polymer alloy made of a combination of polyester and acrylic with alumina trihydrate as a filler. Colors and patterns approximate the appearance of soft stone. Color-matched adhesives and sealants are available to make seams and to join sinks to countertops.

Solidex is an acrylic-modified polyester available in 14 colors: eight solids and six granite patterns.

Surell, once known as 2000X, is a fully densified (air is removed from the mixture before it is cast) polyester resin compound with mineral filler. A variety of pastel colors is available, as are veined and granite patterns.

Because these materials require special tools and highly technical skills, you cannot make or install these countertops yourself; you must use a fabricator. Warranties specify that the material must be properly installed. Make sure that the craftspeople who will be making and installing your countertop have had prior experience with the material, and that the material is ordered from one run, for consistency of color. Most manufacturers offer technical seminars for installers, but with a few exceptions they do not require attendance.

You should also provide the fabricator with the manufacturers' templates for sinks and cooktop cutouts. (Be sure to keep the cutouts after the countertop is installed; they may be useful in case of repairs later on.)

Some tips about installing synthetic solid-surface countertops:

- If a full-height backsplash is planned, it should be installed before the countertop.
- If you are using ¾-inch sheets, unsupported overhangs should not exceed 12 inches; if you are using ½-inch sheets, they should not measure more than 6 inches.
- A solid underlayment is not recommended; rather, the material should "float" on the substrate. It should be supported every 18 inches, within 3 inches of cutouts and at all seam joints.
- There should be at least 3 inches from cutouts to seams or edges. Cutouts should be made on-site, although partial cutouts can be made before the countertop is installed.
- Edges should be prefit, sanded, and cleaned before seaming is done.
- At least ⅛ inch of clearance should be allowed for wall-to-wall installations, and ¹⁄₁₆ inch around appliances, to provide room for the materials to expand when heated.
- Aluminum conductive tape should be installed around cooktops and grills to disperse heat. With a drop-in range, heat strips should be used around the openings.

CERAMIC TILE

More expensive than laminates but less expensive than solid-surface materials and stone, tile is an elegant, versatile countertop surface. Not only is it burn-, scorch-, and blister-resistant, but it is also virtually moisture-proof. A true work surface, tile allows you to cut and prepare foods directly upon it with no need for insulating or other protective devices. Its colors are stable and do not fade over time.

Tile is available in a greater variety of colors than solid-surface materials offer, but unlike those, they can be installed by a skilled do-it-yourselfer as well as by a professional.

Tile can help you create a highly personalized kitchen. Be aware, however, that custom-designed patterns and handpainted backsplashes can add significantly to your cost, particularly if the tiles happen to be set on the diagonal, which requires a good deal of cutting. A less expensive method of achieving such a personalized effect is to create stock patterns or murals using painted tiles already available from manufacturers.

Before you choose colors, patterns, sizes, and textures, however, buy a few samples of the actual tile and see how they look in your kitchen. Real samples are far more reliable indicators than photos of tiled countertops in printed brochures.

The chief disadvantage of tile actually stems from one of its great strengths: the tremendous variety of colors and patterns available can be very confusing. Prices range dramatically, too. You can spend between $5 and $20 per square foot for a tile countertop installation. Not all types of tile are appropriate for countertops, however, and knowing some of the differences will help narrow the choices.

In the past, the look of grouting in a tile countertop was displeasing to some people; others had previous experience with grout that had cracked, stained, or mildewed. Another objection to tiled countertops was that because the grout is slightly recessed, the countertop does not provide a completely flat, even work surface.

In fact, although tile is resistant to stains, grout, if left untreated, is not. Grout joints should be treated with an acrylic joint sealer or an oil furniture polish to help them resist soil.

However, technology has not passed tile by. In recent years, new adhesive techniques and improvements in grouting have been introduced. As a result, tile can be installed more quickly and easily than in the past. Besides traditional Portland cement grouts, latex-modified and epoxy grouts have appeared on the market. Grout is also available in a variety of colors now, so that it, too, can be used as a design accent.

Although some tile is made by hand, much is machine-made (see chapter 9). Because the more precise installation that machine-made tile makes possible is of greater concern in planning countertops than it might be in creating flooring or decorative treatments such as backsplashes and borders, it is the machine-made type that most countertop installers prefer.

The American National Standards Institute (ANSI) has developed standards for materials as well as for the installation of ceramic tile. ANSI classifies tile into three groups, based on surface finish—glazed, unglazed, and special finish; and into four categories

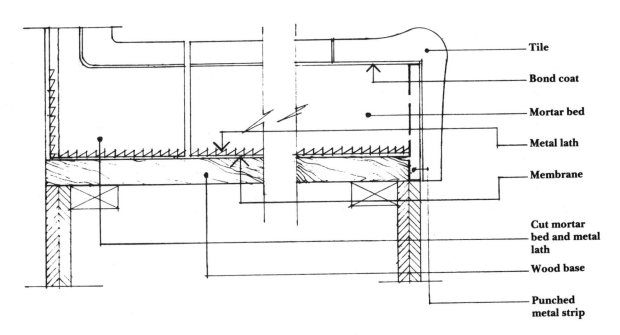

Tile

Bond coat

Mortar bed

Metal lath

Membrane

Cut mortar bed and metal lath

Wood base

Punched metal strip

Figure 10.1   Tile Counters: Conventional Mortar Installation

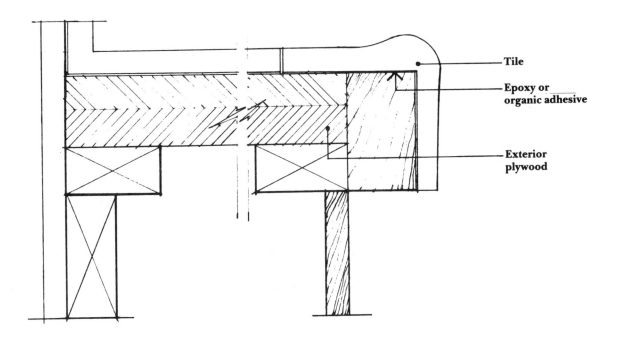

Tile

Epoxy or organic adhesive

Exterior plywood

Figure 10.2   Tile Counters: Thin-set Installation

of permeability—nonvitreous, semivitreous, dense-bodied vitreous, and impervious.

The four main categories of tile are glazed wall tile, quarry tile, paver tile, and ceramic mosaics. Most tile can be used for countertops, although quarry tile, which can be sealed, is not recommended because of its porousness; it will absorb food stains. However, nonvitreous or semivitreous tile can be sealed to protect against stains and water absorption; special sealers are available in tile supply stores. Generally, glazed tile is better than unglazed tile for a countertop.

Glazed Wall Tile. This is a nonvitreous tile with a glaze. Though inappropriate for floors, it is highly suitable for countertops. It is usually about ¼ to ⁵⁄₁₆ inch thick and comes in 4¼-by-4¼-inch and 6-by-6-inch squares.

A subcategory of glazed wall tile is *decorative thin wall tile,* which has handpainted or silk-screened designs fired into the glaze. It should be used for decorative purposes only—for example, backsplashes—because it lacks the structural strength of conventional glazed wall tile.

Ceramic Mosaics. These are smaller tiles, often 2-by-2-inch squares, generally ¼ inch thick. They are available glazed or unglazed, but the glazed versions are better for countertops. They come in square, hexagonal, and rectanguar shapes, and often come mounted on large sheets.

Paver Tile. This looks like ceramic mosaics, only the face area is larger than 6 square inches. Sizes range up to 12-inch squares or 4-by-6-inch or 4-by-8-inch rectangles, in ⅜- to ⅝-inch thicknesses. Usually used for floors, paver tile can be used for countertops if it is glazed. Two drawbacks are that fewer trim pieces are available for this type of tile, and that light-colored porcelain pavers tend to stain.

Quarry Tile. This is a semivitreous or vitreous clay tile, usually left unglazed. It comes in squares of more than 6 inches and thicknesses of ½ to ¾ inch. As we have noted, it is not recommended for countertops.

Imported tile is described in different terminology. For example, *Monocottura* refers to tile that is baked once, with the bisque and glaze fired at the same time. Some American manufacturers are now producing

this type of tile, and it is highly suitable for countertops.

Other types of nonvitreous wall tiles are Cottoforte and white-body earthenware, both of which take color easily and are highly decorative.

Trim pieces, such as coves, bullnose, radius, corner, and base pieces (see section on edge treatments, page 139), are important because they give the countertop a finished appearance, as well as providing decorative accents. These pieces can also be used in conjunction with other kinds of materials for a more customized look. Trim pieces should be ordered together with the tile for the countertop and (if appropriate) for the backsplash, because the color is more likely to match that way.

Shipping cartons should have manufacturers' grade stamps on them because this shows that the tile conforms to ANSI standards for porosity, color, and appearance. A blue label means "standard grade," or that the tile has passed all requirements. A yellow label means "second grade," or that the tile has passed all requirements but has minor flaws in its appearance. An orange label denotes decorative thin wall tile, and that the tile should not be used as a horizontal surface. These grade stamps should not be confused with the markings on Italian tile cartons, where red printing denotes first-choice tiles and blue or green second-choice tiles.

Installing Tile

If you're not changing the basic configuration of your kitchen, you can install tile directly over the existing countertop surface, whether it is laminate or tile.

First the existing top must be sandpapered to make it rough; then it should be wiped clean. If the countertop includes a sink, it must be removed. Since the new countertop will raise the sink slightly, the pipes may need to be extended.

In a new installation, the carpenter must first cut a plywood counter that will receive the tile. Marine plywood is an excellent choice (although it is expensive) because its use will reduce the possibility of movement, swelling, and moisture problems. The thickness of the counter should be adjusted to the thickness of the tile. That is, if the countertop is to be a standard 1½ inches thick, and the tile is ¼ inch thick, then the plywood should be 1¼ inches thick.

For a new installation, sink and appliance cutouts are made when the plywood base for the tile is being installed. Your contractor should check for proper fit before the tile is installed. Cutouts should be at least 2 inches away from the wall or backsplash. The bottom edge of the front tile trim should allow for sufficient clearance for a dishwasher or compactor to be installed beneath it.

The thin-set, or adhesive, technique is used far more frequently for countertop installations than "mud" (see chapter 9). Exceptional cases generally involve antique or Mexican tiles.

The tile is applied directly to the plywood base. First the front trim pieces are installed; then the rest of the tile is installed, working from front to back. Some tiles come with "spacers" so that joints between them will be equal in size. If there is any special cutting to be done, the tile cutter will do it before laying the tile.

The adhesive has to dry and firm up for at least a day before grout can be applied. Grout is pressed into the joints, and the film is removed from the tile with a damp sponge. When the remaining grout haze is dry, it is cleaned off with a soft, dry cloth.

Backsplashes are often installed 4 to 6 inches, or one or two tile heights, up the wall, but today it is more common to see a full-height backsplash that extends from the countertop to the bottom of the wall cabinet.

Grouts and Grouting

Making the small joints that look best in a countertop usually requires using nonsanded grouts (see chapter 9). If you have a small kitchen, it makes sense to use a grout color that is similar to the tile color. A contrasting grout creates the sense of a checkerboard pattern, which will be interesting but usually too busy for a small space. Very dark grouts tend to take on water stains, so medium or neutral shades are a better choice.

Grout should be sealed only after it has hardened and fully cured. Damp curing may be needed in hot, dry climates. Since this requires several days after tile installation, make an allowance for this in planning the construction schedule.

THE NATURAL STONES

Marble

Many designers refuse to use marble in the kitchen because it is so porous and stains so easily. Oils can easily permeate and stain it, while such liquids as lemon juice, vinegar, and alcohol will burn the polish off. Even with care, it requires frequent cleaning and polishing. Marble is also an expensive material—as much as five times as expensive as a laminate countertop—and customization such as bullnosed edges and cutouts can boost the cost even more.

That said, you should be aware that if you are drawn to the material because of its rich veining and smooth, sensuous texture, certain types of marble are more suitable for countertops than others.

Instead of using a polished marble, employing white Carrara marble with a honed finish might be more practical for the kitchen. It, too, is a high-maintenance material, however. It needs to be oiled and waxed to maintain its patina and reduce the chances of its staining, and scrubbed with a fine steel wool. Using pads or trivets under pots and hot dishes is also a necessity, for it can easily be scorched.

Marble is rated according to its relative strength/fragility, on a scale developed by the Marble Institute of America. Those marbles ranked A and B are the most solid and the soundest, require less maintenance, and produce less waste in cutting than C- and D-rated marble. Marble with a relatively large amount of veining tends to be weaker than its lesser-veined counterparts. Generally, the marbles that are the most colorful and decorative are also the most fragile. This is an important consideration, since the whole slab of countertop will have to be replaced if it suffers a major break.

Ironically, the most fragile marbles are also the most expensive. White Carrara marble, on the other hand, not only is plentiful and ages gracefully but is also less expensive than other marbles.

An alternative is to use marble tiles as the countertop material. Their standard size is 12 by 12 by ⅜ inches, but other widths, lengths, and depths are readily available. Marble tiles can also be used as a decorative element for backsplashes. They, too, are highly porous but are less costly than solid marble. If you use marble tile, care must be taken in creating a front-edge treatment, such as a bullnose with ceramic tile or wood.

Since marble shades are not easily matched, and color variations are unpredictable, choosing a marble on the basis of a small sample (as you might reasonably do for a laminate or synthetic solid-surface material) can lead to problems. Instead, you should visit the fabricator with your designer or contractor to see what a larger slab will really look like before you decide to order it.

Like stainless steel, granite, and solid-surface materials, a marble countertop requires a template before it can be fabricated. This will give the cutter the exact pattern needed and eliminate inaccuracies that might occur if measurements alone are specified. Templates are normally made of brown wrapping paper, cardboard, or masonite boards. All cutouts must be prepared to the minutest fraction.

Countertops are not always made with only one slab of marble. Two or more pieces of marble may be joined for a large installation. If you're considering using a large piece, make sure it will fit through your doorway, as well as into your elevator, if required.

Typically, a marble countertop is furnished in a minimum thickness of 1¼ inches. But other configurations are possible with materials of different thicknesses. A ¾-inch counter can be glued to a ¾-inch edge treatment, for example, to achieve the appearance of a 1½-inch counter.

Be aware that the countertop should be supported if there is to be an overhang. If there is an overhang greater than 12 inches, plywood extending from the subcounter should be used for support.

Granite

Granite has many excellent qualities that most people mistakenly attribute to marble. It is practically impervious to heat, so hot pots and dishes can be placed directly on its surface. It doesn't scratch or scar, so food can be cut or chopped directly on its surface. Because it is dramatically less porous than marble, it is also virtually stain-resistant.

Granite is not entirely perfect, however. It is susceptible to grease stains. Some suppliers seal the stone with a protective coating to prevent stains from butter, grease, bacon, and chicken fat, although many do not.

Besides its great durability and ease of maintenance, granite has a rich texture and color that imbues it with timeless aesthetic appeal. Although a range of colors is available, the darker hues are the most commonly found. Granite can be supplied with a polished finish, a thermal finish (which feels rough-textured), or a honed finish (which has a matte appearance).

Slabs can measure 4½ feet wide and up to 9 feet long. For larger installations, such as an island or peninsula, more than one piece will be used. Because the seams will show, the fabricator should take pains to plan a configuration that places them in the most inconspicuous places on the countertop.

The graining pattern in granite is generally more consistent than in marble, so you can rely more easily on a small sample in making your choice. Look for purity of grain, clarity of color, and amount of veining (like marble, granite with more veining tends to be weaker). Beware of seaming and cracks, and be sure to ask about iron content, since this can cause rusting.

Another advantage granite has over marble is that slabs of 1¼- to 1½-inch thickness can overhang base cabinets by as much as 18 inches without support, although this assumes that the base cabinets are of good quality. Granite slabs that are only ¾ inch thick need support brackets, because the thinner material snaps more easily.

Granite's biggest drawback is its potential for breakage, because it is so brittle. Cutouts, for example, should be 2¾ to 3 inches from the edge of the countertop surface, all the way around it.

A template should be used in fabricating a granite countertop. Depending on the supplier, cutouts will be made in the shop or during the installation process. Both the fabricator and the installer must be highly skilled with granite; there is no room for errors or adjustments during installation.

Granite is the most expensive of countertop materials. The price results primarily from the high cost of quarrying and delivering it. As with marble, customization adds significantly to the cost. Bullnose edges are more expensive than rounded or beveled edges, for example. (See "Design on the Edge," below.)

Island installations are always more expensive than regular countertops because they require four finished sides. Angle cuts and corner cuts also add to the cost, as do acquiring larger slabs and using thick-.nesses of more than 1½ inches.

OTHER COUNTERTOP ALTERNATIVES

Butcher Block

The term *butcher block* refers to maple or other hardwoods (predominantly oak) that are laminated together in strips. Butcher block complements both country and contemporary kitchen styles, although it is not appropriate for all areas of the kitchen. While it can serve as an excellent chopping board or food preparation area, it should not be used near sink areas. Moisture will lift the material in time, and heat and light through a window at the sink will dry it out and fade it over time.

If your designer or contractor specifies butcher block, ask two key questions. First, what type of wood is to be used? The harder the wood, the better it will ward off cutting and scratching damage. Second, how will the butcher block resist damage from water and heat—that is, how will the wood be finished? If the countertop is *not* going to be used for chopping or other food preparation, it can be sealed with a urethane sealer, for example. Otherwise, if the wood is to be prefinished, it will need a nontoxic lacquer finish and penetrating sealer. No oiling will be necessary. For unfinished woods, the countertop must be finished by oiling. Proper maintenance will consist of oiling it weekly with a mineral oil. It must also be protected from any standing water and food remains.

Stainless Steel

As a countertop material, stainless steel is still relatively rare but is steadily increasing in use by people who want their kitchens to look like a professional cook's.

Stainless steel is a costly material, far more expensive than laminates or butcher block, about on a par with natural stone. Besides its "high-tech" appearance, it is resistant to stains and heat and easy to maintain. However, there are drawbacks: It does scratch, and because it is a noisy material, it should have a wood underlining to absorb some of the sound. It

also reflects light more than a matte or wood surface would, so extra care must be taken with the kitchen's lighting plan to avoid glare.

A stainless steel countertop should be made of the heaviest-gauge steel. It can be ordered from a restaurant supply source and custom fabricated for your kitchen.

Although you may not find natural stone, wood, or steel materials appropriate for the entire kitchen, dramatic design accents can be created by using them in select areas.

DESIGN ON THE EDGE

What sets a good kitchen apart from a great kitchen are the details. Countertop edge treatments present an opportunity to create an elegant, dramatic, whimsical, or other type of feeling, highly personalized to reflect your own taste. However, before you and your designer or contractor let your imaginations fly, there are some edge basics to learn. Generally, these edges will be produced before, rather than during, the installation process. They can be divided into the following six categories:

Self-edge. This is the most basic kind of edge treatment, the one we all grew up with. It is a simple configuration of two pieces joined to each other at a 90-degree angle. With a color-through laminate, this type of edge need not be visually boring. It can be done in two tones, for example.

Double Radius. Also referred to as a double round-over, this type of countertop has rounded edges on the top and bottom.

Bullnose. This countertop, as the name implies, is completely rounded. It is also referred to as a 180-degree wrap.

Waterfall. Think of this as half of a bullnose; the top edge is rounded, but the bottom is not.

Chamfered Edge. Here the edge is beveled, or pared off, at a 45-degree angle, leaving a spot for a line of contrasting material.

Ogee. This kind of edge is cut to reveal a concave curve, which, like the chamfered edge, can be filled with a contrasting material.

Edge treatments can mix different materials creatively. Adding a "stripe" of a stock wood or of laminate edge molding is the simplest way of achieving a

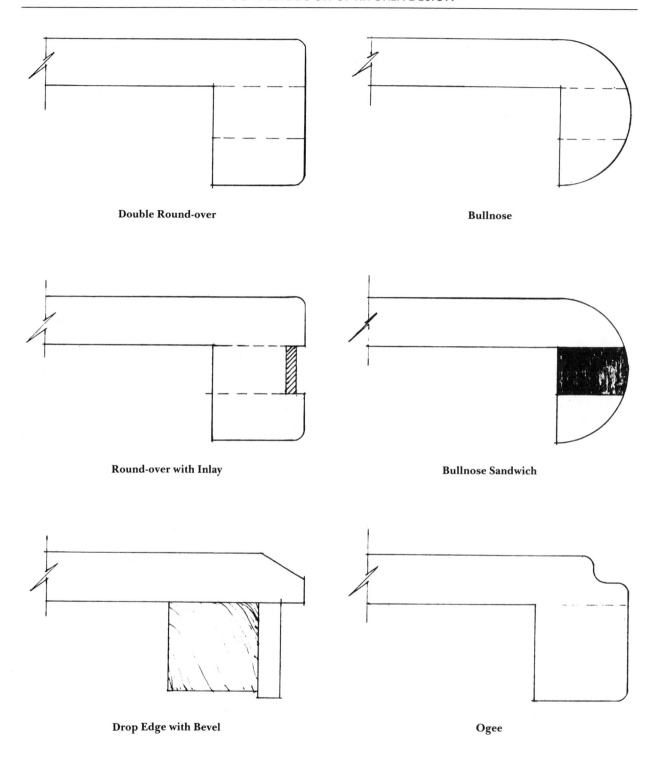

Double Round-over

Bullnose

Round-over with Inlay

Bullnose Sandwich

Drop Edge with Bevel

Ogee

**Figure 10.3   Solid Surfaces: Decorative
Edge Treatments**

**Figure 10.4   Solid Surfaces: Decorative
Edge Treatments**

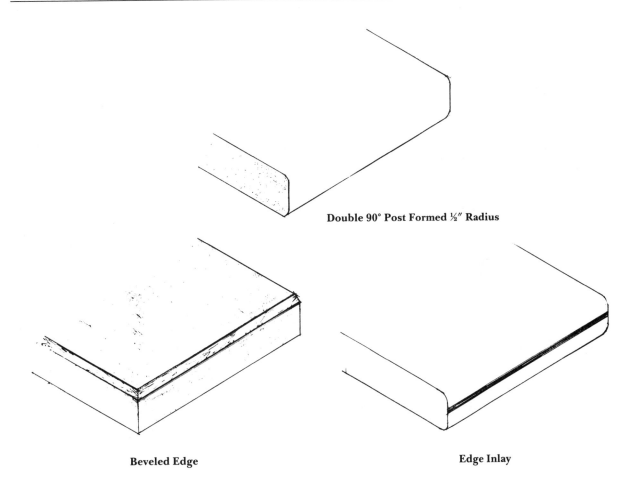

Double 90° Post Formed ½″ Radius

Beveled Edge

Edge Inlay

Figure 10.5   Decorative Edge Details
Laminates

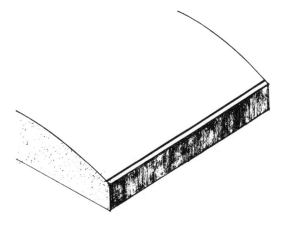

Sloped Edge

Figure 10.6   Decorative Edge Details
Laminates

little design flair in the countertop. Here are just a few of the many other possibilities:

- a plain laminate double-radius top with a "skirt" of mosaic tile
- a round-over with laminate, veneer, or solid-surface inlay
- a bullnose "sandwich" with a central contrasting color or material, possibly with a checkered inlay
- a quarter-round accent strip in a routed edge
- a triple half-round edge
- a cloverleaf-shaped edge
- triple grooves routed into the edge
- rounded trim tile edging a solid-surface countertop

Countertop Measurements

Countertops are usually 1½ inches thick, consisting of ¾ inch of countertop surface attached to ¾ inch of particleboard or plywood underlayment. Standard countertop height is 36 inches.

Countertops usually overhang cabinets by ¾ to 1 inch. That means that if your base cabinets are 24 inches deep, the countertop will be 25 inches. There are design implications here. If a tall cabinet is also 24 inches deep, for example, it will look more harmonious if it is pulled out from the wall so that it will be flush with the countertop overhang.

The overhang should also relate to the depth of a drawer base cabinet or the thickness of the molding on base cabinet doors. In these cases, the overhang can be greater than 1 inch for a more customized appearance.

Overhangs also affect appliance-width clearances. In double-checking these clearances, the space should be measured from countertop to countertop, not from cabinet to cabinet.

Backsplashes can cover the entire wall between the countertop and wall cabinet, or they can run 4 to 6 inches up the wall.

11

Floor Plans That Work
—and Why

There is no such thing as a perfect kitchen plan, because designers and contractors must work with so many limitations. Apartments and townhouses tend to have small, galley-shaped kitchens, whereas the kitchens in older homes usually have multiple entries that often cannot be changed. Personal preferences dictate design limitations as well. If you cannot work with a drop-in range/oven combination, for example, you immediately eliminate one possible space saver.

The plans presented here were *real* solutions to *real* design challenges. None are perfect, but they are striking, imaginative, and highly functional examples of how space planning and design was geared to match the needs and preferences of a variety of households.

1. Opening Up a Small Apartment Kitchen

THE CHALLENGE

The basic plan in the galley-shaped, 8-by-10-foot kitchen in this condominium apartment contained a workable triangle between the sink (on one wall) and the range and refrigerator (at opposite ends of the opposite wall), and efficient counter space.

But with only one access, the galley was a "dead end," and the hallway to the rest of the apartment was tunnel-like and depressing.

WHY THE PLAN WORKS

1. The design solution involved closing off the coat closet behind the kitchen on the hallway side, and opening it on the kitchen side. This created an alcove for the refrigerator and allowed for a second entry to and from the kitchen.

A cabinet measuring 24 inches deep and 21 inches high was placed over the refrigerator. Three vertical dividers provide storage for cutting boards, serving trays, and storage bags. The right side of the cabinet is for the storage of oversize objects—punch bowls, woks, and other items that are seldom used.

2. The plan also involved moving the sink and dishwasher to the left of the counter (opposite the new hallway entry), and moving the range and micro-wave to the right, with a 3-inch filler and countertop at the right for safe fire clearance to the wall. This

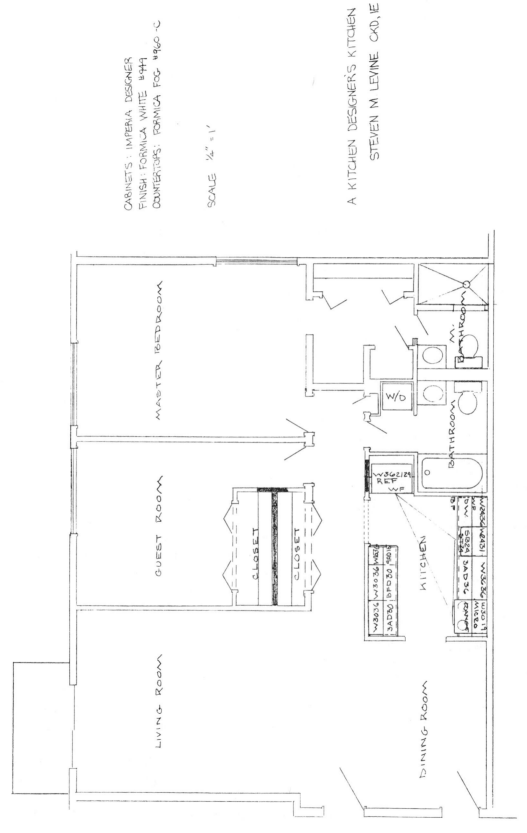

CABINETS: IMPERIA DESIGNER
FINISH: FORMICA WHITE #949
COUNTERTOPS: FORMICA FOG #960-C

SCALE ½" = 1'

A KITCHEN DESIGNER'S KITCHEN
STEVEN M LEVINE CKD, 1E

Figure 11.1   Enlarging a Small Apartment Kitchen

provided 2 feet of counter to the left of the sink and 3 feet to the right, sufficient for both food preparation and cleanup.

3. The plan also works because there is one continuous countertop now on the hallway/kitchen wall side of the kitchen, with ample wall and base cabinet storage.

(Design credit: Charles River Kitchens, Needham, MA)

2. Making a Townhouse Kitchen Smaller to Add More Space

THE CHALLENGE

The original plan for this townhouse kitchen combined the worst of all possible worlds: limited overall space of 11 by 12 feet that featured a paltry 30-inch work space between the sink and the range, a 14-foot round-trip hike from the sink to the longest work counter, inadequate storage, no eating area, and no possibility of repositioning the exterior doors or windows.

WHY THE PLAN WORKS

1. The design solution added three new walls and reduced the overall width of the room for more storage, more countertop, a breakfast bar, and a more efficient work triangle. A wall is positioned 25 inches back from the counter edge, allowing for the cabinet depth of 24 inches and a 1-inch counter overhang.

2. The counter-to-counter distance was reduced to 42 inches. The new width of the room is 38 inches smaller than in the original plan. A new row of cabinets created an additional 76 inches of available wall storage space.

3. The refrigerator was moved across the room and to the left of the sink. A side panel and 24-inch cabinet above the refrigerator were added for tray and cutting-board storage.

4. The sink was moved slightly to the right of the window center, to add more work space between the sink and the refrigerator: 46 inches versus 30 inches in the old plan.

5. The range and microwave were positioned across from the sink.

6. Two new pantry cabinets were placed in the kitchen along with the new 37½-inch return walls. A

breakfast bar for two is positioned in a corner to the left of the narrow pantry.

(Design credit: Charles River Kitchens, Needham, MA)

3. A Double Island Defines a Kitchen in Open Space

THE CHALLENGE

The kitchen in this large house was to be incorporated into a 30-by-50-foot "great room" addition to the existing home. The chief dilemmas were as follows: how to define the kitchen space as distinct from the balance of the space, which was to be used for a living/dining/entertainment room; how to light it properly, considering that the space had a 21-foot vaulted ceiling; how to provide ample storage with little wall space; and how to make the spacious kitchen both efficient and workable for more than one cook.

WHY THE PLAN WORKS

1. A cable-suspended light bridge incorporating recessed down-lighting helped define the space. Its angled shape mirrors the shape of the larger of two islands in the plan. The larger island defines the space for working, with a cleanup sink, dishwasher, and compactor. The dining counter is set at an upper level of this working island, which also serves as a buffer to the people seated at the table in the living/dining/entertainment room.

2. The smaller island is devoted to food preparation, with a separate sink and cooktop. It also creates a compact work triangle, whose perimeter measures a comfortable 18 feet between the primary range, food preparation sink, and the refrigerator.

3. There is ample counter space for food preparation along the wall: 4 feet on either side of the primary range, 2 feet on one side of the smaller island, and approximately 6 feet on the other side of the smaller island. Two people can easily work in this kitchen.

4. Storage for dishes is provided in the base cabinet next to the dishwasher, and for glasses in the wall cabinet next to the primary range. A built-in spice rack is convenient for both cooktops. A walk-in pantry is concealed behind the cabinet doors that are located between the ovens and the refrigerator.

5. The kitchen's height configurations are appro-

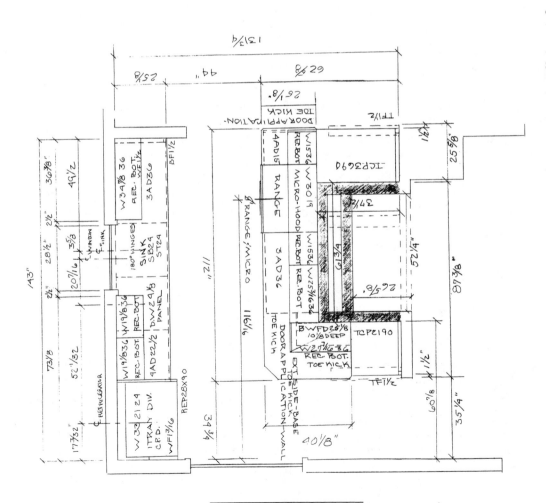

Figure 11.2   Improving the Efficiency of a Townhouse Kitchen

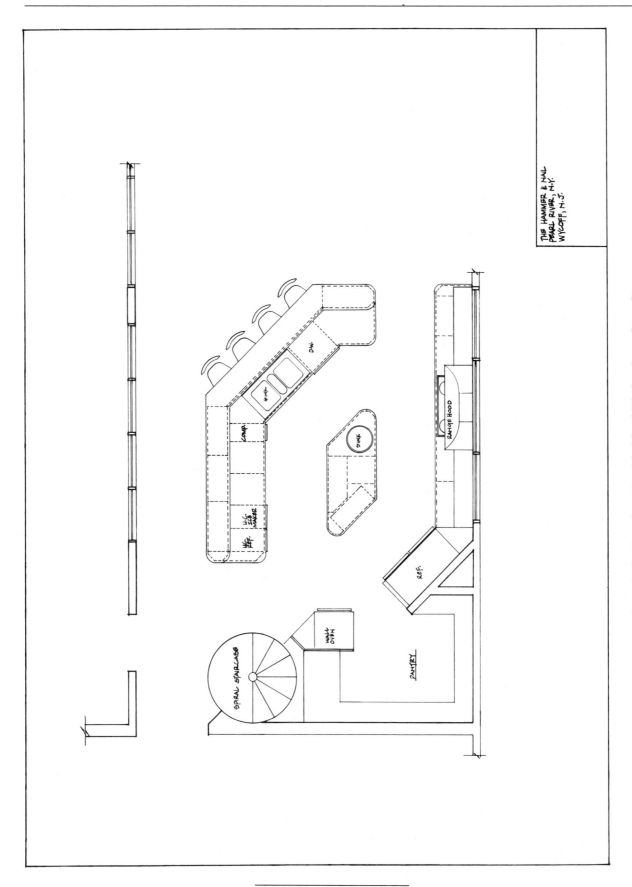

THE HAMMER & NAIL
PEARL RIVER, N.Y.
WYCOFF, N.J.

SPIRAL STAIRCASE

WALL OVEN

PANTRY

REF.

RANGE HOOD

SINK

D.W.

SINK

COMP.

MIC
&
WARMER

REF.

Figure 11.3   Creating a Double-island Kitchen in an Open Space

priate; all the tall elements—the refrigerator, the tall cabinets, and the wall ovens—are located at one end of the layout.

(Design credit: The Hammer & Nail, Wyckoff, NJ)

4. Creating Multiple Working Spaces in a Vacation Home

THE CHALLENGE

This seaside vacation home was designed for a family of seven that often doubles in size on weekends. Multiple cooks enjoy entertaining, from sit-down dinners to beachfront barbecues. There were two design constraints: the site was small and narrow, and the kitchen had to provide views of the ocean.

WHY THE PLAN WORKS

1. The modified U shape allows for a compact path between sink, island range, refrigerator, and ovens, yet provides ample work and storage space so several people can work comfortably together.

Measurements are the following: 4 feet, 8 inches from sink to range; 3 feet from range to refrigerator; 7 feet, 6 inches from refrigerator to sink. The kitchen itself is 16 feet, 8 inches wide and 20 feet, 6 inches long. Adjacent to the kitchen is a walk-in office/laundry center that measures 6 feet, 6 inches by 15 feet.

2. There is a dynamic, highly functional relationship between the sink and the angled peninsula breakfast bar. The breakfast bar is also designed to double as a buffet server for the dining room.

3. Additional dining space is accommodated at a table in the kitchen, which has easy access to the refrigerator, and to buffet space atop the base cabinets between the refrigerator and the office/laundry area.

4. Ample continuous counter space is provided for work: a total of 44 feet, not counting the island. (The island might have served multiple functions by including a second sink and a second dishwasher, and by moving the range to the breakfast bar. Since the kitchen was built, the homeowners have agreed that there should have been two dishwashers.)

5. The island is rounded so that it does not pose a safety hazard to people working or conversing in the kitchen.

(Design credit: Salustro Partnership/Architects and Planners, Watchung, NJ)

5. Kitchen, New Deck "Open Up" 30-Year-Old Tract House

THE CHALLENGE

The owners of this 30-year-old suburban Colonial-style tract home wanted an updated, open feeling. They wanted to be able to view the new deck and their backyard when they opened their front door. They also wanted the kitchen eating area to be separate from the work area. The existing kitchen was small, but the homeowners did not want to expand the house substantially.

WHY THE PLAN WORKS

1. Several of the homeowners' concerns were addressed by moving the kitchen from where it had been (in what is now largely the laundry area) and adding a glassed-in breakfast room to the back of the kitchen. This allowed the view to the deck and backyard.

2. The kitchen was doubled in size, to 16 by 17 feet, plus the 6-by-12-foot breakfast room. It functions well because there is a compact work flow from the refrigerator to the sink (5 feet), from the sink to the range (4 feet), and from the range to the refrigerator (5 feet).

3. The 5-by-7-foot center island is a functional food preparation center and includes the range and secondary sink. The island also serves to separate the work areas from the dining area.

4. The refrigerator is easily accessible for people in the breakfast room.

5. The plan allows for an efficient use of space considering that there are so many entries to the kitchen: from the main hall, the dining room, the family room, and the deck. A good traffic pattern has been established between the family room, the kitchen, and the dining room. What otherwise might have been wasted space along the wall next to the entry to the family room is devoted to a planning center. Tall storage space is provided along the 6-foot-wall opposite the secondary sink in the island.

6. In addition to the work space at the island, there is sufficient work/landing/cleanup space along the sink/refrigerator wall, with 2 feet on one side of the sink, and 3 feet between the sink and refrigerator.

(Design credit: Salustro Partnership/Architects and Planners, Watchung, NJ)

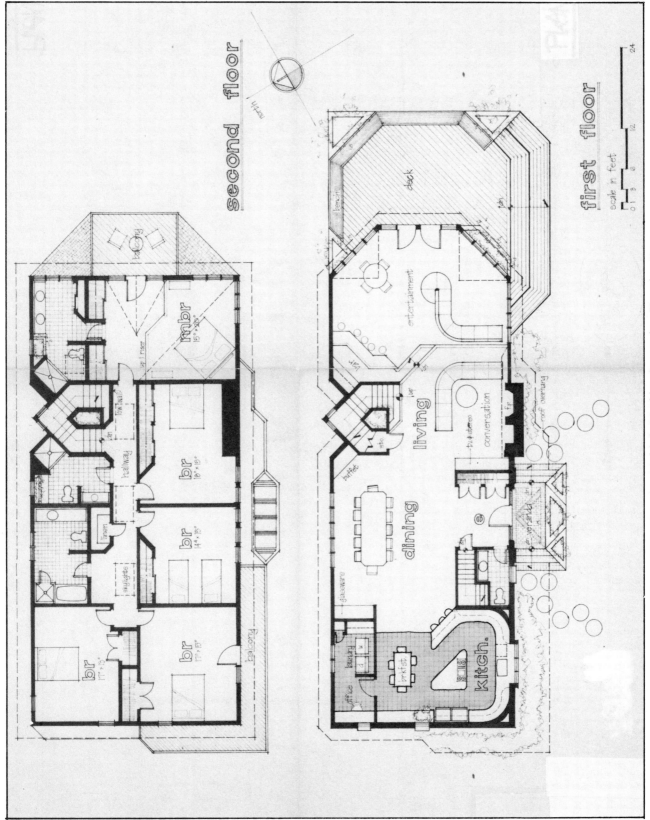

Figure 11.4 Creating Multiple Working Spaces in a Vacation Home

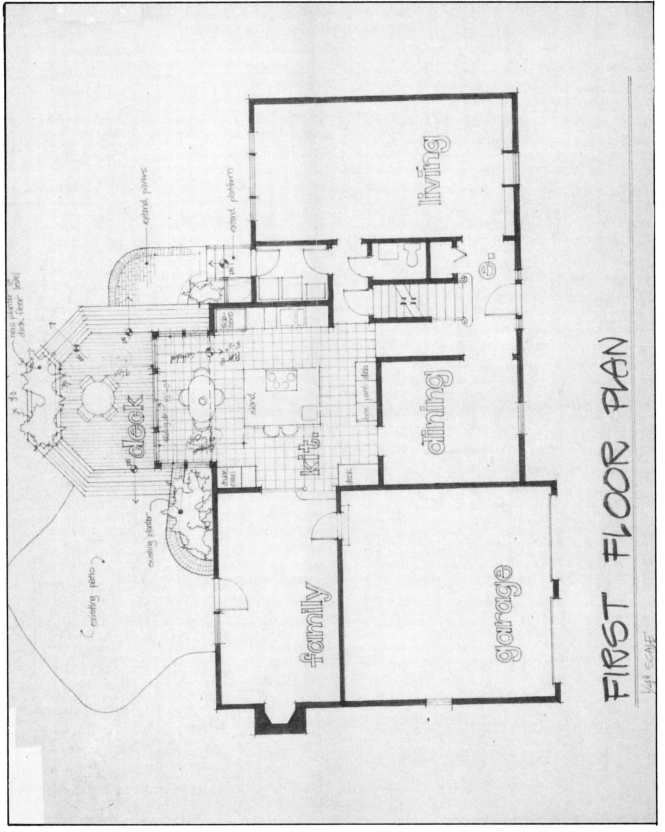

FIRST FLOOR PLAN

1/4 SCALE

Figure 11.5   Transforming a Thirty-year-old Tract House Kitchen

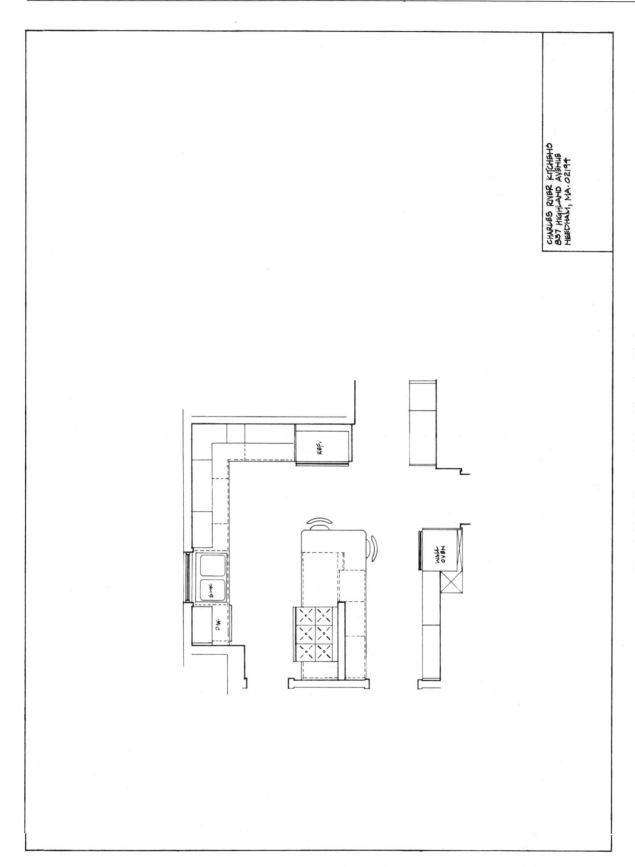

CHARLES RIVER KITCHENS
857 HIGHLAND AVENUE
NEEDHAM, MA. 02194

REF.

SINK

D.W.

WALL OVEN

Figure 11.6   Reorganizing a Victorian Kitchen

6. Reorganizing a Victorian Kitchen for Gourmet Cooks

THE CHALLENGE

The kitchen in this old Victorian house was spacious but poorly organized. The original plan included the dangerous placement of the range at the end of a cabinet run, directly under a window. What little counter space was available was not continuous, and it was usually used for storing items that overflowed from the too-few cabinets. The homeowners, gourmet cooks, wanted a commercial-style range, two kinds of ovens, and an eating area within the kitchen.

WHY THE PLAN WORKS

1. While the remodeled kitchen is still an L shape with a peninsula, as the original was, the room was enlarged by 30 inches in width and 24 inches in length, and the peninsula was turned into a multi-purpose space. The peninsula shape was retained because an island would not have fit (the room is 14 feet, 2 inches wide at its narrowest point and 14 feet, 1 inch long).

2. The new six-burner commercial range not only is aesthetically appealing but has been safely installed, with a 50-inch-high knee-wall behind the range that shields it from the view of diners seated at the breakfast bar in the peninsula. A suspended hood with a heavy-duty exhaust fan with 950-cfm capacity was installed over the range. Since the range is placed to the right end of the peninsula, the rest of the counter surface can be used for preparing food on the kitchen side and for eating on the "social" side. A 12-inch-wide counter maintains an extra-safe margin for heat, regardless of the range's design for side-wall zero-clearance.

3. The refrigerator is placed to the right of the sink, providing for right-hand hinging.

4. All the household's primary daily cooking, baking, and storage needs are available in the base and wall storage at the primary work counter. Tall pantry storage and an oven cabinet replace the desk in the original plan. The new kitchen provides roughly twice as much wall cabinet storage as there was in the original kitchen.

5. Although not depicted, skylights above the cabinets along the sink wall brighten the kitchen dramatically.

(Design credit: Charles River Kitchens, Needham, MA)

7. Expanding a Small, Dark Art Deco Kitchen

THE CHALLENGE

Although this five-bedroom Art Deco–style home was architecturally striking, its kitchen was small and poorly lit. A small lean-to type of addition had previously been connected to the side of the kitchen to serve as an entry and mud room, but looked awkward. The goal was to create a large kitchen with a better traffic flow, a task made more difficult because the kitchen entry was the family's most-used entry to the home.

WHY THE PLAN WORKS

1. The mud room is still a major entry and has been upgraded to provide a buffer area from the cold. A pocket door separates the kitchen from the mud room.

2. The food preparation area is separated from the cleanup area, which is placed in the large L-shaped space. The preparation area is just a few steps between the prep sink, the cooktop, and the refrigerator, yet despite this compactness, it still has sufficient work space for multiple cooks and for the requirements of entertaining.

3. Four counter stools in the half-circle extending from the island provide comfortable space for informal meals. A hot-water dispenser is conveniently placed in the island sink.

4. Because it's used infrequently, a separate freezer is located on the half-circle wall. Glass-doored wall cabinets mounted on the curved wall contain china, while the base cabinets store larger and less frequently used serving pieces.

5. The microwave is mounted to the left of the refrigerator, which makes food defrosting and reheating convenient. Microwave ware is stored in the base cabinet below.

6. Large-scale entertaining is facilitated with a second dishwasher and two additional sinks.

7. The kitchen is flooded with light through an 18-

foot window wall. New lighting includes both over- and under-cabinet fixtures as well as recessed cans.

(Design credit: kitchen interior design, Michael De Giulio, CKD, De Giulio Kitchen and Bath Design; architect, Stuart Shayman, Wilmette, IL)

8. An Elegant Pass-Through Is Structural and Efficient

THE CHALLENGE

This 1960 French Normandy home had elegance and charm, but the kitchen did not. It was small, broken up into separate areas, and dark. The goal was to create a space that was open and flowing, as well as to provide sufficient work space for more than one cook. Bearing walls had to be removed, so the space required restructuring.

WHY THE PLAN WORKS

1. One of the more striking elements of this plan is the separation of the kitchen and breakfast area. On the kitchen side is a cooktop with ample work space around it, attached to a raised pass-through counter that serves the breakfast area. The classical columns and elliptical arches, which maintain the Normandy style of the kitchen, are all structural elements. The arches hide the new 12-inch steel I-beam that supports the second floor, and the columns encase the steel posts that support the I-beam.

2. The ovens are placed on a wall of tall cabinets that wrap around a corner, and, among other functions, house a laundry chute. The peninsula's counter area opposite the ovens provides landing space for oven-cooked dishes.

3. The microwave is placed in a tall cabinet adjacent to the pass-through countertop; microwave ware is stored here. A 3-foot countertop work space has been provided between the microwave and the cooktop.

4. A desk area is centered below an existing window to allow for natural light and views to the outdoors.

5. Aisle space is a comfortable 4 feet, so that the cooks' paths aren't impeded by one another or by the open doors of appliances and cabinetry.

(Design credit: Michael De Giulio, CKD, De Giulio Kitchen and Bath Design, Wilmette, IL)

9. Moving a Kitchen Without Making Structural Changes

THE CHALLENGE

This English Tudor home underwent a complete redesign of the kitchen, eat-in area, and family room. The existing kitchen was located at the rear of the house, but the homeowners wanted to relocate it to the front, thereby creating a new adjoining family room overlooking the backyard.

WHY THE PLAN WORKS

1. The old kitchen has now been replaced by the new family room. Although there was extensive demolition of the existing walls, no major structural changes took place. The entrance to the attached garage was relocated to allow the creation of an eat-in area undisturbed by an access door to the garage. This door, the rear entrance vestibule, and the door at the rear stairs are grouped in the same circulation space.

2. The new kitchen is a basic L shape, housing wall ovens and the refrigerator along one wall and the sink and dishwasher along the other. The work space is supplemented by a 4-by-6½-foot island that includes a cooktop. The ovens are placed in a corner next to the refrigerator, and there is landing space for them on the island.

3. The kitchen cabinets were custom-made and have a 6-inch-high base below the cabinet, which, in some cases, conceals a storage drawer.

(Design credit: Dennis A. Myland, AIA, Montclair, NJ)

10. Angling for More Usable Space in an Old Farmhouse Kitchen

THE CHALLENGE

There's usually not a lot of "elbow room" in a kitchen of this small size, but this plan shows that even an 8-by-11-foot space can serve a small family comfortably. While the kitchen doesn't provide enough space to create an eat-in area, the dining room adjoins the kitchen, and no structural changes were required to execute the plan.

WHY THE PLAN WORKS

1. The key to creating more usable space in this modified U plan is the angled range, which allows for

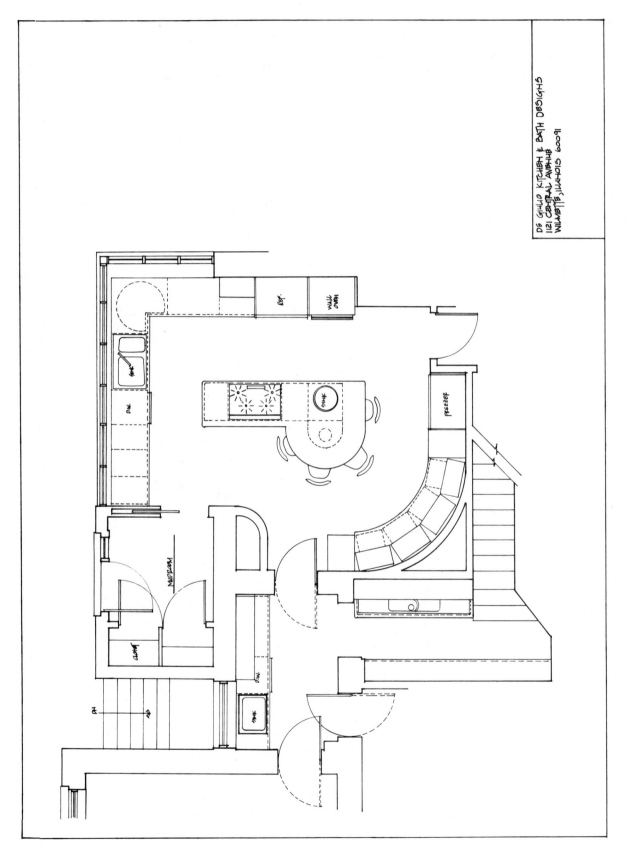

Figure 11.7A   Expanding a Small, Dark, Art Deco Kitchen

Figure 11.7B   Cabinetry for a Curved Wall

Figure 11.7C   Utilizing Natural and Artificial Light

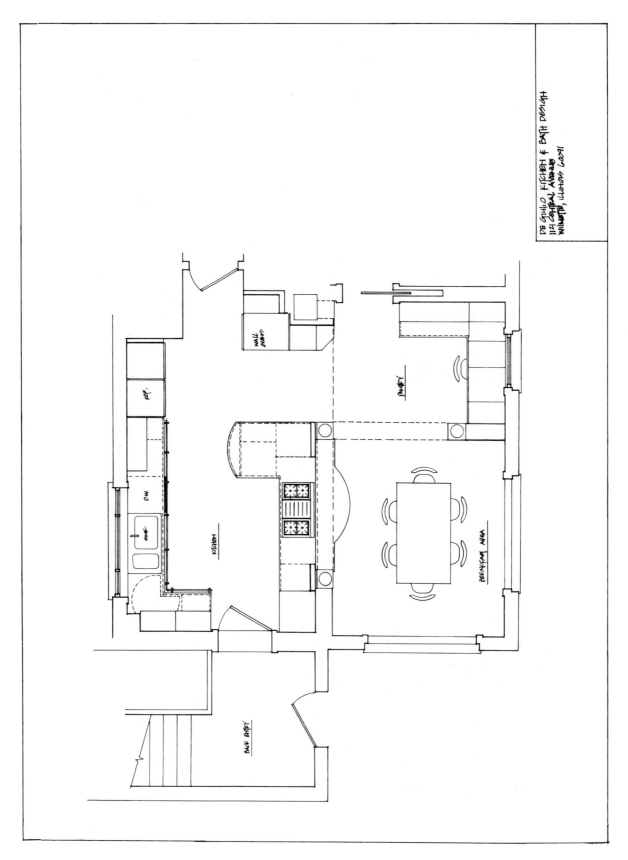

Figure 11.8A Constructing the Elegant Pass-through

Figure 11.8B   The Classic Columns Conceal Steel Beams

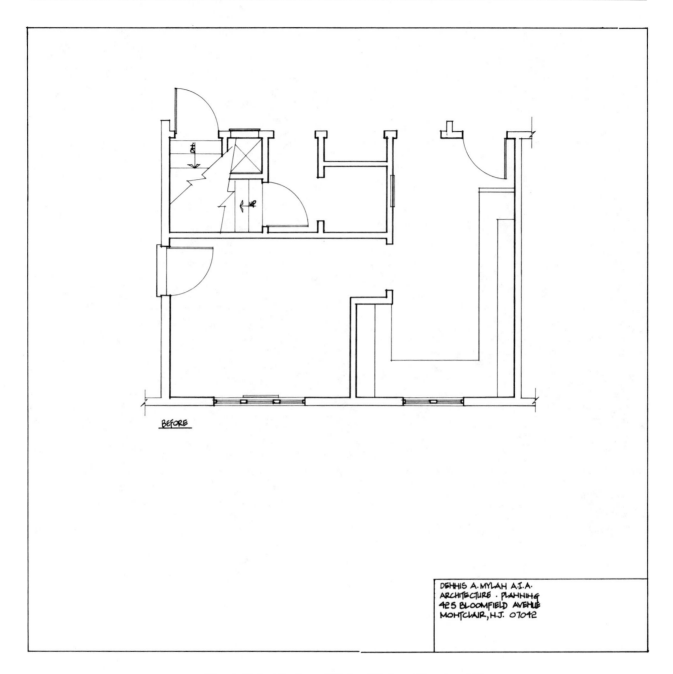

BEFORE

DENNIS A. MYLAN A.I.A.
ARCHITECTURE · PLANNING
425 BLOOMFIELD AVENUE
MONTCLAIR, N.J. 07042

Figure 11.9   Moving a Kitchen Without Structural Changes

A   Before

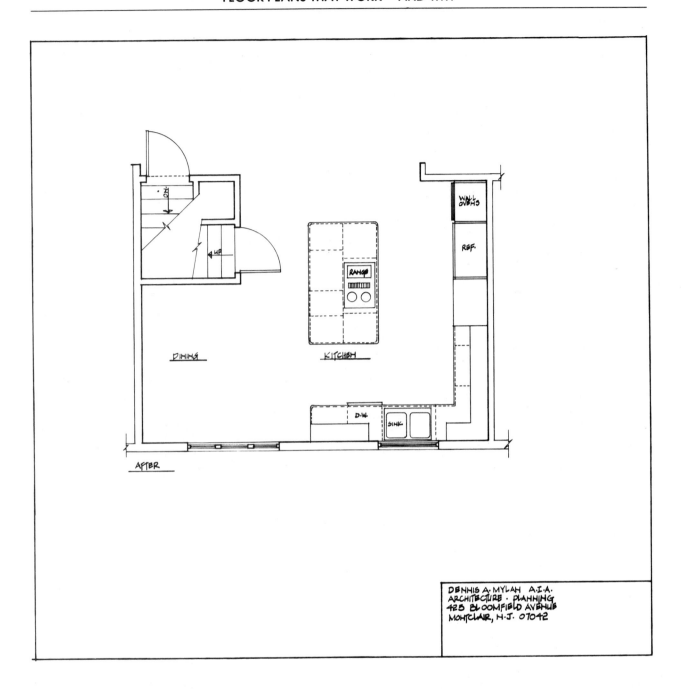

DINING

KITCHEN

RANGE

WALL OVENS

REF.

D·W

SINK

AFTER

DENNIS A. MYLAN A.I.A.
ARCHITECTURE · PLANNING
423 BLOOMFIELD AVENUE
MONTCLAIR, N.J. 07042

B   After

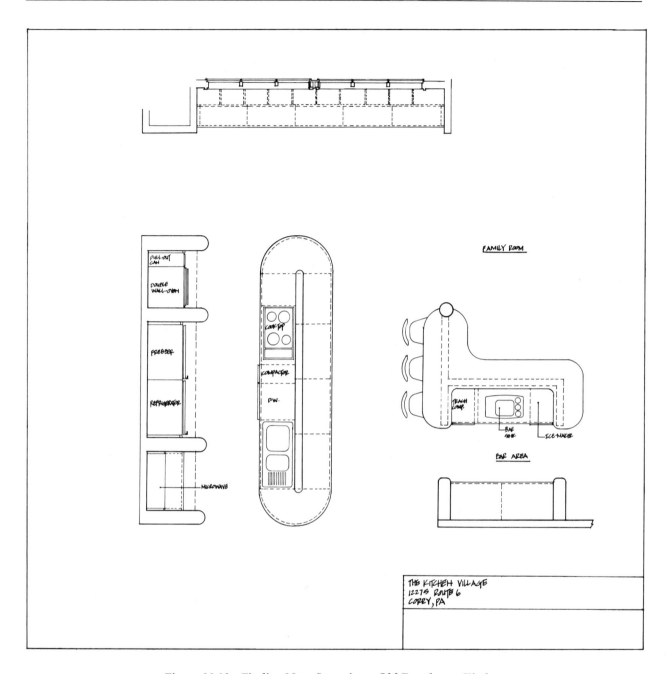

Figure 11.10   Finding More Space in an Old Farmhouse Kitchen

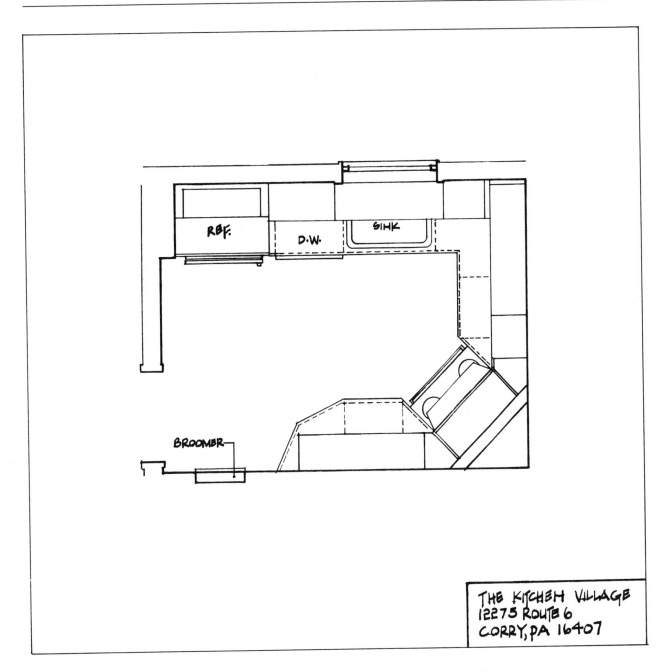

Figure 11.11 Clustering Appliances in a "Super Island"

good countertop work space on either side of it, as well as between it and the sink.

2. The microwave is recessed into a stairwell that still leaves sufficient headroom clearance. It is also convenient to the refrigerator.

3. The wall behind the refrigerator is furred out 4 inches to allow for the door to open more than 90 degrees. This capability makes it easier to retrieve foods in the crisper, for example.

4. One stud-wall cavity is fitted with a pantry closet front and a pegboard for hanging brooms, mops, and dustpans.

(Design credit: Connie Edwards, CKD, the Kitchen Village, Erie, PA)

11. Clustering Appliances and Work Space in a 15-Foot "Super Island"

THE CHALLENGE

The openness of this floor plan and the views in this lakefront home addition may be architecturally striking, but they presented several dilemmas. Among them: where to position appliances, how to provide sufficient storage, how to overcome the lack of wall space, and how to define the open space without obstructing the sense of openness, light, and views which the homeowners valued.

WHY THE PLAN WORKS

1. A 15-foot island contains the sink, dishwasher, compactor, and cooktop; generous cabinet storage is provided in half-round cabinets and base cabinets. The island also helps define the space. The cook can interact with people gathered at the separate snack bar/serving island opposite the "super island"; it also provides a transition to the family room.

2. Measuring 15 feet, 9 inches, the wall on the other side of the "super island" houses a refrigerator and separate freezer, easily accessible for the cook, with a microwave and double wall ovens flanking them.

3. The lack of shallow and easily accessible wall cabinets is offset with the placement of 12-inch "floating" cabinets under the windows overlooking the lake. No more than countertop height, these are actually wall cabinets, rather than base cabinets, that have been attached to the wall below the windows. Under-cabinet lighting reinforces the "floating" appearance.

4. Sufficient aisle space is provided between the snack counter and the "super island" to allow for traffic to flow comfortably to the family room. The ample space also permits diners to be seated or to stand and leave the table without feeling cramped.

(Design credit: Connie Edwards, CKD, the Kitchen Village, Erie, PA)

APPENDIX A:
Important Organizations

American Arbitration Association
140 West 51st Street
New York, NY 10020
Tel. (212) 484-4000

American Gas Association
1515 Wilson Boulevard
Arlington, VA 22209
Tel. (703) 841-8400

American Home Lighting Institute
435 Michigan Avenue
Chicago, IL 60611
Tel. (312) 644-0828

American Institute of Architects
1735 New York Avenue N.W.
Washington, D.C. 20006
Tel. (202) 626-7300

American National Standards Institute (ANSI)
1430 Broadway
New York, NY 10018
Tel. (212) 354-3300

American Plywood Association
P.O. Box 11700
Tacoma, WA 98411
Tel. (206) 565-6600

American Society of Heating, Refrigerating, and Air
   Conditioning Engineers
1791 Tullie Circle N.E.
Atlanta, GA 30329
Tel. (404) 636-8400

American Society of Interior Designers
1430 Broadway
New York, NY 10018
Tel. (212) 944-9220

Association of Home Appliance Manufacturers
20 North Wacker Drive
Chicago, IL 60606
Tel. (912) 984-5816

Building Officials and Code Administrators
   International
4051 West Flossmoor Road
Country Club Hills, IL 60477-5795
Tel. (312) 799-2300

Ceramic Tile Institute
700 North Virgil Avenue
Los Angeles, CA 90029
Tel. (213) 660-1911

Consumer Education Research Center
350 Scotland Road
Orange, NJ 07050
Tel. (800-USA-0121)
(For booklet: "Consumers Guide to Home Repair
   Grants and Subsidized Loans")

Council of Better Business Bureaus
4200 Wilson Boulevard
Arlington, VA 22203
Tel. (703) 276-0100

Environmental Protection Agency
401 M Street S.W.
Washington, D.C. 20460
Tel. (202) 382-2090

EPA Drinking Water Hotline
Tel. (800-426-4791)
(Brochure: "Is Your Drinking Water Safe?"—an
   introduction to contaminants included in the Safe
   Drinking Water Act)

EPA Indoor Air Division, Office of Air and
   Radiation (Brochure: "The Inside Story: A Guide
   to Indoor Air Quality")

Federal Trade Commission
Office of Consumer/Business Education
6th Street and Pennsylvania Avenue N.W.
Washington, D.C. 20580
Tel. (202) 326-3650

Hardwood Plywood Manufacturers Association
1825 Michael Faraday Drive
Reston, VA 22090-2789
Tel. (703) 435-2900

Home Owners Warranty Corporation
P.O. Box 152087
Irving, TX 75015-2087
Tel. (214) 402-7600

Home Ventilating Institute
30 West University Drive
Arlington Heights, IL 60004-1893
Tel. (312) 394-0150

Kitchen Cabinet Manufacturers Association
P.O. Box 6830
Falls Church, VA 22040
Tel. (703) 237-7580

Maple Flooring Manufacturers Association
60 Revere Drive
Northbrook, IL 60062
Tel. (708) 480-9138

Marble Institute of America
33505 State Street
Farmington, MI 48024
Tel. (313) 476-5558

National Association of the Remodeling Industry
1901 N. Moore Street
Arlington, VA 22209
Tel. (703) 276-7600

National Fire Protection Association
(National Electrical Code)
1 Batterymarch Park
Quincy, MA 02269
Tel. (617) 770-3000

National Kitchen and Bath Association
687 Willow Grove Street
Hackettstown, NJ 07840
Tel. (908) 852-0033

National Oak Flooring Manufacturers Association
P.O. Box 3009
Memphis, TN 38173
Tel. (901) 526-5016

National Sanitation Foundation
3475 Plymouth Road
P.O. Box 1468
Ann Arbor, MI 48106
Tel. (313) 769-8010

Remodelors Council
National Association of Home Builders
15th and M Streets N.W.
Washington, D.C. 20005
Tel. (202) 822-0200

Tile Council of America
P.O. Box 326
Princeton, NJ 08542-0326
Tel. (609) 921-7050

Water Quality Association
4151 Naperville Road
Lisle, IL 60532
Tel. (708) 505-0160

APPENDIX B:
Adapting for the Elderly and the Handicapped

ABLEDATA
Adaptive Equipment Center
Newington Children's Hospital
181 East Cedar Street
Newington, CT 06111
Tel. (800-344-5405)
(Data bank of manufacturers; printouts by category
   with product descriptions)

American Association of Retired Persons (AARP)
Consumer Affairs Department
1909 K Street N.W.
Washington, D.C. 20049
Tel. (202) 728-4355
(Booklet: "The Do-Able Renewable Home")

American National Standards Institute (ANSI)
1430 Broadway
New York, NY 10018
Tel. (212) 354-3300
(Specification A117.1-1986: "For Making Buildings
   and Facilities Accessible to and Useable by
   Physically Handicapped People")

Dwyer Products Corporation
Calumet Avenue
Michigan City, IN 46360
Tel. (219) 874-5236
(Manufacturer; catalog available)

Eastern Paralyzed Veterans Association
75-20 Astoria Boulevard
Jackson Heights, NY 11370-1178
Tel. (718) 803-EPVA
(Booklets: "Building Design Requirements for the
   Physically Handicapped" and "Wheelchair House
   Designs")

The Hygeia Group
555 Westbury Avenue
Carle Place, NY 11514
Tel. (516) 997-8150
(Distributor; catalog available)

Institute for Technology Development
Advanced Living Systems Division
428 North Lamar Boulevard
Oxford, MS 38655
Tel. (601) 234-0158
(Brochure: "Enabling Products: A Sourcebook")

National Association of Home Builders
National Research Center
400 Prince Georges Center Boulevard
Upper Marlboro, MD 20772-8731
Tel. (301) 249-4000
(Booklets: "Fire-Safe, Adaptable Demonstration
   House," "Home Modifications for the Elderly,"
   and "Directory of Accessible Building Products")

National Council on the Aging
600 Maryland Avenue S.W.
Washington, DC 20024
Tel. (202) 479-1200

UCLA/USC Long-Term Care Center
32144 CHS
10833 Le Conte Avenue
Los Angeles, CA 90024-1687
Tel. (213) 825-9111
(Booklet: "National Directory of Home
   Modification and Repair Programs")

Whirlpool Corporation
Administrative Center
Benton Harbor, MI 49022-2692
Tel. (616) 926-3164
(Booklets: "Designs for Independent Living" and
   "Tools for Independent Living")

APPENDIX C:
CONSUMER REPORTS
RATINGS

THE RATINGS

Individual brands and models are rated based on the estimated quality of the tested product samples. The Ratings order is derived from laboratory tests, controlled use tests, and/or expert judgments. The Ratings offer comparative buying information that greatly increases the likelihood you will receive value for your money.

When using the Ratings, first read the introduction preceding each chart, then the notes and footnotes in order to find out about the features, qualities, or deficiencies shared by products in the test group.

The first sentence in the introduction to each Ratings chart tells you the basis of the Ratings order. Sometimes groups of products may be listed alphabetically or by price when the quality differences are so small as to be not worth considering. Usually, however, Ratings are "listed in order of estimated quality." That means Consumers Union's engineers judged the brand (or product type) listed first to be the best, the one listed next to be second best, and so on. Sometimes, rated products are about equal to one another and are therefore listed in a special fashion, perhaps alphabetically and within brackets.

Prices

The prices are listed as published at the time of the original report. Whenever possible, it pays to shop around and buy from the dealer or source that offers the best price and also provides satisfactory servicing arrangements.

Ratings of top-freezer refrigerators

As published in a **November 1989** report (model currency updated, February 1991). Listed in order of estimated quality. Bold rules separate distinct differences in overall performance. Brackets indicate essentially identical overall performance.

① Price. The estimated average price, based on what Consumers Union paid and on a price survey during a six-month period. All prices include automatic ice-maker, either as factory installed or as a kit (with a kit, you may have to pay for installation labor).

② Annual energy use. These costs, based on energy-consumption tests, are more representative than figures on the "Energy Guide" labels in the stores. CU used a more stringent test than the government requires for that label, and used the current national average rate of 7.7 cents per kilowatt-hour. Estimates are based on a 37°F refrigerator and a 0° freezer and assume that energy-saver (anticondensate) heaters are on for six months and off for six. Energy use does not include operation of the ice-maker. Figures for the *Montgomery Ward* are deceptively low because we could not get the freezer to 0°.

To determine what the annual dollar cost of operation in your area might be, multiply your electric rate (in cents per kilowatt-hour) by the number of kilowatt-hours used by the model and divide by 100.

③ Temperature balance. The ability of a model to maintain 37° in the refrigerator and 0° in the freezer. Only the *Ward* could not achieve that ideal balance.

④ Temperature uniformity. The degree to which temperatures varied throughout refrigerator and freezer main space and doors.

⑤ Temperature compensation. How well did each model compensate for changes in room temperature? Tests simulated a winter vacation, when you might turn the thermostat down from 70° to 55°, a hot summer day when your kitchen might go from 70° to 90°, or a fall day when temperatures might drop from 90° to 70°.

Better ◉ ◑ ○ ◒ ● Worse

Brand and model	Price (and range) ①	Cost	Kilowatt-hours ②	Balance ③	Uniformity ④	Compensation ⑤	Reserve capacity ⑥	Meat-keeper ⑦	Crisper humidity ⑧	Ice-making ⑨	Noise ⑩	Overall convenience ⑪	Dimensions (H x W x D), in. ⑫
Amana TC20M/Ⓡ TC20Q	$865	$79	1026	◉	◑	◉	◉	◉	○	◑	○	◑	68 x 32¼ x 32¼
Ⓓ Sears Kenmore 79061	776	84	1094	◉	○	◑	◑	◑	◑	○	◑	◑	66¼ x 32¾ x 30¼
General Electric TBX21ZL	949	84	1089	◉	○	◑	○	◉	◑	◑	○	○	66¼ x 31¼ x 31¾
Maytag RTD21A	818	89	1154	◉	○	◒	○	◉	◑	◉	○	◉	66¼ x 31½ x 33¼
Whirlpool ET20DKXV/Ⓡ ET20DKXX	795	84	1094	◉	○	◑	◑	◑	◑	○	◑	○	66¼ x 32¾ x 30¼
Jenn-Air JRT1214/Ⓡ JRT216	842	89	1154	◉	◑	◑	◑	◉	◉	◑	◑	◑	66½ x 31½ x 31¾
Caloric GFS207-1	740	84	1094	◉	◑	◑	◑	◑	◑	◑	◑	○	66¼ x 32¾ x 30¼
Hotpoint CTX21GL	723	84	1089	◉	◑	◒	○	◑	●	◑	○	◑	66¼ x 31¼ x 31¾
Frigidaire FPCE21TFWO/Ⓡ FPCE21TN	806	86	1116	◉	○	○	○	○	○	○	◑	○	66¾ x 31¼ x 30½
Ⓓ Montgomery Ward HMG21974	759	89	1154	○	◑	◑	◑	◉	◉	◉	◑	◑	66½ x 31½ x 31¾
Gibson RT21F9WT3B/Ⓡ RT21F9WX	825	83	1077	◉	◑	◑	◑	◑	◑	◑	◑	◑	66¾ x 31¼ x 31½
KitchenAid KTRF20KT/Ⓡ KTRS 20KW	856	91	1182	◉	○	◑	◑	○	●	◑	◑	◑	66¼ x 32¾ x 29¼
Kelvinator TMK206ENOW/ Ⓡ TGK 2105N	631	83	1077	◉	●	◑	◑	◑	◑	◑	◑	◑	66¾ x 31¼ x 30¾
Magic Chef RB21JN-4A/Ⓡ RB 21KN4A	797	101	1308	◉	◑	◑	◑	◑	◑	◑	○	○	66¼ x 31¾ x 31¾
Admiral NT21K9/Ⓡ NT21L9	794	101	1308	◉	◑	◑	●	◉	◑	○	○	○	66¼ x 31¾ x 32½

❻ Reserve capacity. How well each model worked under the most severe conditions—a possible indication of how it will perform after components have aged.

❼ Meat-keeper. Meat and cold-cuts are best kept at temperatures between 30° and 35°. Some meat-keepers were actually warmer than the center of the refrigerator.

❽ Crisper humidity. How well this area retained moisture—important if you don't want lettuce and such to dry out.

❾ Ice-maker. Scores reflect the amount (in pounds) of ice made per day, frequency of ice-making cycles, and size of storage bin.

❿ Noise. The opinion of a listening panel, plus measurements with a sound level meter, as the compressor came on and while it ran.

⓫ Overall convenience. CU gave each model a 70-point convenience inspection. How clear and logical were the controls? How easy was it to clean? Unique features are listed in the Advantages (or Disadvantages) column.

⓬ Dimensions. Height, width, and depth to next highest quarter inch as measured by CU. Door hinges and handles are included.

⓭ Depth, door open. Use this figure to determine clearance needed in front of refrigerator to open the door 90 degrees.

⓮ Side clearance. Extra space needed on hinge side of door to remove crisper.

⓯ Capacity. CU's measurement of usable storage space. Manufacturers claimed capacities, which are certified by AHAM, are 25 to 35 percent higher (see Features table). This does not include shelf retainers and nooks and crannies that never get used. Total volume is without (and with) automatic ice-maker. The *Jenn-Air* and *Sears* came with ice-maker installed.

⓰ Shelf area. CU's measurement of usable area—always less than that advertised by the manufacturer.

Depth, door open, in.	Side clearance	Capacity, cu. ft. Refrigerator	Freezer	Total	Shelf area, sq. ft.	Advantages	Disadvantages	Comments
61	0	10.1	4.6	14.7 (13.7)	25.2 (24.0)	C,E,F,H,L	c	G,N,O,R
59¾	19½	11.1	4.1	(15.2)	(23.1)	A,B,E,F,I,J,M	h,m,n	P,R
60	19	10.0	5.4	15.4 (14.6)	23.7 (22.9)	C,E,G,J,L,P,R	g,i,q	B,G,H,I,R
61¼	22½	10.5	5.4	15.9 (14.7)	28.1 (26.8)	A,B,C,E,F,J,L, M,P,Q,S	c,j,q,s	B,C,H,P,R,T
59¾	22½	10.6	4.7	15.3 (14.4)	26.5 (25.5)	A,B,E,F,I,L	g,h,m	H,P,Q,R
61½	22¾	11.2	4.1	(15.3)	(25.1)	B,C,E,F,J,T	e,j,o,p,t	F,S,U
59¾	23¾	10.5	4.9	15.4 (14.8)	25.1 (24.3)	A,B,E	g,m,q,r	A,L,P,R
60	0	10.9	5.5	16.4 (15.6)	24.2 (23.5)	C,G,J,L	g,i,o,p,q	A,B,R
59¾	0	10.4	5.1	15.5 (14.9)	26.7 (25.9)	C,E,F,J,L,O,R	d,h,i,k,l, o,p,s	H,I,S
61½	21	11.3	5.4	16.7 (15.8)	27.7 (26.7)	B,C,E,J,T	a,j,o,p,r,t	I,J,S
60	0	10.9	5.0	15.9 (15.3)	23.4 (22.6)	E,F,G,H,K,O,R	b,d,g,i,k, l,o,p,r	E,I,K,M,Q,S
58¾	12½	9.6	4.6	14.2 (13.5)	22.9 (22.0)	A,D,J,M,N,S	f,h,m,o,r,s	B,C,D,R
59¼	0	10.9	5.0	15.9 (15.3)	23.3 (22.6)	G,O,R	b,d,f,g,i, k,l,o,p,q,r	F,K,S
61	19½	10.1	5.6	15.7 (14.6)	26.4 (25.3)	B,C,E,F,J	e,j,o,q	A,G,S
61	24½	10.3	5.5	15.8 (14.9)	26.7 (25.7)	B,C,E,J	e,j,o,q	A,G,S

Ⓡ *indicates that, according to the manufacturer, model has been replaced by an essentially similar model.*
Ⓓ *indicates that model has been discontinued. The information has been retained to permit comparisons.*

Specifications and Features

All have: • Adjustable glass shelves in the refrigerator main space. • Reversible, textured steel doors. • Four rollers. • Leveling provisions. • Anticondensate, "energy-saver" switch. • Door stops.
Except as noted, all have: Controls to maintain 37°F in refrigerator and 0 in freezer. • Plastic seamless liner. • At least one 40-watt light in refrigerator. • 1-yr. warranty on parts and labor for entire unit. • 5-yr. warranty on sealed refrigeration unit. • 2 crispers, one or both with seals.

Key to Advantages

A–Energy-saver switch has light or red bar to remind you anticondensate heater is on.
B–Controls easy to reach.
C–Meat-keeper has temperature control; judged moderately effective.
D–Has porcelain-on-steel liner, meat-keeper, and crispers; judged easy to use and clean.
E–Adjustable snuggers or fingers in refrigerator or freezer door shelves keep small items upright.
F–Some refrigerator door shelves or door-shelf bins removable and adjustable.
G–Some refrigerator or freezer door-shelf guards are removable for easy cleaning.
H–Has refrigerator shelf that can also serve as can dispenser or defrost area.
I–Has at least 1 deep door shelf for gallon container.
J–Has extra-deep freezer door shelves.
K–Has freezer door area for frozen cans.
L–Has ice-cube tray storage shelf if ice-maker is not installed.
M–Has light in freezer.
N–Freezer vents judged less vulnerable to spills than others.
O–Has rear condenser coils; needs less cleaning than bottom-mounted coils.
P–Freezer shelf is adjustable for more than 2 positions.
Q–Has locks on refrigerator wheels.
R–One crisper is larger than other, offering more flexibility.
S–Some drawers mounted on rollers for easier handling.
T–Anticondensate heater very effective.

Key to Disadvantages

a–Freezer temperature could not be made cold enough.
b–Refrigerator temperature varied much more than average under stable conditions.
c–Freezer warmed more than most during defrost.
d–Exterior sweated more than others with anticondensate heaters on in moderate humidity.
e–Markings on energy switch could be confusing.
f–Butter door will not stay open by itself.
g–Lacks butter tray.
h–Freezer shelf not adjustable.
i–Drip pan cannot be removed and therefore is very hard to clean.
j–Condenser judged very hard to clean.
k–Requires a minimum 3-inch clearance on top, 1 inch on bottom.
l–Optional ice-maker very difficult to install.
m–Drip pan has to be lifted up over wire brace and could spill.
n–Handle had to be installed with a Torx-head screwdriver.
o–Crisper drawers lack adequate stops.
p–Crisper shelf-support can be easily dislodged when opening crisper drawers.
q–Door-shelf retainer lets 2-liter soda bottle topple out when door is abruptly opened.
r–Gap under a refrigerator door-shelf retainer lets small items fall through.
s–Gap under freezer door-shelf retainer lets small items fall through.
t–Position of energy-saver switch is not immediately obvious.

Key to Comments

A–Neither crisper has seals.
B–Meat-keeper has seals.
C–Light bulb is shielded well.
D–Porcelain-on-steel liner has 10-year warranty.
E–"Picture-frame" door trim.
F–Door trim accepts optional door panel.
G–Has white handles.
H–Has brown door-seal gaskets.
I–Has almond-colored door interior.
J–Freezer sticker describes food storage times.
K–Had 60-watt bulb in refrigerator.
L–1-year warranty for parts (not labor).
M–10-year warranty on compressor.
N–Has separate wine-bottle holder.
O–Has vertical divider in freezer.
P–Has 2 lights in refrigerator.
Q–Lacks egg-storage provision.
R–Leveling is done by adjusting rollers.
S–Leveling is done by separate leveling legs; that prevents rolling.
T–"Buy-back" 10-year warranty on sealed refrigeration system if purchased in 1989.
U–See comments on model availability in Features table.

Features of refrigerators

As published in a **May 1991** report.

① Brand and model. Models tested and a selection of other models of similar design and capacity. Brands are listed alphabetically; within brands, in order of increasing price. Except for tested models (marked with •), information is based on CU's interpretation of literature from manufacturer and from the Association of Home Appliance Manufacturers.

② Price. Retail price, or suggested retail as quoted by the manufacturer.

③ Energy cost. From a model's Energy Guide sticker, this is an annual figure, based on U.S. Department of Energy test protocols and the 1988 average electricity rate of 8.04 cents per kilowatt-hour. (Energy costs in the Ratings are based on our test protocols and the 1990 rate of 7.9 cents per kWh.)

④ Claimed capacity. Volume as given by the manufacturer and certified by AHAM. Capacity listed in the Ratings is more realistic, however.

⑤ Claimed shelf area. The total claimed area. Again the Ratings give a more realistic figure.

⑥ Shelves. The number and type of shelves in each compartment. A **p** indicates a partial-width shelf; all others are full-width. The number of drawers (or baskets) in the freezer is noted, too.

Better ● ◖ ○ ◑ ● Worse

Brand and model	Price	Energy cost	Refrigerator, cu. ft.	Freezer, cu. ft.	Total, cu. ft.	Claimed capacity	Claimed shelf area, sq. ft.	Crisper humidity control	Ice & water dispensers	Electronic monitor or controls	Gal.-container door rack	Refrig: Main space, glass	Refrig: Door, aluminum	Refrig: Door, plastic	Refrig: Main space, glass	Refrig: Main space, wire	Freezer: Main space, plastic	Freezer: Drawers	Freezer: Door, plastic	Comments
Admiral																				
• CDNS24V9	$1199	$105	15.2	8.2	23.5	27.6		—	✓	—	✓	4	—	5	3	—	1p	1	5	D,E,J,K,L,P
BDNS24-9	1199	105	15.1	8.4	23.6	28.1		—	✓	—	✓	4	—	5	3	—	1+1p	1	5	A,B,D,E,J,P
Amana																				
• SZD27K	1700	105	16.9	9.8	26.7	28.3		✓	✓	—	✓	3+2p	—	4+3p	—	3	—	1	6	A,C,E,F,H,K,L,O
• SZDE27K	1900	105	16.9	9.8	26.7	28.3		✓	✓	✓	✓	3+2p	—	4+3p	—	3	—	1	6	A,C,E,F,H,K,L,O
Frigidaire																				
• FPCE24VWL	999	106	14.7	9.3	24.0	26.3		✓	✓	—	—	4	3	—	—	1	2p	3	5	A,E,F,I,K
FPCE24VF	999	90	14.7	9.3	24.0	29.9		✓	—	—	—	4	3	—	—	5	—	1	6	A,E,F,I,K
GE																				
TFX27RL	1550	113	16.7	9.9	26.6	28.8		—	✓	—	✓	4	—	5	—	3	—	1	5	A,C,D,F,H,K
• TFX27VL	1600	106	16.7	9.9	26.6	29.9		—	✓	—	✓	4	—	5	—	3	—	1	5	C,D,E,F,H,J,K
TFX27EL	1650	121	16.7	9.9	26.6	29.9		✓	✓	✓	✓	4	—	5	—	3	—	1	5	A,C,D,F,H,K
• TFX27FL	1850	125	16.7	9.9	26.6	29.8		✓	✓	—	✓	4	—	5	—	3	—	1	5	A,C,D,F,G,H,J,K
Hotpoint																				
• CSX27DL	1400	106	16.7	9.9	26.6	28.8		—	✓	—	✓	4	—	5	—	3	—	1	5	A,C,D,H,J,K
CXS27CL	1650	125	16.7	9.9	26.6	29.8		✓	✓	✓	✓	4	—	5	—	3	—	1	5	A,C,D,F,G,H,J,K
Jenn-Air																				
• JRSD246	1750	105	15.3	8.2	23.5	27.5		✓	—	—	✓	4	—	5	—	4	—	1	5	A,E,H,J,K,P
Kelvinator																				
• FMW240EN	899	106	14.7	9.3	24.0	26.4		✓	—	—	—	4	5	—	—	3	2p	1	5	A,K,Q
KitchenAid																				
• KSRS25QW	1649	109	15.2	9.8	25.0	27.2		✓	—	✓	✓	5	4	—	1	1	—	3	5	A,C,E,K,N
Maytag																				
RSD24A	1430	90	15.2	8.6	23.8	30.4		✓	—	—	✓	4	—	5	—	4+1p	—	1	6	A,D,E,F,H,J,P
• RSW24A	1700	100	15.2	8.3	23.5	29.0		✓	✓	—	✓	4	—	5	—	4	—	1	5	A,D,E,F,H,J,P
Montgomery Ward																				
24894	—	102	15.1	8.7	23.8	28.7		—	—	—	✓	4	—	5	5	—	—	1	6	D,E,J,N,P,S
• 24902	1200	123	15.1	8.5	23.6	28.1		—	✓	—	✓	4	—	5	3	—	1p	1	5	D,E,J,N,P,R
RCA																				
• MSX27XL	1550	121	16.7	9.9	26.6	29.9		✓	✓	✓	—	4	—	—	—	3	—	1	5	C,D,F,H,J,K,L
Sears Kenmore																				
• 50771	1385	113	16.6	9.9	26.5	27.6		—	✓	—	✓	4	—	5	—	3	—	1	5	A,C,E,F,J,K,M,S
51791	—	125	16.6	9.9	26.5	27.5		—	✓	—	✓	4	—	5	—	3	—	1	5	A,C,E,F,G,J,K,M,S
Whirlpool																				
• ED27DQXW	1625	113	16.4	10.2	26.7	25.6		✓	✓	—	✓	4	—	4	—	1	—	4	5	C,D,E,J,K,L,M,N
White Westinghouse																				
• RS249M	949	106	14.7	9.3	24.0	29.5		✓	—	—	—	4	4	—	—	2	2p	2	5	A,D,E,K,Q

Key to Comments

A–Door-trim frame and/or optional door panels are available.
B–Optional ice-cream maker available.
C–Ice dispenser delivers crushed ice or cubes (selectable).
D–Has separate snack drawer.
E–Has wine rack.
F–Has separate storage dishes.
G–Has Refreshment Center door within refrigerator door.
H–Freezer shelf is adjustable.
I–Has dispenser jug on refrigerator door shelf.
J–Has "bookend" or other type of shelf snugger to hold small containers on refrigerator door shelf.
K–Some refrigerator door shelves/bins are adjustable.
L–Some freezer door shelves are adjustable.
M–Shelves slide out for easy access.
N–Freezer has quick-freeze shelf.
O–Freezer has shelf for juice cans.
P–Refrigerator door shelf not deep enough to hold gallon container comfortably.
Q–Refrigerator's main space also has 1 plastic shelf.
R–Model has been discontinued but may still be available in some stores.
S–Model has been discontinued, and replaced: **Ward 24894** by **24824,** $900; **Sears 50771** by **51771,** $1530; **Sears 51791** by **51781,** $1729.

Ratings of refrigerators

As published in a **May 1991** report. Listed in order of estimated quality. Ratings should be used with Features table. Bracketed models had essentially identical overall performance and are listed alphabetically. The *Amanas* are essentially the same except for controls and defrost systems.

1 Brand and model. Consumer's Union bought large, top-of-the-line models with a factory-installed automatic ice-maker and a dispenser in the door for ice water. If you can't find a model, call the company.

2 Price. Estimated average price based on national retail selling prices or prices quoted at retail in recent months. Price does not include plumbing hardware.

3 Annual energy use. Based on CU's energy-consumption tests with refrigerators set for 37°F and freezers set for 0° and assuming any anticondensate heater ("energy saver") is on for six months. Temperature criteria are more stringent than those specified in government test protocols. Figures do not include the operation of ice-maker or ice and water dispensers. Costs are based on the 1990 national average electricity rate of 7.9 cents per kilowatt-hour. To determine the cost in your area, multiply your electric rate (cents per kWh) by the number of kilowatt-hours the model uses per year.

4 Temperature balance. A model's ability to maintain and set temperatures: 37° in the refrigerator and 0° in the freezer.

5 Temperature uniformity. The degree to which temperatures varied throughout the refrigerator and freezer main space and doors. Normally, the dairy compartment in the door runs several degrees warmer and the meat-keeper several degrees cooler than the main space.

6 Temperature compensation. How well each model could compensate for changes in room temperature. Tests simulated a winter vacation, with the household thermostat turned down from 70° to 55°; a hot summer day, when a kitchen might go from 70° to 90°; and a fall day when temperatures might go from 90° to 70°.

7 Reserve capacity. How well each model worked under severe conditions, a possible indicator of how it will perform after components have aged.

8 Meat-keeper temperature. Fresh meat and coldcuts are best kept at temperatures between 30° and 35°.

9 Crisper humidity. These judgments show ability to retain moisture and effectiveness of humidity control, if any.

10 Ice and water dispensers. Scores reflect the coolness of five successive 10-ounce tumblers of water and how well ice was dispensed into glasses.

11 Ice-making. Scores reflect the quantity of ice produced per day, which ranged from 3½ to 5 pounds. CU also took into account the frequency of ice-making cycles and the size of the ice bin.

12 Noise. Scores reflect listeners' judgments and readings taken with a sound-level meter.

13 Overall convenience. CU inspected each model with a checklist, covering details about controls, door handles, lighting, layout of shelves, and much more. Especially important: how easy the controls were to read and set and how easy the refrigerator was to clean.

14 Dimensions. CU measurements to the next highest quarter-inch, door hinges and handles included. Depth, with the refrigerator door open at a 90-degree angle, measured from 49 to 50½ inches.

15 Side clearances. How much space is needed between the hinge side of an open door and an adjacent right-angled wall to remove a crisper, say, or pull out shelves and bins. First figure is for main compartment, second for freezer door.

16 CU-measured capacity. The usable internal volume, to the nearest tenth of a cubic foot. CU's figures are smaller than manufacturers' (see Features table) because they do not include shelf retainers, crannies that never get used, and other unusable space. The freezer volume does not include room taken by the ice-maker.

17 CU-measured shelf area. Again, CU's measurements are more realistic than those of manufacturers.

◉ ◓ ○ ◒ ● Better ⟷ Worse

		Energy use		Temperature												Capacity, cu. ft.						
Brand and model	Price	Annual cost	Kilowatt-hours	Balance	Uniformity	Compensation	Reserve capacity	Meat-keeper	Crisper humidity	Ice & water dispensers	Ice-making	Noise	Overall convenience	Dimensions (H × W × D), in.	Side clearances, in.	Refrigerator	Freezer	Total	CU-measured shelf area, sq. ft.	Advantages	Disadvantages	Comments
Amana SZD27K & SZDE27K	$1490/1780	$116	1464	◉	◓	◉	◓	◉	◉	○	◓	○	◓	68½ x 35¾ x 35¾	5/12	11.3	5.4	16.7	24.8	C,D,E,G,H,I,J,O,P,R,S,W,Y	—	*C,D,G,I,J,M,O,T,W*
General Electric TFX27VL	1475	115	1460	◉	○	○	○	◉	◓	◉	◉	○	◓	69¾ x 36 x 32¾	12/11	11.4	5.3	16.7	23.1	C,E,G,H,K,O,U,W	a,h	*B,E,F,I,N,P,U*
Hotpoint CSX27DL	1320	115	1460	◉	○	○	○	◉	◓	◉	◉	○	◓	69¾ x 36 x 32¾	12/11	11.9	5.3	17.2	22.0	C,E,G,H,K,U,W	a,h	*B,N,P,U*
Sears Kenmore 50771	1385	115	1460	◉	○	○	○	◉	◓	◉	◉	○	◓	69¾ x 36 x 32¾	12/11	11.5	5.2	16.7	21.5	A,C,F,G,H,O,U,W	a,h	*B,I,J,N,U,AA*
RCA MSX27XL	1490	123	1560	◉	○	○	○	◉	◓	◉	◉	○	◓	69¾ x 36 x 32¾	12/11	11.4	5.3	16.7	23.1	C,E,G,H,K,O,U,W,X	a	*B,N,P,U*
Whirlpool ED27DQXW	1520	124	1566	◉	◓	◓	○	◉	◓	◓	◓	○	◓	69½ x 35½ x 34	10½/11	10.6	5.1	15.7	22.0	A,B,C,D,F,G,H,I,K,M,W	j	*B,E,G,I,J,K,T*
KitchenAid KSRS25QW	1535	114	1440	◉	○	○	◓	◓	◒	◓	◓	○	◓	69½ x 35½ x 32¼	12/11	10.9	5.0	16.0	24.3	A,C,F,G,I,L,M,W	j	*B,D,E,G,I,J,K,O,S,T,X*
General Electric TFX27FL	1685	133	1680	◉	○	○	◒	◉	◓	◉	◉	○	◓	69¾ x 36 x 33¼	12/11	11.1	5.3	16.4	23.0	C,E,G,H,K,O,U,W,X	a,h	*B,E,F,N,P,U,V*
Admiral CDNS24V9	1065	109	1380	◉	◓	○	○	○	●	◓	◉	○	○	67 x 36 x 31¼	17/11	11.3	4.7	16.0	22.5	C,H,K	f,i,l	*B,D,H,I,L,O*
Jenn-Air JRSD245	1355	107	1356	◉	◒	◒	◓	◉	●	◓	◓	◓	◓	67 x 36 x 30¾	17/11	10.6	4.7	15.3	23.3	C,E,H,I,L	f,i	*B,C,G,H,I,J,L,O,R*
Maytag RSW24A	1580	107	1356	◓ [1]	◒ [1]	◒	◓	○ [1]	●	◓	◓	○	◓	67 x 36 x 31½	17/11	10.4	4.7	15.1	25.0	C,E,H,I,K,L,O,Q,V	d,i	*B,E,G,H,I,J,O,R,Z*
Montgomery Ward (Signature 2000) 24902	1220	125	1584	◉	○	○	○	◒	●	○	◉	◓	○	67 x 36 x 30¾	17/11	11.3	4.8	16.1	23.7	H,K,M,Q	f,i,k,l	*A,B,E,H,I,K,L,Y*
Frigidaire FPCE24VWL	1100	116	1472	◉	◒	○	○	◓	◓	◓	○	◒	○	66¾ x 36 x 32	6½/9	10.5	4.9	15.4	22.0	C,F,H,I,N,O,T	b,e,f,g,m	*E,G,I,O*
Kelvinator FMW240EN	1235	116	1472	◉ [2]	◒	○	○	◓	○	◓	○	◒	○	66¾ x 36 x 32½	6½/9	10.2	5.8	16.0	22.7	T	b,c,e,f,m	*E,Q*
White Westinghouse RS249M	1000	116	1472	◉	◒	○	○	◓	○	◓	○	◒	○	66¾ x 36 x 32¼	6½/9	10.2	5.2	15.4	24.2	F,K,T	b,c,e,f,m	*H,I*

[1] *Repositioning meat-keeper and utility drawer may improve or worsen temperature performance.*

[2] *Freezer on two samples could not reach zero in some tests because absence of baskets allows inlet air ducts to be blocked.*

Features in Common

All have: • Adjustable glass shelves in refrigerator. • Temperature-controlled meat-keeper. • Anticondensate heating, judged effective in controlling exterior condensation. • At least 1 crisper drawer, at least partly sealed. • Bulk-storage drawer in bottom of freezer. • Door-shelf retainers, bins, or both, that are easily removed for cleaning. • 4 rollers on base, the front pair adjustable for leveling. • Parts and labor warranty for at least 1 year on entire unit, 5 years on sealed refrigeration system.

Except as noted, all: • Can maintain 37°F in refrigerator, 0° in freezer. • Have adjustable shelves/bins on refrigerator door. • Have textured steel doors. • Have plastic seamless liner. • Have door stops. • Met 1990 U.S. Energy Dept. efficiency requirements.

Key to Advantages

A–Controls are easy to reach.
B–Some refrigerator shelves slide forward for easier access.
C–Refrigerator door has removable bins whose height can be adjusted.
D–Freezer door has removable bins whose height can be adjusted.
E–Height of some freezer shelves adjustable.
F–Freezer baskets slide for easier access. (On **White-Westinghouse** and **Frigidaire,** baskets can be removed to convert space to shelves.)
G–Refrigerator door has at least 1 shelf that can easily fit 1-gallon milk containers.
H–Bookend-type "snugger(s)" on refrigerator door shelves keep small containers upright (**Frigidaire** uses plastic fingerlike tabs).
I–2 crisper drawers.
J–Sliding freezer shelf for cans.
K–Separate deli/utility drawer.
L–Some drawers are on rollers.
M–Fast-freezer shelf above ice-maker.
N–Juice-dispenser jug on inside of door.
O–Comes with microwaveable containers for storing, heating, and serving.
P–Beverage area on door shelf has separate temperature control.
Q–Separate ice and water dispenser lock-outs.

R-**SZDE27K** has electronic touchpad controls and electronic monitor.

S-Crisper's humidity controls very effective.

T-Has rear condenser coils; need cleaning less often than bottom-mounted coils but refrigerator must be moved from wall to clean.

U-Defrost drain-tube opening easily accessible for cleaning.

V-Locks on rollers to curb rolling.

W-Lets user select cubes or crushed.

X-Electronic monitor and diagnostic system.

Y-Dispenser area has night light, which can be set to turn on automatically after dark.

Key to Disadvantages

a-Upper shelf area of freezer door warmed more than most during defrost.

b-Lacks separate On/Off control arm for ice-maker; ice bin must be physically removed to stop ice-maker.

c-Butter door will not stay open by itself.

d-Ice and water dispensers difficult to operate.

e-Requires at least 3-inch clearance on top and 1 inch on bottom for air circulation.

f-Lacks door stops.

g-Doors are smooth, not textured; may show smudges more readily.

h-Drip pan cannot be removed; hard to clean (but water may evaporate faster).

i-Condenser wrapped in metal "shroud," which curbs dust but makes cleaning hard.

j-Drip pan must be lifted over a wire brace; hard to remove.

k-Lacks adjustable shelves on refrigerator door.

l-Crisper drawers lack adequate stops.

m-Ice dispenser can be activated even when freezer door is open; ice can fall to floor.

Key to Comments

A-Tested model manufactured in 1989 (1990 version not available at time of tests). Did not meet 1990 government energy-efficiency requirements.

B-Meat-keeper is sealed.

C-Standard door trim accepts optional decorator door panels.

D-Has white handles.

E-Has brown (or tan) door-seal gasket.

F-Has almond-colored door interior.

G-Crisper(s) have humidity control.

H-Chart in freezer lists food-storage times.

I-Has wine rack.

J-Has 2 lights in refrigerator.

K-Has 2 lights in freezer.

L-Has separate leveling legs to prevent rolling.

M-Entire cabinet, not just doors, is textured.

N-Has metal interior liner.

O-5-year warranty on liner except door.

P-Limited lifetime warranty on plastic drawer material.

Q-1-year $100 freezer food-loss protection.

R-Second-year parts-only warranty.

S-Sixth-through-tenth-year parts-only warranty on sealed refrigeration system.

T-Unlike other models that circulate hot refrigerants, these models have an electric "energy saver" anticondensate heater, judged effective in controlling exterior condensation. (**Whirlpool** and **KitchenAid** have light to remind you that heater is on.)

U-Company claims meat-keeper control can convert meat-keeper to spare crisper.

V-Has door-within-door Refreshment Center.

W-**SZDE37K** has 5-year warranty on electronic parts.

X-Glass butter dish, not plastic.

Y-Model has been discontinued but may still be available in some stores.

Z-For models sold in 1991, company warranties sealed refrigeration system until Dec. 31, 1999.

AA-Model has been discontinued and replaced by **51771** ($1530 suggested retail), which company says is essentially similar.

Microwave ovens

Which have been most reliable?

Microwave ovens' track record for repairs is much better than that of other relatively new electronic gizmos such as VCRs and CD players. Only 1 in 20 microwave ovens purchased since 1985 has ever needed a repair. That's what Consumers Union learned when its readers were asked in the 1988 Annual Questionnaire for their repair experiences.

Data were gathered on nearly 22,000 midsized microwave ovens, all bought new from 1985 to 1988, most with electronic touch controls. The data were used to calculate the Repair Indexes for 14 brands.

Brands at the top of the chart have had a much better repair record than those at the bottom, as measured by the percentage of respondents whose ovens needed at least one repair. Differences of less than three points aren't meaningful. Since appliances tend to need more fixing as they age, the data were adjusted for differences in age among models of different brands.

Note that the data apply only to brands—individual models may fare better or worse than the brand as a whole. And the data are historical in nature, indicating only how reliable a brand has been in the past. A brand's past doesn't inevitably predict a model's future. Still, you can improve your odds of getting a reliable oven by choosing from brands near the top of the chart.

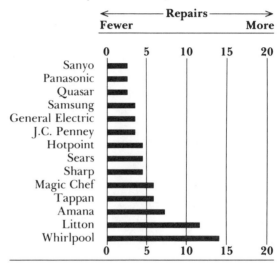

Repair index by brand

Fewer ← Repairs → More

Sanyo
Panasonic
Quasar
Samsung
General Electric
J.C. Penney
Hotpoint
Sears
Sharp
Magic Chef
Tappan
Amana
Litton
Whirlpool

Guide to Key Microwave-Oven Features

1 Brand and model. Models tested (marked with •) and a selection of their brandmates, with each brand's models listed in order of increasing price. Based on the manufacturers' specifications, the untested models have the same basic construction and should perform similarly to the tested ones. When a manufacturer has more than one basic design, the models that are similar are bracketed. Except as noted, all have wood-grain finish, electronic controls with 5 to 10 power levels, and a timer with a maximum setting of 99 minutes and 99 seconds.

2 Price. Suggested retail, as quoted by the manufacturer, or the average price (indicated by *) when a range was quoted. + indicates shipping is extra. Microwave ovens are heavily discounted; the prices CU paid are noted in the Ratings, but keep in mind that the shoppers didn't price-shop.

3 Cooking stages. A stage is a specific set of time and power-level (or temperature and power-level) commands. Every microwave oven can execute at least one; many can remember a number of stages and perform them in sequence. CU counts only actual cooking stages in this tabulation, not (as manufacturers sometimes do) delays, pauses, or defrost time.

4 Sensor. This registers moisture escaping from the food and signals the microwave oven to go into a programmed final cooking sequence.

5 Turntable. Since no microwave oven distributes its energy with absolute uniformity, many foods should be turned now and then to help reduce uneven heating. A turntable helps, at the cost of some interior capacity.

6 Delay start. This lets you program an oven to turn on by itself at a future time. An unimportant feature in an appliance renowned for speed.

7 Defrost assistance. Built-in prompting or programming that automatically varies the power as food defrosts. Defrosting, assisted or solo, still requires food to be turned periodically.

8 Defrost/cook. In this two-stage mode, the oven is set to automatically defrost and then go on to a cooking program. In some cases, this feature will increase the number of programmable stages that are possible with the oven.

9 Preprogrammed recipes. The oven's instructions list foods that are keyed to specific, built-in settings. There may be only a few such settings, but the manufacturer may note many foods that can be cooked at each setting.

10 User-programmable recipes. This feature allows programs of your own to be entered into an oven's memory for future use.

11 Temperature probe. A slim temperature sensor you insert into the food, making it easier to cook large dishes such as casseroles to just the right temperature. When the interior of the food reaches the programmed temperature, the oven signals and, usually, cycles into a Hold or Keep-warm phase. For best results in roasts or meatloaf, the probe should be inserted at an angle.

12 Mounting hardware. C indicates hardware is included for mounting under-cabinet; W, for wall mounting; O, under-cabinet hardware is optional.

13 Warranty. The basic terms for the whole unit and the coverage on the magnetron, as stated by the manufacturer. Any additional terms are noted under special features. Most warranties explicitly include labor for the initial period, whether in factory service centers or by arrangement with dealers, and are for carry-in service.

Key to Other Features

A–Each press of a command button gives a short period of high-power cooking.
B–Has 100 power levels.
C–Unit comes with shelf.
D–Braille adapter kit available as option.
E–Has mechanical controls, with continuously variable power levels and a 35-minute timer.

F–Has mechanical controls, with 5 power levels and a 30- or 35-minute timer.
G–Cabinet finished in white, **GE JEM30WH, Whirlpool MW3601XS;** in silver, **Sanyo EM380, Sears 88426 & 88628;** in grey, all **Frigidaires.**
H–Warranty provides for in-home service.
I–Has unrestricted 90-day exchange or refund warranty.

Better ◀——————▶ Worse

Brand and model	Price	Cooking stages	Sensor	Turntable	Delay start	Defrost assistance	Defrost/cook	Programmed recipes	User-programmable recipes	Temperature probe	Mounting hardware	Warranty, basic/mgntrn.	Other features
Amana													
MS4T/R M84TMA	$190*	3	—	—	—	✓	✓	—	—	—	—	1/5 yr.	A
• M86P/R M86PMA	225*	4	—	—	✓	✓	✓	✓	✓	—	—	1/5	A
D Frigidaire													
D MC83OL	184*	1	—	—	—	—	—	—	—	—	O	1/10	F,G,H
D MC85OL	194*	1	—	—	—	✓	—	—	—	—	O	1/10	G,H
D MC87OL	209*	2	—	—	✓	✓	—	✓	—	—	O	1/10	G,H
D • MC89OL	279*	2	—	—	✓	✓	✓	✓	—	—	O	1/10	G,H
General Electric													
JEM20H	204*	2	—	—	—	✓	✓	—	—	—	O	1/10	H,I
JEM22H	234*	2	—	—	—	✓	✓	✓	—	—	O	1/10	H,I
• JEM30WH	234*	2	—	—	✓	✓	✓	✓	—	—	O	1/10	A,C,G,H,I
• JEM31H	244*	2	—	—	✓	✓	✓	✓	—	—	C	3/10	A,C,H,I
Goldstar													
ER653MA	300	3	—	✓	✓	✓	—	—	—	—	—	2/7	—
ER654M/	300	3	—	✓	✓	✓	✓	—	—	—	—	2/7	—
• ER654S/R WM11M	320	3	✓	✓	✓	✓	✓	—	—	—	—	2/7	—
Hotpoint													
REM10F/R REM29H	169*	1	—	—	—	—	—	—	—	—	C	1/5	E,I
D • REM30F	194*	2	—	✓	—	—	—	—	✓	—	C	1/5	C,I
J.C. Penney													
• 5545/R Cat. No. 863-0444	210	3	—	✓	✓	✓	—	—	—	—	—	1/4	A
Magic Chef													
• M151OP/R	219	2	—	✓	—	✓	✓	✓	✓	—	—	1/5	H
Panasonic													
NN5368A/R NN5360A	199	2	—	✓	✓	✓	—	—	—	—	—	1/5	—
• NN5508A/R NN5500A	219	3	—	✓	✓	✓	✓	—	—	—	—	1/5	—
• NN5808A/R NN5700A	249	3	✓	✓	✓	✓	✓	—	—	—	—	1/5	—
Quasar													
D MQ6658W	210	2	—	✓	✓	✓	✓	✓	—	—	O	1/5	—
D MQ6668W	220	3	—	✓	✓	✓	✓	✓	—	—	O	1/5	—
D MQ6678W	240	3	—	✓	✓	✓	✓	✓	✓	—	O	1/5	—
• MQ6698W/R MQ1108	280	3	✓	✓	✓	✓	✓	✓	—	—	O	1/5	—
Samsung													
D • MW5710	216	4	—	✓	✓	—	✓	✓	✓	—	—	1/8	A
Sears													
D Cat. No. 88425	250+	2	—	✓	—	—	—	—	—	—	W	1/5	A,B
D Cat. No. 88426	250+	2	—	✓	—	—	—	—	—	—	W	1/5	A,B,G
D • Cat. No. 88627	290	4	—	✓	✓	✓	✓	—	✓	—	W	1/5	A,B
D Cat. No. 89628	300+	4	✓	✓	✓	✓	✓	—	✓	—	W	1/5	A,B,G
Sharp													
• R4A70/R R5H82	230*	3	—	✓	✓	✓	—	✓	—	—	—	2/7	A
D R4A80	240*	3	✓	✓	✓	✓	—	—	—	—	—	2/7	A
• R4P80	270*	3	✓	✓	✓	✓	—	✓	✓	—	—	2/7	A
D R4H80/R R4K82	300*	3	✓	✓	✓	✓	—	—	✓	—	—	2/7	A
Tappan													
561246	164*	1	—	—	—	—	—	—	—	—	O	1/10	F,H
562278	189*	3	—	—	—	✓	✓	—	—	—	O	1/10	H
562478	209*	3	—	—	—	✓	✓	—	✓	—	O	1/10	H
• 562897/R 562990	259*	2	—	—	—	✓	✓	✓	✓	—	O	1/10	H
Whirlpool													
D MW3200XS	170	1	—	—	—	—	—	—	—	—	O	1/5	F,H
D MW3500XS	210	4	—	—	—	✓	✓	—	✓	—	O	1/5	D,H
D MW3600XS	230	6	—	—	✓	✓	✓	✓	✓	—	O	1/5	H
D • MW3601XS	230	6	—	—	✓	✓	✓	✓	✓	—	O	1/5	C,G,H

R indicates that, according to the manufacturer, model has been replaced by an essentially similar model.

D indicates that model has been discontinued. The information has been retained to permit comparisons.

Ratings of midsize microwave ovens

As published in a **March 1989** report (model currency updated February 1991).

Guide to the Ratings

Listed in order of estimated quality based on performance, convenience, and features. Except as noted in Comments, most models would rank about the same when estimated quality is based mainly on performance with no regard for features and little for convenience. Quality differences between closely ranked models were slight.

❶ **Brand and model.** Consumers Union tested one and sometimes two full-featured, mid-size models of major brands. Most brands, however, offer cheaper models with fewer features; those that should perform similarly to the ones tested are in the Features table on page 179.

❷ **Price paid.** The price CU paid for each oven, which is usually less than the maker's suggested retail price (see the Features table). + indicates that shipping is extra.

❸ **Size.** Measurements allow for protrusions and are rounded to the next highest quarter-inch. All models should fit in the 15 inches between countertop and wall cabinet. Many of the ovens can be attached to the bottom of a cabinet (see Features table).

❹ **Capacity.** Manufacturers' figures, which are usually within one-tenth of a cubic foot of the oven's usable capacity as measured by CU. Exceptions: models with turntables, which reduce usable capacity. The *Magic Chef*, the only model that can operate without its turntable, was measured without it and was still among the smallest in usable capacity.

❺ **Power.** Defined by manufacturers in terms of magnetron wattage, a rough measure of heating speed. More power usually cooks faster, but that's not always so, as a comparison between this column and the next, heating speed, reveals.

❻ **Heating speed.** Based on CU's tests in heating measured amounts of water. The speediest model can cook about 30 percent faster than the slowest one. Besides magnetron power, those differences may be to due to food location and orientation, which we varied to get the best results.

❼ **Reheating.** CU heated up the standard plate of cold "leftovers"—a scoop of mashed potatoes, 24 green beans, and a quarter-pound slice of meat loaf—using a model's reheat program, if any, or manufacturer's instructions. The lower a model's score, the less evenly it heated food. With two plates of food in ovens with shelf, CU got good results if the dishes were staggered and occasionally swapped.

❽ **Defrost assistance.** The best at defrosting meat loaf were not especially convenient or fast because the best results are obtained by slowly lowering the power and by turning the food. That can be done with any microwave. The scores in this column reflect the amount of built-in help the model provides. Those aids include automatically lowering or cycling oven power and pauses or beeps to remind you to turn the food. Models with a turntable often did a better job, but not always. Turning the food is advisable, even on models with turntables, and it's easiest on those that provide a reminder beep.

❾ **Popping corn.** CU used a popular brand of corn that comes in a special bag for microwave use. Even the best poppers left from 34 to 164 unpopped kernels. Most of the others left up to 214. The model that left more than 350 unpopped was judged below average. CU also tested popping performance with corn in a special plastic container. The two methods yielded nearly opposite results.

❿ **Space efficiency.** Exterior dimensions correspond only loosely to interior size. CU calculated each model's space efficiency, the ratio of its capacity to its exterior size. Models with a turntable scored lower than those without.

⓫ **Display prompts.** High-scoring models give more than standard information; they volunteer in words what step to program next. The friendliest asks "Time?", "Start?", or "Code?" to help you program.

⓬ **Display clarity.** Top scores went to models with display characters that were unusually bright and large.

⓭ **Control panel.** All have electronic tough pads that give audible signals when programmed. The best controls were uncluttered, with good contrast for lettering and logical placement of the functions.

⓮ **Number pad.** CU gave extra points to number-pad layouts similar to that on a push-button phone. Models lost points for a "countup" system of entering numbers, which is more difficult to use than the direct-entry method.

⓯ **Instruction manual.** The best were complete and clear, with lots of pictures. CU especially disliked manuals with instructions for models other than the one purchased.

⓰ **Noise.** All have a fan that operates when the oven is in use. The best were unobtrusive; the worst, annoying.

⓱ **Door opening.** CU prefers an easy-to-grasp handle on the door rather than a push-button release on the frame, which makes it less convenient to open the door with one hand. All doors swing to the left.

⓲ **Window visibility.** A coarse screen on the oven's window, especially if combined with a dim interior light, can make it hard to see inside. The *Magic Chef* offers about the worst visibility we've seen on any microwave oven.

Better ● ◑ ○ ◐ ● Worse

① Brand and model	② Price paid	③ Size (H x W x D) in.	④ Capacity, cu. ft.	⑤ Power, watts	⑥ Speed	⑦ Reheating	⑧ Defrost assistance	⑨ Popping corn	⑩ Space efficiency	⑪ Display prompts	⑫ Display clarity	⑬ Control panel	⑭ Number pad	⑮ Instruction manual	⑯ Noise	⑰ Door opening	⑱ Window visibility	Advantages	Disadvantages	Comments
General Electric JEM31H	$225	11½ x 23½ x 12½	.9	700														E,F,	h	B,C,E
Quasar MQ6698W /R MOS1108	250	11¾ x 23½ x 12¼	.9	700									[1]					E,G,I	f,h	C
General Electric JEM30WH	225	11¼ x 23¾ x 12½	.9	600														E,F	d,j	B,E
Amana M86P /R M86PMA	189	12½ x 20¾ x 12½	.8	600														A,E,I	g,k	A
Samsung MW5710	169	12½ x 20¾ x 13½	.9	600														A,E,F,I	k	A,B
Hotpoint REM30F	200	11¼ x 24 x 12½	.8	600														—	d,l	B,E
J.C. Penney 5545 /R Cat. No. 863-0444	179+	13 x 23 x 15½	1.0	600														A,D,F	e,k	—
Sharp R4P80 /R R4K82	280	12½ x 20¾ x 16	1.0	600														D,E,F,G	f	F
Tappan 562897 /R 56-2990	177	12¼ x 23 x 13	.8	650														E,H	f,l	D
Whirlpool MW3601XS	240	12 x 22½ x 13	.8	650														—	f,l	C,E
Sharp R4A70 /R R5H82	200	12½ x 20½ x 15½	1.0	600									[1]					C,D,E,F	f,m,n	—
Frigidaire MC890L	240	12¼ x 23 x 12¾	.8	700														E,H	f,l	D
Panasonic NN5808A /R NN5700A	215	11¾ x 20¼ x 14½	.8	600									[1]					G,H	f	C
White Westinghouse KM485L	225	12¼ x 23 x 12½	.8	700														E	c,f	—
Panasonic NN5508A /R NN5500A	189	11½ x 20¼ x 14¼	.8	600									[1]					E	f,j	C
Sears Kenmore Cat. No. 88627	189+	11¾ x 21¾ x 13¼	.8	650														F	b,f,i	C
Goldstar ER6545S /R WM11M	199	13 x 21¾ x 15½ [2]	1.0	650				○[3]										G,H	a,e	·
Magic Chef M151OP /R M1514T	177	13¼ x 20½ x 14¼	.8	600														B,E	d,f,l	C,D

[R] indicates that, according to the manufacturer, model has been replaced by an essentially similar model.

[D] indicates that model has been discontinued. The information has been retained to permit comparisons.

[1] Number pad uses count-up system.

[2] Vents on top of oven; requires additional inch or so of clearance.

[3] Manufacturer warns against popping corn, but gives instructions on how to do it.

Specifications and Features

All have: • At least 5 power levels, a sufficient number for any cooking task. • Oven on-times of 4 to 7 seconds per cycle at lowest setting, 7 to 19 seconds at medium. • Touch pads that provide audible signal when programmed. • Displays that show time of day when oven isn't in use. • Interior light that goes on when oven is operating and window in door for viewing food. • Weight between 32 and 46 pounds.

Except as noted, all: • Can be used as kitchen timers. • Drew between 1100 and 1360 watts. • Have reduced power settings that cycle from 18 to 22 percent of the time at the lowest setting, and 53 to 60 percent at Medium. • Made a good 2-pound meat loaf, using temperature probe if provided, in 25 to 35 minutes. • Operate on high power unless otherwise instructed. • Have a defrost setting that varies power level. • Have provision for keeping minor spills in oven from running onto counter or floor.

Key to Advantages

A–Percentage of full power at low setting—12 percent—judged best.

B–Turntable is recessed into oven floor; switch is provided to use oven without turntable rotating. Indicator shows when turntable is on or off.

C–Made very good meat loaf in only 20 minutes.

D–Oven could accommodate an average-sized turkey without touching the walls or ceiling.

E–Oven has built-in programs for cooking or reheating; some ovens require entering weight of food.

F–Has control for quickly entering fixed, short cooking time at high power. Multiple pushes of pad increase time with some.

G–Has sensor-controlled cooking or reheating.

H–Has control for increasing or decreasing the degree of "doneness" with automatic cooking.

I–Has memory for one or more user-programmed recipes.

181

Key to Disadvantages

a–Did poor job in cooking microwavable pizza and brownies because metal turntable caused bottom of foods to be undercooked. Turntable has high lip; placing food to utilize maximum available space judged awkward.

b–Energy distribution when baking potatoes worse than other models; overall energy distribution, somewhat worse than others.

c–When oven display is used as a kitchen timer, oven light and blower operate.

d–Percentage-on at lowest reduced power settings is relatively high, above 30 percent.

e–Percentage-on at medium power setting is relatively high, about 63 percent.

f–Requires service personnel to change interior light bulb.

g–Although light bulb is accessible, manufacturer warns that it is not "customer serviceable."

h–Oven draws 1460 watts, more likely than most others to overload a branch circuit.

i–Setting power levels above 10 percent requires punching two digits.

j–Manufacturer does not provide recipe book with oven, a slight disadvantage.

k–Full power level must be programmed for each use.

l–Lacks defrost setting that automatically varies power.

m–Cannot be used as a kitchen timer.

n–Cooking time can be set only to the nearest 10 seconds; somewhat less precise than other models where precision is to nearest second.

Key to Comments

A–Meat loaf made using temperature probe not as good as that made by estimating cooking time.

B–Making good meat loaf using manufacturer's recommended setting took about 40 minutes; somewhat longer than most others. Except for the **Magic Chef**, all could be set at a higher level, which should cut time.

C–Manufacturer's defrosting instructions include turning the food for uniform defrosting.

D–Separate On/Off switch must be pushed to operate oven and turn it off; most other ovens do not require switching.

E–Manufacturer has free hotline to provide extensive consumer information.

F–This model would have ranked considerably lower if basic performance was the primary criterion and features were not considered.

Ratings of microwave/convection ovens

Ratings should be read in conjunction with the information on Features as published in a **September 1989** report (model currency updated February 1991).

Guide to the Ratings

Listed by groups in order of estimated quality, based on cooking, convenience, and features. Except where separated by a bold rule, difference among closely ranked models were slight. See also the Features information.

1 Brand and model. We tested full-feature ovens. Most have a fan to circulate the hot air. Tappan sells an oven that uses a different technology, supplying *thermal* heat only; Panasonic sells both kinds.

2 Price. Manufacturer's suggested retail. Discounts are often available. * indicates price is approximate; + indicates that shipping is extra.

3 Power. The wattage of the magnetron, as stated by manufacturer. More power usually (but not always) cooks faster.

4 Dimensions. Height, width, and depth, rounded to next higher quarter-inch. Protrusions are included in the measurements. Note that these ovens have vents at the back, so they can't stand flush against the wall. Some also have vents on top, which require clearance.

5 Exterior. Simulated wood (S) is still very popular, but white (W) and gray (G) are available too.

6 Claimed capacity. Manufacturers' figures for oven space in cubic feet.

7 Usable capacity. Useful oven space in cubic feet. Turntables or trays that must be used were in place when CU measured.

8 Heating speed. With each oven at full power, CU checked how much each oven had heated half a liter of water after two minutes microwaving and one liter after 8½ minutes microwaving. The slowest oven here took about 45 percent longer than the fastest. Note that where the food is placed in the oven can affect heating speed.

9 Defrosting. We defrosted one-pound packages of frozen ground chuck, using each oven's defrost program or following the manufacturer's instructions. Then we checked for uniformity. The best oven left no icy spots and didn't cook any part of the meat.

10 Reheating. In microwave mode, CU heated a standard plate of cold leftovers (a slice of meatloaf, a scoop of mashed potatoes, and a half-cup of green beans), using each model's reheat program or following the manufacturer's instructions. The more evenly the food was heated, the higher the score. The models that have a moisture sensor consistently did very well, even when the amounts of the foods on the plate were varied.

11 Instructions and recipes. Cooking with these combination ovens requires learning new techniques. The literature that came with many of the models made that task needlessly difficult. Some instruction books were poorly organized. Some focused mainly on microwave cooking, with little mention of cooking in heat and combination modes.

12 Ease of use. How easily can each oven be programmed without reference to instructions or guides? Helpful: prompts in the display that suggest the appropriate programming sequence, and an uncluttered control panel.

13 Space efficiency. Based on the ratio of usable capacity to overall size. Turntables are space-consuming; models with that feature generally scored lower here than those without.

14 Noise. These scores are for combination cooking only; differences in noise levels were less noteworthy during microwave-only and heat-only cooking. Models judged poor cycled noisily several times a minute.

Specifications and Features
All: • Are countertop models. (Built-in or under-cabinet kits are optional for some; see Features information.) • Can hold a 6-pound roasting chicken. • Draw 1345–1688 watts. • Weigh 46–66 pounds. • Were fairly quiet at full microwave power. • Broil at 450–500°F. • Have door with screened window that swings open to the left. • Have interior light that goes on when oven is operating. • Have provision for keeping minor spills from leaking onto the counter. • Make audible signal when cooking is finished. • Show time of day on electronic display when oven is not in use. • *Except as noted, all:* • Have electronic touch pad that beeps as it is programmed. • Have at least 5 microwave power levels. • Can be programmed for up to 99 minutes and 99 seconds for microwave, heat, and combination cooking. • Can preheat to selected temperature and hold that temperature for at least 30 minutes. • Were fairly quiet when cooking with heat only. • Have 4 basic combination-cooking programs with 1 microwave power level and varying oven temperatures. • Have 1 broil setting. • Have minimum temperature setting at 200°F. • Hold two 8¼-inch luncheon plates or one 11¾ x 7½ x 1¾-inch glass baking dish. • Hold 5- to 9¼-pound hamburgers on pan or rack or 5 to 9 bread slices on tray, turntable, or floor. • Have push-button door release. • Have stainless-steel interior. • Have interior light that goes on when door is opened. • Come with use-and-care booklet and recipe book that cover all modes of cooking. • Function as timer.

Key to Advantages

A–2-step programming for full-power cooking.

B–Specific temperature settings on touch pads made programming of oven heat very easy.

C–100°F minimum oven-temperature setting.

D–150°F minimum oven-temperature setting.

E–Can be programmed for up to 199 minutes and 99 seconds in heat and combination modes.

F–Can be programmed for up to 4 hours in heat mode.

G–Can be programmed for up to 9 hours and 99 minutes in heat and combination modes.

H–Large, easy-to-read characters in electronic display.

I–Display alternates between oven temperature or power level and time countdown.

J–Took less time than most to bake biscuits.

K–Took less time than most to defrost meat.

L–Took less time than most to combination-cook 6-pound chicken.

M–Held a 12½-pound turkey easily.

N–Took less time than most to combination-cook meat loaf.

O–Took less time than most to broil hamburgers.

P–Broil area can hold 16 quarter-pound burgers.

Q–Oven-width rack slides out and locks in position.

R–Oven-width broil pan slides out and locks in position.

S–Quieter than most in heat mode.

T–Oven door has handle.

U–Nonstick interior finish was easy to wipe.

V–The word "hot" flashes in display when door is opened after preheating.

W–Cookbook judged better than most.

Key to Disadvantages

a–Has count-up buttons for setting time, judged less convenient than full keypad.

b–Keypads don't beep when pressed.

c–Programming power levels above 9 percent requires touching 2 keypads.

d–Cooking time can be set only to nearest 10 seconds, rather than to nearest second.

e–Has only 3 microwave power levels.

f–Doesn't beep when preheat temperature has been reached; displays a small symbol.

g–300°F minimum oven-temperature setting.

h–No setting between 100° and 320°F.

i–Confusing power-level symbols in display.

j–Kitchen timer less convenient to set than most.

k–Code for programming moisture sensor not on oven itself; user must refer to instructions.

l–Ceramic oven tray must be removed for convection-only cooking.

m–Changing quantities when using programmed recipe feature confusing.

n–Broil pan lacks drain insert.

o–Broil pan must be removed to turn food.

p–Broil pan must be purchased separately.

q–No pan for baking; small baking sheet must be purchased separately.

r–Small turntable holds only 4 bread slices.

s–Holds only one 8¼-inch luncheon plate.

t–Can't hold 11¾-x-7½-x-1¾-inch baking dish.

u–11¾-x-7½-x-1¾-inch baking dish fits only one way.

v–Took longer than others to defrost ground chuck using automatic defrost.

w–Took longer than others to combination-cook 6-pound chicken.

x–Took longer than others to combination-cook meat loaf.

y–Took longer than most to bake biscuits.

z–Took longer than others to bake bread and broil hamburgers.

aa–For best results when baking bread, top of loaf must be shielded with aluminum foil partway through baking.

bb–Must be taken to shop to replace interior light.

cc–Oven has exposed element on floor; easy to spill on and difficult to clean under.

dd–Oven can't cook in stages.

ee–Oven can't cook in stages in convection or combination modes.

ff–No automatic preheat for broil.

gg–No kitchen timer.

hh–Poor view through oven window.

Key to Comments

A–Push buttons instead of keypad controls.

B–Light does not turn on when door is opened.

C–Oven fan turns on when door is opened.

D–Temperature probe didn't operate properly during convection cooking in one sample.

E–250°F minimum, oven-temperature setting.

F–Holds preheat oven temperature for 15 minutes.

G–Combination cooking is preprogrammed for microwave power level and oven temperature, depending on selected cooking time.

H–Has two basic preprogrammed combination-cooking settings, each with different microwave power level and oven temperature.

I–Microwave power level is preprogrammed for basic combination cooking; user can change oven temperature.

J–Has two basic preprogrammed combination-cooking settings; user can change oven temperature but not microwave power level.

K–Has one basic preprogrammed combination-cooking setting; user can change both oven temperature and microwave power level.

L–Broil pan can be used to bake some foods.

M–Has oven-width rack, which can't slide out.

N–Oven can be set so turntable doesn't revolve.

O–Splash trivet that fits over turntable prevents juices from cooking, but juices are inaccessible for basting.

P–Oven floor can hold 16 bread slices, but all don't cook well when microwaving.

Q–Continuous-clean finish on rear oven wall; other walls are stainless steel.

R–Door handle stiff on our sample.

Legend (rating scale): ● ◑ ○ ◐ ● — Better → Worse

Brand and model	Price	Power	Dimensions (H x W x D), in.	Exterior	Claimed capacity, cu. ft.	Usable capacity, cu. ft.	Heating speed	Defrosting	Reheating	Instructions, recipes	Ease of use	Space efficiency	Noise	Advantages	Disadvantages	Comments
Sharp Carousell II R9H80 /R R9H81	$539*	700	14¾ x 24¾ x 18	G	1.5	0.9	●	●	◐	◑	◑	○	○	A,B,C,K,M,N,O	s,bb.	D,F,J
General Electric JET342G001	434*	700	15¼ x 24 x 18½	S	1.4	1.4	◑	◑	◑	◑	◑	●	◑	G,M,P,R,S,T,V,W	k,w,y	L,M,P
Montgomery Ward 8288	330	650	15 x 22 x 19¾	S	1.3	1.3	◑	●	●	●	◑	○	◑	A,B,D,K,L,M,N	bb	F,J
Whirlpool MC8991XTO	422*	700	15 x 22 x 19¾	W	1.3	1.3	◑	◑	●	○	◑	○	◑	D,E,H,K,M,O,Q	x,bb,dd	K
Panasonic Dimension 4 NN9807 /R NN9850	580	700	15½ x 24 x 18½	S	1.4	0.9	◑	◑	●	○	○	●	◑	G,M,P,Q,S,W	a,s,y,z,bb	L
Amana RMC720 /R RMC720A	380	700	14¼ x 21¾ x 16¼	S	1.0	1.0	◑	◑	◑	◑	◑	●	◑	A,K,R,S,X	b,s,u	M
Samsung Multi Chef MW6790C	375*	650	14 x 22¼ x 18	S	1.0	0.9	◑	○	○	●	◑	○	○	B,G,J,K,T,V	n,o,q,ee	E,M,R
Goldstar ER930C	430	650	14¼ x 21¾ x 16	S	0.9	0.5	◑	◑	◑	◑	◑	◑	◑	B,I,J,O,T	j,r,s,t	F,H
Tappan Micro-Bake 565897 (thermal)	399	700	15½ x 23½ x 17¼	S	1.3	1.1	○	◑	○	○	○	◑	◑	A,F,M,O,S,T,U	a,aa,cc,dd,ff,hh	E,G,L,M
J.C. Penney Cat. No. 863-2879 /R Cat. No. 863-0071	360+	650	14¼ x 21¾ x 16	S	0.9	0.5	●	●	●	●	◑	◑	◑	B,I,J,O,T	j,r,s,t	F,H
Sears Kenmore 88963	450	750	15¾ x 24¼ x 19¼	G	1.3	1.3	◑	●	●	●	◑	○	○	H,K,T	c,j,l,m,o,p,q,bb	I,M
Brother Hi Speed MF3200	649	650	15 x 21¾ x 19¾	W	0.9	0.5	○	○	○	○	◑	○	◑	C,J,N,O	a,d,f,h,i,j,r,s,t,v,bb	A,C,I,N,O,Q
Magic Chef M71C10	439	600	15 x 21¾ x 19¾	S	0.9	0.5	◑	○	◑	◑	◑	○	○	H,K,N	a,d,e,f,g,r,s,t, bb,dd,gg	B,I,N,O,Q

/R indicates that, according to the manufacturer, model has been replaced by an essentially similar model.
/D indicates that model has been discontinued. The information has been retained to permit comparisons.

185

Guide to Key Microwave/Convection Oven Features

1 Number of cooking stages. A stage is a set of commands: time and power-level or time and oven-temperature. Two or more stages allow the flexibility of sequential cooking. All but the **Magic Chef, Samsung, Tappan,** and **Whirlpool** allow you to set an automated cooking sequence of different modes—for example, heat-only followed by microwave-only.

2 Number of racks. Most come with a rack or two. If there's a turntable or tray, the rack generally stands on that.

3 Turntable. Since microwave ovens don't distribute energy with absolute uniformity, many foods need turning now and then. A turntable makes that convenient, but at the cost of usable capacity.

4 Broil pan. Helpful for making hamburgers. Typically, it includes a drain insert that allows juices to drip down into the pan. Most can double as baking pans.

5 Guide card. A plasticized card with abbreviated instructions for frequent tasks. It saves you the bother of referring to the instruction book.

6 Guide on oven. Printed instructions that help you program the cooking—again, saving you the bother of referring to the instructions.

7 Moisture sensor. Allows automated microwave cooking without the need to set power level or cooking time. This useful feature measures moisture escaping from the food (which must be covered for the sensor to work properly). When the sensor detects a certain moisture level, it shuts off the oven. It's especially helpful for warming leftovers.

8 Temperature probe. You insert the slim probe into the food; when the inside of the food reaches the set temperature, the oven signals and shuts itself off or cycles into a keep-warm phase. (For best results, insert the probe at an angle.)

9 Audible preheat signal. Cooking with heat sometimes requires preheating the oven. This feature beeps when it's time to place the food in the oven.

10 Delay start. Lets you program an oven to turn itself on at a future time. Unimportant for microwave use, where cooking is fast anyway. Note that many foods shouldn't be left sitting too long in an oven at room temperature.

11 Defrost assist. To ease defrosting, some ovens can automatically lower or cycle microwave power. Some also pause or beep to remind you to turn the food.

12 Defrost/cook. An automatic two-stage mode. The oven defrosts, then automatically switches to a cooking program. In some cases, this feature increases the number of programmable stages that are available.

13 Keep warm. A separate program to keep food in the oven warm after a cooking program.

14 Mounting hardware. Optional kits allow some ovens to be built in (B) with a trim kit or mounted under a cabinet (C).

15 Warranty. Number of years that the oven/magnetron are covered. Most warranties are for carry-in service and include labor throughout the basic-warranty period. In addition, **GE** allows you to return the oven for exchange or refund during the first 90 days. Some warranties (for **GE, Sharp,** and **Whirlpool**) provide for service in your home.

Key to Other Features
A–Tray for oven floor.
B–Separate reheat sensor setting.
C–Separate, preprogrammed reheat setting.
D–Degree of doneness setting for automatic cooking.
E–Shortcut setting for fixed, short microwave cooking time at full power.
F–Shortcut setting for cooking time for full microwave power; multiple touches of keypad increase the time. Setting also extends time at lower microwave power levels and for convection and combination cooking (but not for automatic cooking programs).
G–Recipes can be programmed in memory. Has 25 preprogrammed recipes.
H–6 automatic cooking programs for a variety of foods.
I–Probe allows automatic cooking of certain foods (primarily meat and poultry).
J–Allows automatic combination cooking of meat and poultry based on weight.
K–Allows automatic combination cooking of certain frozen foods based on weight.
L–Special convection setting leaves turntable stationary.
M–Separate fine-tuning switch in addition to doneness setting for automatic cooking.
N–2 broil settings.
O–Slow-cook feature.
P–Child lock-out feature.
Q–Baking sheet.
R–Splash trivet fits over turntable; insulating mat is used between wire rack and metal pan for combination cooking.

Brand and model	Cooking stages	Racks	Turntable	Broil pan	Guide card	Guide on oven	Moisture sensor	Temperature probe	Audible preheat signal	Delay start	Defrost assist	Defrost/cook	Keep warm	Mounting hardware	Warranty, yr.	Other features
Sharp Carousel II R9H80/[R] R9H81	4	2	✓	—	✓	✓	✓	✓	✓	✓	✓	—	B	2/7	B,F,H,I,O
General Electric JET 342G001	2	1	—	✓	✓	—	✓	✓	✓	✓	✓	—	B	1/5	I,N
Montgomery Ward 8288	4	2	—	✓	✓	✓	✓	✓	✓	✓	✓	—	—	1/7	A,I,Q
Whirlpool MC8991XTO	1	2	—	—	✓	✓	—	✓	✓	✓	✓	✓	—	1/10	A,D,O,Q
Panasonic Dimension 4 NN9807/[R] NN9850	3	2	✓	✓	—	✓	✓	✓	✓	✓	✓	—	B	1/5	D,J,K,N
[D] Quasar MQ8798H	3	1	—	—	—	✓	✓	✓	✓	✓	✓	—	B	1/5	B,J
Amana RMC 720/[R] RMC720A	3	1	—	✓	—	✓	✓	✓	✓	✓	✓	—	B	1/5	C,Q
Samsung Multi Chef MW6790C	2	1	—	✓	✓	—	—	✓	✓	✓	✓	—	—	1/8	N
Goldstar ER930C	2	2	✓	—	—	✓	—	✓	✓	✓	✓	✓	—	2/8	E
Tappan Micro-Bake 565897	1	1	—	✓	✓	✓	—	✓	—	—	✓	—	—	1/10	—
J.C. Penney Cat. No. 863-2879/[R] Cat. No. 863-0071	2	2	✓	✓	—	✓	—	✓	✓	✓	✓	✓	C	1/5	E
[D] Sears Kenmore 88963	3	1	—	✓	✓	✓	✓	✓	✓	✓	✓	✓	—	1/5	A,E,G,P
Brother Hi Speed MF3200	3	1	✓	—	✓	✓	✓	✓	✓	✓	✓	✓	—	2/8	D,H,L,M,R
Magic Chef MC71C10	1	1	✓	✓	—	✓	—	✓	—	—	—	—	B	1/5	L,R

[R] indicates that, according to the manufacturer, model has been replaced by an essentially similar model. The information has been retained to permit comparisons.

[D] indicates that model has been discontinued.

Ratings of large microwave ovens

As published in a **November 1990** report (model currency updated February 1991). Listed in order of estimated quality based on cooking performance and convenience features.

❶ Brand and model. CU tested mostly top-of-the-line models. Many brands offer lower-cost models of similar construction. If you can't find a model, call the company.

❷ Price. Estimated average price, based on prices paid and on prices quoted in recent months.

❸ Dimensions. Rounded to next highest quarter inch. Some models require extra clearance for vents.

❹ Usable capacity. For most models, this is close to or the same as the labeled capacity. An asterisk marks turntable models, whose claimed capacity is much larger than usable capacity because the manufacturer counts the space outside the turntable. The *Magic Chef's* turntable is flush-mounted and can be switched off, so little space is wasted.

❺ Usable floor space. As measured by CU. Asterisk marks turntable models; measurement is diameter of the largest round casserole that can sit on turntable. With the *Magic Chef's* turntable off, usable floor space becomes 14½-x-13 inches.

❻ Power. The claimed output of the magnetron (microwave generator), in watts. The small differences between models had little bearing on relative performance. Heating speed, noted in the next column, is a more meaningful expression of power output.

❼ Heating speed. Derived from measurements of the time required to heat quantities of water placed in the center of each oven's floor; other locations might provide different results. To boil a liter of water, the fastest models would take 8½ minutes; the slowest, 10½ minutes.

❽ Leftovers. Using the most-automated settings, CU warmed up dinners. The results are composite judgments of average temperature, temperature uniformity, and cooking time. Models with a moisture sensor were the most convenient, but didn't always perform best.

❾ Defrosting. CU used the most-automated defrost settings to thaw one-pound packages of frozen ground beef. CU favored ovens that calculate power level and time once you enter weight. Highest scores went to those that thawed the beef fastest without cooking it, and did so with the least intervention.

❿ Quiche. A hard test—cooking a pastry crust, eight bacon strips, and beaten eggs and cheese. CU found big differences in evenness and time.

⓫ Popcorn. CU used a microwave popcorn high-rated in the June 1989 issue, popped it following package directions, measured the volume of popped kernels, then counted unpopped and burned kernels. The best models, which have special popcorn settings, burned few or no kernels and made 12 cups. The worse burned up to 40 percent of the kernels and made 8 cups.

Rating legend: ⊙ = Better ← → ● = Worse (⊙ ◑ ○ ◐ ●)

❶ Brand and model	❷ Price	❸ Dimensions, H x W x D, in.	❹ Usable capacity, cu. ft.	❺ Usable floor space, W x D, in.	❻ Power, watts	❼ Heating speed	❽ Leftovers	❾ Defrosting	❿ Quiche	⓫ Popcorn	Brownies	Melted cheese	Baked potatoes
✓ Sharp R-5H81/R R-5H82	$297	14½ x 24½ x 19	1.2*	16*	700	◑	◑	◑	⊙	⊙	◑	◑	⊙
D Sears Kenmore 89447	300	15½ x 23 x 18½	1.0*	15¼*	750	○	◑	○	⊙	◑	○	◑	⊙
Panasonic NN-7809/R NN7800	289	14 x 23½ x 16¾	1.0*	15*	700	◑	⊙	◑	◐	◑	○	◑	⊙
General Electric JE1465H/R JE1465J	298	14 x 23½ x 15¼	1.5	16½ x 13¼	700	◐	○	○	○	⊙	◑	○	⊙
D Magic Chef M41F-10P	292	15½ x 22 x 15½	0.8*	13*	700	○	◑	◑	◑	◐	◑	●	⊙
D Whirlpool MW8900XS	359	15¼ x 24 x 15½	1.3	16¼ x 13¾	700	○	⊙	◐	○	◐	◐	◑	◑
Jenn-Air M166	356	15½ x 22 x 16	1.1	14½ x 12¾	625	○	◑	◐	○	○	◑	●	⊙
Amana RSB460P	331	14½ x 21¾ x 17¾	1.2	13¼ x 15½	700	○	⊙	◑	○	○	○	○	⊙
Hotpoint RE1450H	280	14½ x 23¾ x 16	1.4	16 x 13¾	700	◐	⊙	○	◐	○	◑	◑	⊙
Tappan 56-4994	300	15½ x 23½ x 17¼	1.2	15½ x 14½	700	◑	○	○	◑	○	○	◑	⊙
D Quasar MQ7 799W	268	14 x 23½ x 15	1.4	16¼ x 13¼	700	◐	⊙	○	○	◑	◑	◑	⊙
Frigidaire MC1385L	315	15½ x 23½ x 17½	1.3	15½ x 14½	700	○	○	○	◐	○	○	●	⊙
Caloric MPS229	248	14½ x 21¾ x 17¾	1.2	13½ x 15½	700	○	◑	○	◐	◑	○	◑	⊙

R indicates that, according to the manufacturer, model has been replaced by an essentially similar model.

D indicates that model has been discontinued. The information has been retained to permit comparisons.

⑫ **Brownies.** The better performers did a workmanlike job. The worst overcooked some areas and left others underdone.

⑬ **Melted cheese.** CU set out nine slices on an oven's floor or turntable. The scores show how uniformly the array melted.

⑭ **Baked potatoes.** All the ovens did a good job of baking four potatoes at a time. Those with a slightly lower score left one or two potatoes a tiny bit over- or underdone.

⑮ **Keypad readability.** Most important: size and contrast of letters, numbers.

⑯ **Display readability.** Higher-scoring displays were large and brighly colored and lit, with good contrast.

⑰ **Programming ease.** A judgment of how conveniently the keypad is laid out and how logical the programming steps are. CU favored models that prompt you by asking for the next command.

⑱ **Interior visibility.** A dim interior light, a coarse screen, or a dark door pane cut down visibility through the door.

⑲ **Noise.** None were intrusive. The best were almost silent.

⑳ **Cleaning ease.** CU likes to see smooth surfaces and rounded edges. A removable glass tray is a plus.

Specifications and Features

All: • Are countertop models. • Operate on full power unless programmed otherwise. • Pause when door is opened. • Can be programmed for 99 minutes and 99 seconds of operation. • Work as a kitchen timer.

All have: • Electronic touchpad control. • Audible signal when buttons are pressed and at end of cooking cycle. • Door that opens to left. • Plastic inner window. • Display that shows time when oven is not in use. • Grounded plug.

Except as noted, all have: • Temperature probe. • Multistage cooking programs. • Auto defrost. • Auto reheat. • Weight of 48 to 57 pounds. • Cookbook. • Optional trim kit. • Plastic outer window. • Blue LED display. • User-replaceable interior light. • Painted metal interior.

Key to Advantages

A–Lighter than others (about 38 pounds).
B–Turntable can be switched off, increasing usable volume (but affecting performance for some jobs).
C–Browning element, or "browner."
D–Lock-out to keep children from operating.
E–Quick-reference instruction card.
F–Timer, unlike others, can serve as kitchen timer even when oven is operating.
G–Beeps when cooked food left inside.
H–Display shows when cooked food left inside.
I–Has moisture sensor.
J–Temperature probe can be thermometer.
K–Memory for user-programmed recipes.
L–Angled plug; oven can be very close to outlet.
M–Display shows power level (**Amana, Whirlpool, Caloric** show all but full power).
N–Excellent display prompts.
O–Very good display prompts.
P–Hands-free (push-button) door opening.
Q–Very accurate temperature probe.

Keypad readability ⑮	Display readability ⑯	Programming ease ⑰	Interior visibility ⑱	Noise ⑲	Cleaning ease ⑳	Advantages	Disadvantages	Comments
○	○	◐	◐	◐	◐	E,I,J,K,M,O,Q,R,S,T	b,g	B,M,O,T
◐	◐	◐	◐	○	○	D,E,H,I,R,T	b,k	A,B,L,N,O,Q,R
◐	○	○	○	○	◐	A,I,M,P,T,U	b,e,g	B,D,G,K,M,Q,R,U
○	◐	◐	◐	◐	◐	A,G,H,I,M,N,R,T	c,f	A,D,J,M,O,R
○	◐	○	◐	◐	◐	B,E,F,L,S	f,g,h	A,H,L,O,R
○	◐	◐	○	◐	○	E,F,G,H,I,L,M,O,R,S	c,d	A,E,I,J,L,O,R
◐	◐	◐	○	◐	○	F,L,O,Q,S	g	A,B,H,I,L,O,S,V
○	◐	◐	◐	○	○	F,J,L,M,S	g	A,C,I,J,M,O,S
○	◐	◐	◐	○	○	G,H,L,O,R,T	d,i	A,B,M,N,R,V
○	◐	◐	◐	◐	○	C,F,H,J,L,M,N,R,T	j	A,B,F,H,L,O,P,Q,R
○	○	○	◐	○	◐	A,I,M,P,T	b,c,e,g	D,G,J,K,M,Q,R,U
○	◐	◐	◐	◐	○	C,F,H,J,L,M,N,Q,T	a,j	A,B,F,H,L,O,P,Q,T
◐	◐	◐	◐	◐	○	F,J,L,M,S	a,g	A,I,J,M,O,Q,R

R–Instruction manual easy to use.
S–Good cookbook.
T–Weight-programmable cooking, defrosting.
U–Fastest at heating.

Key to Disadvantages
a–Instruction manual hard to use.
b–Interior light not user-replaceable.
c–Potatoes did not bake as well with sensor on.
d–No multistage cooking programs.
e–Count-up keypad, a slight disadvantage.
f–Temperature probe less accurate than most.
g–No visual end-of-cycle signal.
h–With turntable switched off, cheese melted very unevenly.
i–No cookbook.
j–Mechanical on/off; slight disadvantage.
k–Must be set to "0" power to use display as kitchen timer.

Key to Comments
A–Removable metal rack.
B–Glass bottom tray.

C–Stainless-steel interior.
D–Green LED display.
E–Orange LED display.
F–Green LED display with yellow prompts.
G–LCD display; dim in well-lit room.
H–Preprogrammed recipes.
I–Glass outer window.
J–Ceramic floor.
K–No temperature probe.
L–Numeric keypad has phone-type layout.
M–Keypad numbers in 1 or 2 rows or columns.
N–Open handle can be fitted with loop for limited-mobility user.
O–Full-sized cookbook.
P–No auto-defrost.
Q–Needs clearance top and/or sides for air vents.
R–Brown sides and top.
S–Black sides and top.
T–Gray sides and top.
U–Discontinued, but may be available.
V–No auto reheat.

REPAIR HISTORY

On the whole, the repair record of microwave ovens has been pretty good when compared with the repair history of other major appliances. According to readers, however, it seems that large ovens such as the ones CU tested have been more likely to need repair than midsize ovens.

In the graph below, CU distilled the experience of some 46,000 readers who gave data in the 1989 Annual Questionnaire about full-size ovens they'd bought new since 1984. Since older ovens are more likely to have needed repairs, CU has standardized the data to eliminate differences due solely to age. The bars in the graph indicate the percent of ovens that have been repaired; differences of less than three points are not meaningful.

Among the most reliable oven brands were *Panasonic, Sanyo, Sharp, Quasar, General Electric,* and *Hotpoint. Whirlpool* was far and away the least reliable brand: Fully a fifth of *Whirlpool* ovens have gone on the fritz at some point.

A few caveats are in order. First, the data are historical, meaning that they are derived from models that are sometimes several years old, and so may not reflect any recent improvement in brand reliability. And the information applies to the brand as a whole—individual models within the brand may have fared better or worse.

Still, the brand histories have remained consistent over time. You improve your odds of finding a trouble-free microwave oven if you stick with brands near the top of the list.

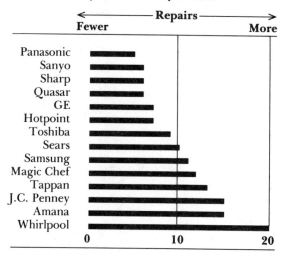

Features of dishwashers

As published in a **May 1990** report.

1 **Brand and model.** Table includes both tested and untested models. According to manufacturers' specifications, untested models have a wash system essentially similar to those tested and should perform similarly. • = model tested. When a manufacturer has more than one wash system in its line, the models that have a similar mechanism are bracketed.

2 **Price.** For tested models, the estimated average, based on prices paid and quoted in a six-month period. For others, the suggested or approximate retail, as stated by the manufacturer. A dash means the manufacturer would not provide a price.

3 **Controls.** Dials (**D**) are mechanical controls. On some models, you must turn dials and push buttons or switches at the same time (**DP**). On others, you use only push buttons (**PB**) to select cycles. Electronic controls (**E**) have solid-state timing circuitry and touchpads for selecting cycles.

4 **Additional cycles.** All dishwashers listed provide a basic Regular or Normal cycle, a Light (one-wash) cycle, and a Rinse-and-Hold cycle. All also allow selection of no-heat drying, an energy-saver.

The **Super/Pots & pans** and **Super/Heavy** cycles may extend the wash periods, add an extra wash, or boost the water temperature.

A **Delicate/China/Crystal** cycle pumps the water more gently than in the Normal cycle.

The **Sani cycle** boosts water temperature above 140°F in the final rinse and, for a few models, on the second wash.

We think only two or three cycles—Normal, Heavy, and perhaps Light—are enough for most homes.

5 **Water-heating switch.** A check here means you can set the dishwasher to boost water temperature for its standard cycle and perhaps for others; that can help the dishwasher do its job adequately if you've lowered the water heater's thermostat. Models without a switch either heat the water routinely or monitor the temperature and provide the boost as needed.

6 **Drying blower.** Common on higher-priced models but not essential. Models with a blower should dry dishes a little better than a comparable model without one.

7 **Time display.** On some, a numbered dial (**ND**) or a digital display (**DD**) shows the time left until the end of the cycle.

8 **Delayed start.** Some machines can be preset to start several hours after you've loaded up and set the controls. That makes it easy to take advantage of off-peak electricity rates.

9 **Rinse-conditioner dispenser.** Injects conditioner into the final rinse to help curb spotting by making water flow in sheets.

10 **Construction.** Porcelain-coated steel (**Po**) resists abrasion better than solid-plastic tubs (**Pl**) but can be chipped.

11 **Door colors.** Most machines come with one or more reversible door panels for a choice of colors.

12 **Convertible/portable version.** These models can be bought now for use as portables and later converted to an under-counter installation.

④ Additional cycles   **⑩ Construction**

Better ● ◐ ○ ◐ ● Worse

❶ Brand and model	② Price	③ Controls	Super/Pots & pans	Super/Heavy	Delicate/China/Crystal	Sani-cycle	Water-heating switch	Drying blower	Time display	Delayed start	Rinse-conditioner dispenser	Tub	Door liner	Door colors	Convertible/portable versions	Comments
Caloric																
• DUS406	$300	DP	✓	✓	—	—	✓	—		—	✓	Po	Pl	3	DCS413	—
DUS409	500	E	✓	✓	—	—	✓	—		✓	✓	Po	Pl	3	—	—
Frigidaire																
• DW4500F	355	DP	✓	✓	—	✓	✓	—		✓	✓	Po	Pl	3	DW4400D	—
DW5500F	540	DP	✓	✓	—	✓	✓	✓	—	✓	✓	Po	Pl	3	—	—
DW6600F	620	E	✓	✓	—	✓	✓	✓	DD	✓	✓	Po	Pl	3	—	—
General Electric																
GSD500L	294	DP	—	—	—	—	—	—		—	✓	Pl	Pl	2	—	—
GSD640L	344	DP	✓	—	—	—	—	—		—	✓	Pl	Pl	2	—	—
GSD1000L	444	DP	✓	—	—	—	—	—		—	✓	Pl	Pl	4	—	E
GSD1100L	444	DP	✓	—	—	—	—	—		—	✓	Pl	Pl	4	—	E
• GSD1200L/Ⓡ GSD1200M	475	PB	✓	—	✓	—	—	—		—	✓	Pl	Pl	4	—	E
• GSD2800L/Ⓡ GSD2800M	552	E	✓	—	✓	✓	—	—	DD	✓	✓	Pl	Pl	4	—	B,E
Hotpoint																
• HDA950G/Ⓡ HDA9509M	340	DP	✓	—	—	✓	—	—		—	✓	Po	Po	4	—	—
HDA1000K	404	DP	✓	—	—	✓	—	—		—	✓	Pl	Pl	2	—	—
• HDA2000G/Ⓡ HDA2000M	380	E	✓	—	✓	—	—	—	DD	—	✓	Pl	Pl	4	—	B
HDA2600K	564	E	✓	—	✓	✓	—	—	DD	✓	✓	Pl	Pl	4	—	B
Jenn Air																
• DU476 Ⓡ DU86	572	DP	—	✓	—	✓	✓	✓	—	—	✓	Po	Po	4	—	L
DU496	765	PB	—	✓	—	✓	✓	✓	—	✓	✓	Po	Po	4	—	L
Ⓓ DU588	849	E	—	✓	—	✓	✓	✓	DD	✓	✓	Po	Po	4	—	L
Kitchen Aid																
• KUDC220T	439	DP	✓	—	—	—	✓	✓	—	—	✓	Po	Po	2	—	—
KUD1220T	519	DP	✓	—	—	—	—	✓	—	—	✓	Po	Po	4	KPD1620T	C
KUDS220T	699	PB	✓	—	—	✓	—	✓	—	—	✓	Po	Po	4	—	C,D,F
• KUDS22ST	718	E	✓	—	—	✓	✓	✓	DD	✓	✓	Po	Po	4	—	A,C,D,F

Ⓡ indicates that, according to the manufacturer, model has been replaced by an essentially similar model.

Ⓓ indicates that model has been discontinued. The information has been retained to permit comparisons.

Key to Comments

A—Systems monitor displays warning codes for a few common malfunctions.

B—Systems monitor displays messages and codes for numerous oversights and malfunctions.

C—Upper wash arm has guard to prevent blockage.

D—Has folding dividers in upper rack for more flexible loading.

E—Cup rack has 1 or 2 fold-down shelves for 2-tier stacking of cups and squat glasses.

F—Upper rack can be raised, lowered, or tilted to change overhead clearance.

G—Has flatware basket in door.

H—Has additional cutlery basket in door.

	Price ②	Controls ③	Super/Pots & pans	Super/Heavy	Delicate/China/Crystal	Sani-cycle	Water-heating switch ⑤	Drying blower ⑥	Time display ⑦	Delayed start ⑧	Rinse-conditioner dispenser ⑨	Tub	Door liner	Door colors ⑪	Convertible/portable versions ⑫	Comments
Magic Chef																
• DU110CA	451	DP	✓	✓	—	—	✓	—	—	—	✓	Po	Pl	3	—	—
Maytag																
WU202/Ⓡ WU204	$489	D	✓	—	—	—	—	✓	—	—	—	Po	Po	4	WC202	M
WU302/Ⓡ WU302	—	DP	✓	—	—	—	—	✓	—	—	—	Po	Po	4	—	M
WU502/Ⓡ WU502	539	DP	✓	—	—	—	✓	✓	—	—	—	Po	Po	4	WC502	M
• WU702/Ⓡ WU704	549	DP	✓	—	—	✓	✓	✓	—	—	✓	Po	Po	4	WC702	D,M
WU902/Ⓡ WU904	635	PB	✓	—	—	✓	✓	✓	—	—	✓	Po	Po	4	—	D,M
WU1000/Ⓡ WU1000	695	E	✓	—	—	✓	✓	DD	✓	—	✓	Po	Po	4	—	D,M
Sears																
• 16485/Ⓡ 16405	299	DP	✓	—	—	—	—	—	—	—	✓	Po	Pl	3	17485	I
Ⓓ 16585	369	DP	✓	—	—	✓	—	—	—	—	✓	Po	Pl	3	—	J
• 16695/Ⓡ 16605	374	DP	✓	—	—	✓	—	—	—	—	✓	Po	Pl	4	—	K
Ⓓ 16785	420	DP	✓	—	—	✓	—	—	—	✓	✓	Po	Pl	4	17785	N
Ⓓ 16875	479	PB	✓	—	—	✓	✓	—	—	✓	✓	Po	Pl	4	—	O
Ⓓ 16985	619	E	✓	—	—	✓	✓	DD	—	✓	✓	Po	Pl	4	—	B,M
Whirlpool																
DU8550XT	399	DP	✓	—	—	✓	—	—	—	—	✓	Po	Pl	2	—	G
DU8700XT	429	DP	✓	✓	—	✓	—	—	—	✓	✓	Po	Pl	2	DP8700T	F,G
• DU8900XT	449	DP	✓	✓	—	✓	—	—	—	✓	✓	Po	Pl	2	—	F,G,H
DU9200XT	499	E	✓	✓	—	✓	—	—	—	✓	✓	Po	Pl	2	—	F,G
• DU9400XT	530	E	✓	✓	—	✓	—	—	—	✓	✓	Po	Pl	2	—	F,G
DU9700XR/Ⓡ 19700XT	659	E	✓	✓	—	✓	—	DD	—	✓	✓	Po	Pl	6	—	F,G,H
White Westinghouse																
• SU550J/Ⓡ SU550N	314	DP	✓	✓	—	—	—	ND	—	—	✓	Po	Pl	3	SC560J	—
SU770J/Ⓡ SU770N	379	DP	✓	✓	—	✓	—	ND	—	✓	✓	Po	Pl	3	—	—
Ⓓ SU980J	—	DP	✓	✓	—	✓	—	✓	ND	✓	✓	Po	Pl	4	—	F,P

I—Replaced by **16405.** Available without utensil basket and cup shelf as **15405,** $318.

J—Replaced by **16505.** Available without utensil basket and cup shelf as **15505,** $367.

K—Replaced by **16605.** Available without utensil basket and cup shelf as **15605,** $387.

L—Manufacturer's literature shows an illustration of a convertible/portable version but gives no model number or details.

M—Discontinued.

N—Discontinued; replaced by **16705.**

O—Discontinued; replaced by **16805,** $501.

P—Discontinued; may be available in some stores.

Ratings of dishwashers

As published in a **May 1990** report (model currency updated February 1991). Listed in order of estimated quality, based on washing ability, energy efficiency, convenience, safety, and other factors. Except where separated by bold rules, closely ranked models differed little in quality.

❶ **Price.** The estimated average retail price, based on prices paid and quoted during a six-month period.

❷ **Washing ability.** Results with Normal/Regular cycle (or closest equivalent two-wash cycle) on test loads smeared with various foods. Each machine washed six loads with 140°F water, six loads with 120° water. CU inspected each load afterward to assess its cleanliness. Judgments here summarize results for both water temperatures. The machines generally didn't get loads quite as clean with 120° water, even if the dishwasher's heater compensated by boosting the water temperature for some parts of the cycle.

❸ **Energy efficiency.** These scores take into account the direct use of electricity for washing and heated drying, along with the cost of heating the water in the water's heater and within the dishwasher.

❹ **Noise.** CU judged the sound each machine made as it ran in a plywood enclosure. A given machine might sound better or worse in your kitchen, but the relative standings should remain the same.

❺ **Cycle time.** Using cooler water often lengthens washing time. That's because most machines need extra time to heat the water.

❻ **Water used.** As measured by CU, for the cycle used in the dishwashing test.

Key to Advantages

A–Has systems monitor that displays a few functions.
B–Has systems monitor with numerous displays for malfunctions or status of cycle.
C–Has hidden touchpad to lock controls from children.
D–Timer dial or digital display shows minutes left in cycle.
E–May be set for delayed start up to 6 hours (**KitchenAid** and **GE**, up to 9 hours; **Sears** up to 12 hours).
F–Upper rack can be adjusted up and down or tilted to change overhead clearance.
G–Bottom of upper rack is terraced with steps to accommodate oversized plates in lower rack.
H–Accepts larger dinner plates (12 inches or more) better than most others.
I–Has no water tower to intrude into main rack; judged to provide more flexibility for loading pots, bowls, and larger items.
J–Accepts very tall glasses better than most.
K–Upper rack (lower rack on **Jenn Air** and **Maytag**) has 1 or 2 fold-down sections for two-tier stacking of cups and squat glasses.
L–Upper rack has pickets for two-tier stacking of cups and squat glasses.
M–Upper rack has adjustable or folding divider props.
N–Has extra covered basket for small items.
O–Has extra utensil basket.
P–Flatware basket(s) has covered sections for small items.
Q–Flatware basket has carrying handle.
R–Automatically drains water for extra protection against accidental overfilling and flooding.
S–Solid-plastic interior and door liner.
T–Solid-plastic door liner.
U–Chassis has wheels or "shoes" to facilitate moving during installation or servicing.
V–Smooth control-panel surface easy to clean.

Key to Disadvantages

a–Did not dry glassware as well as most others (**KitchenAid**, with 120° water; **Sears**, with 140° water).
b–Did not dry flatware as well as most others (**Caloric**, with 120° water; others, at both water temperatures).
c–Timer isn't accessible. Canceling a cycle takes a minute or two. **GE** also dumps its detergent when cycle is canceled.
d–On our sample, it was difficult to avoid shortening first fill when advancing the timer dial to Start.
e–Has signal lights rather than timer; only gives rough indication of progress through the cycles.
f–Timer dial does not give a clear indication of when cycle is over.
g–Cannot take glasses as tall as most others.
h–Certain areas in tub and door occasionally required cleaning during CU's tests.
i–Flatware basket lacks carrying handle.
j–On CU samples, lower rack moved somewhat stiffly, dragging along tub sides.
k–Door latch moved stiffly on CU sample.
l–External fiberglass insulation blanket lacked protective sheath; may fray if not handled carefully during installation.

Key to Comments

A–Has electronic timer; even so, you can cancel cycle quickly.
B–Regular cycle includes only 1 wash phase, not 2 as in most machines, or was otherwise limited. CU ran tests using Heavy wash to get a more comparable wash-and-rinse cycle.
C–Rack design is opposite the norm: Upper rack holds larger plates and pots, lower holds cups and glasses.
D–Has removable flatware rack mounted inside door.
E–Some water may splash out if you open door quickly during wash cycle.
F–Requires 20-amp circuit.
G–Warranty includes parts and labor for 5 years.
H–Manufacturer warrantees only parts; labor is responsibility of dealer.
I–Manufacturer recommends minimum water temperature of 140°, but overall washing performance suffered only slightly with 120° water.

Key to ratings (Washing ability, Energy efficiency, Noise):
● Better ◐ ○ ◑ ● Worse

① Price ② Washing ability ③ Energy efficiency, 140°/120° water ④ Noise ⑤ Cycle time, 140°/120° water ⑥ Water used

Brand and model	Price ①	China	Flatware	Glasses	Energy efficiency 140°/120° ③	Noise ④	Cycle time 140°/120° water ⑤	Water used ⑥	Advantages	Disadvantages	Comments
KitchenAid KUDS22ST	$718	●	●	◐	◐/◐	◐	75/80 min.	9½ gal.	A,D,E,F,I,M,P,V	—	A
Magic Chef DU110CA	451	●	●	◐	○/◐	◐	80/110	11½	E,G,Q,S	f	
Maytag WU702 /R WU704	549	●	●	◐	◐/◐	○	75/80	11½	I,J,K,M,P,U	j,l	C,E,F
Jenn Air DU476 /R WU486	572	●	●	◐	●/○	○	80/100	12	I,J,K,M,P,U	j,l	C,E,F
KitchenAid KUDC220T	439	●	●	◐	◐/●	○	80/80	12	I	a,l	—
General Electric GSD2800L /R GSD2800M	552	◐	●	○	◐/●	◐	80/80	10	B,C,D,E,G,J,K,P,Q,R,S,V	—	A
[D] Sears 16985	619	●	●	◐	◐/○	◐	70/85	10½	B,C,D,E,F,J,K,M,N,O,P,R,T,U	—	A,G
Sears 16695 /R 16605	374	●	◐	◐	◐/○	◐	70/115	10½	K,N,O,P,U,T	a,d	—
General Electric GSD1200L /R GSD1200M	475	◐	◐	○	○/◐	◐	85/100	10½	G,J,K,P,Q,S	c	—
Frigidaire DW4500F	355	◐	○	◐	○/○	◐	70/70	11½	E,F,G,H,K,L,P,Q,T	h	B
Whirlpool DU8900XT	449	●	○	◐	◐/○	◐	75/110	10½	E,F,O,T,U	b	B,D
Whirlpool DU9400XT	530	●	○	◐	◐/○	◐	70/105	10½	C,E,F,T,U,V	b,e	A,B,D
White Westinghouse SU550J /R SU550N	314	◐	◐	◐	○/◐	◐	75/75	11½	D,G,L,Q,T	h,l	B
Caloric DUS406	300	◐	◐	○	○/○	○	75/85	11½	N,T	b,g,i	B,H
Hotpoint HDA2000G /R HDA200M	380	○	◐	●	◐/●	◐	75/85	10½	B,D,H,P,Q,S,V	—	A
Sears 16485 /R 16405	299	◐	◐	○	○/◐	○	75/75	11½	I,K,N,O,T	g,k	I
General Electric GSD600L /R GSD640L	305	○	◐	●	◐/●	○	75/75	11½	H,Q,S	—	—
Hotpoint HDA950G /R HDA9509M	340	◐	●	○	◐/◐	●	70/80	10	H,Q	b,g,l	—

R indicates that, according to the manufacturer, model has been replaced by an essentially similar model.
D indicates that model has been discontinued. The information has been retained to permit comparisons.

195

Electric & gas ranges

As published in **February 1989** report.
Which have been most reliable?

Frequency of repair data from *Consumer Reports'* Annual Questionnaire reveals that electric ranges have been more reliable than gas models. Self-cleaning ranges of either type have been less reliable than manual clean models.

Readers provided data on more than 33,000 freestanding ranges purchased from 1982 to 1988—27,808 electric ranges (enough to assess the reliability of all the tested brands except *Gibson*) and 5864 gas ranges (enough to calculate reliability for four brands, only two of which are among those tested).

The graph gives an idea of what percentage of brands'

self-cleaning ranges have ever required repairs. Differences of four index points generally can be considered meaningful. The difference in reliability between the two top electric brands—*Hotpoint* and *General Electric*—and the worst—*Magic Chef*—is not as striking as the difference among gas ranges, where *Caloric* has had a much worse record than *Tappan,* the best gas brand.

The data apply only to brands, not specific models, and to how those brands have behaved in the past. Still, readers' experiences have been remarkably consistent over the years. You have a much better chance of avoiding repair headaches if you choose a brand that has a low Repair Index.

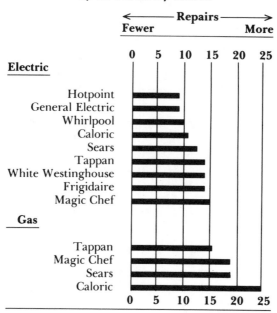

Repair index by brand

Guide to Features

❶ Brand and model. The table includes both tested and untested models. Manufacturers' specifications show untested models are similar in construction to those tested; they should be similar in performance. Features, which can affect convenience and cleaning ease, are likely to vary. • indicates model tested.

❷ Price. The approximate retail price, as quoted by manufacturer. Discounts are usually available (see prices quoted to CU shoppers in Ratings). + indicates shipping is extra.

❸ Oven window. A plus only if you can see inside clearly. Dark glass cuts the view.

❹ Black-glass door. A common feature. Some models have a window, too.

❺ Cooktop light. A nice night light, but otherwise unnecessary in a well-lit kitchen.

❻ Clock. All have a clock and timer and can be set to bake or self-clean automatically. The clock/timer can be analog (A), digital/mechanical (DM), or digital/electronic (DE).

❼ Drip bowls. They catch spills around burners and can be cleaned at the sink or in the dishwasher. Porcelain (P) is easier to clean than chrome (C) and can be cleaned in the oven during the self-clean cycle. The chrome ones, however, may speed up cooking.

Electric

Brand and model	Price	Oven window	Black-glass door	Cooktop light	Clock	Drip bowls	Comments
General Electric							
JBP24GK / Ⓡ JSP24GN	$499-539	—	✓	—	A	P	—
• JBP26GJ / Ⓡ JSP26GN	559-599	✓	✓	—	A	P	—
JB450GK / Ⓡ JSP-450	599-639	✓	✓	—	DE	P	—
JB550GJ / Ⓡ JSP550GN	669-699	✓	✓	✓	DE	P	A
Frigidaire							
Ⓓ RE34BA	540	—	✓	—	A	C	—
Ⓓ REG36A	600	✓	—	—	A	P	—
Ⓓ • RSE37BA	550	—	✓	✓	A	C	—
Gibson							
• CEC4S6WS /	—	✓	✓	—	DM	C	—
Whirlpool							
Ⓓ RF365BXV	549	—	✓	—	A	C	—
Ⓓ RF385OXP	639	✓	—	—	A	P	—
• RF376PXP /	659	✓	✓	—	A	P	—
Ⓓ RF390PXV	659	✓	✓	—	DE	P	—
Ⓓ RF395PXV	749	✓	✓	✓	DE	P	—

Gas

Brand and model	Price	Oven window	Black-glass door	Cooktop light	Clock	Drip bowls	Comments
General Electric							
Ⓓ JGBP24GEJ	$579-639	—	✓	—	A	C	—
Ⓓ • JGBP26GEJ	649-699	✓	✓	✓	DM	C	—
Ⓓ JGBP28GEJ	679-729	✓	✓	✓	DE	C	B
Roper							
• F8958 / Ⓡ FGS395V	659-699	✓	✓	✓	DE	C	C
Hardwick							
• CPG9841W579A / Ⓡ CPJ-9841-K689 DG	—	✓	✓	✓	DE	C	—
Sears							
Ⓓ • 73781	—	✓	✓	—	DE	C	C
Ⓓ 73581	709+	✓	✓	—	DE	C	—
O'Keefe & Merritt							
306758	550-560	—	✓	—	A	—	—
• 307988 / Ⓡ 307989	700	✓	✓	✓	DE	C	—
Tappan							
Ⓓ 302758	550-560	—	✓	—	A	—	—
Ⓓ 303658	630-640	—	✓	✓	DM	C	—
Ⓓ • 303988	700	✓	✓	✓	DE	C	—

Ⓡ indicates that, according to the manufacturer, model has been replaced by an essentially similar model.

Ⓓ indicates that model has been discontinued. The information has been retained to permit comparisons.

Key to Comments
A—Has "power saver" coil element, which allows heated portion to match pot size.

B—Has brushed-chrome cooktop; doesn't chip but difficult to keep clean and may become discolored with use.

C—One oven rack folds in two for storage.

Ratings of electric and gas ranges

As published in a **February 1989** report (model currency updated February 1991).

Guide to the Ratings

Listed by type; within type, listed in order of estimated quality based mainly on how well each model baked, broiled, and self-cleaned, how easy the cooktop was to clean, and oven and broiler capacity. Bracketed models were judged equal and are listed alphabetically. Ratings should be used in conjunction with the Features table.

❶ **Brand and model.** These are the top-rated models (or replacements) from the 1987 reports. All are 30-inch free-standing models from the middle or top of each manufacturer's line.

❷ **Price.** The average quoted to CU shoppers. The manufacturer's suggested retail price, shown in the Features table, is often discounted. Prices are for white; colored exteriors may cost extra. + indicates shipping is extra.

❸ **Dimensions.** All are 30 inches wide and have a cooktop 36 inches above the floor. Overall height and depth vary by a few inches. Height is to the top of the backguard; depth includes any projections at back. Dimension in parentheses is depth with door open. Height can be increased a bit by extending the leveling legs. Figures are rounded to next highest quarter inch.

❹ **Oven capacity.** Important to those who bake on both shelves at once or who need maximum space for, say, a turkey. Shelf supports and broiler reduce useful space. Differences in height (up to 2¼ inches) account for most of the variance.

❺ **Baking.** CU used a white cake mix, baking four layers and then two layers. Once the optimum shelf and pan locations were ascertained, most models baked perfect cakes—moist, light, and nicely browned. Only the *Whirlpool* could be faulted, for overbrowning the two layers on its top shelf.

❻ **Broiling.** Effective broiling area on the electrics was larger than on gas models. Those with the best scores delivered a tray of 16 burgers that were well done on the outside and rare inside. Those that scored a notch lower broiled fewer burgers judged excellent.

❼ **Self-cleaning.** Electric models have shown a slight edge over gas models through the years. All need to have door frames cleaned before the self-cleaning cycle is started. All left some residue around the front of the oven cavity and inside the door. After self-cleaning, an ashy residue needs to be wiped out with a damp sponge.

The high temperatures reached during self-cleaning can cause hot spots on the range's exterior. Details are called out in the Ratings. Families with children, beware.

The self-cleaning feature adds $50 to $100 to the price of an electric model, $100 to the price of a gas model. Running the cycle is cheap—about 55 cents worth of electricity or 35 cents worth of gas.

❽ **Cooktop cleanability.** CU judged the ease of cleaning under the cooktop, the backguard, drip bowls, and venting area. The *Whirlpool* boasts the most features that make cleaning easy, hence its high score. The *Roper* and the similar *Sears* gas models had the fewest such features as well as a vent that gets particularly dirty and is difficult to clean.

❾ **Cooktop-cleaning features.** All but the electric *GE* have a cooktop that props up; a few also come out for cleaning at the sink. Under-the-cooktop cleaning is greatly eased if that space is uncluttered with hardware and there are deep spill wells. A curved, seamless backguard eliminates another area where grime can build. Note that all gas models share a design that makes cleaning more difficult: The oven vent emerges between the backguard and the cooktop. (Most electrics vent through one of the burner elements.) Porcelain drip bowls are easier to clean.

Specifications and features

All: • Have push-to-turn surface burner controls. • Have porcelain cooktop, painted sides, and black glass door. • Broil in the oven. • Have two oven shelves with a safety stop. • Have oven light. • Have storage drawer that can be removed to expose the floor. • Can be preset for baking and self-cleaning.

Except as noted, all: • Have shiny metal drip bowls under burners. • Cooktops prop up for cleaning. • Oven doors can be removed for cleaning. • Have door lock that requires manual latching before self-cleaning. • Offer choice of self-clean durations. • Oven interiors are dark gray; appear clean despite minor soiling. • Have oven window that has only fair visibility and that gets hot during self-cleaning. • Have oven light that lights when door opens and is easy to replace. • Have porcelain enameled broiler pan and insert. • Have white storage drawer. • Don't let 12-quart pot sit well on back burner. • Manufacturers provide toll-free phone number. • Have 1-year warranty on parts and labor. • Simmered successfully in CU tests.

All electric ranges: • Operate at 120/240 volts or 120/208 volts. • Have 28-inch and 26-inch removable surface elements. • Have indicator lights to show what's in use. • Have 60-minute analog timer. • Have dial-type controls on backguard. • Use both bake and broil elements when baking. • Get hot (130°–160°F) behind oven door handle and at rear vent (140°–180°F) during self-cleaning.

All gas ranges: • Require 120-volt electric supply. • Have dial-type burner controls mounted at front. • Have automatic spark-igniter for burners and separate glow-type igniters for oven/broiler. • Have removable, aluminum surface burners. • Vent oven at rear of cooktop. • Get hot at control panel (160°–200°F) and at rear vent (200°–235°) during self-clean.

Except as noted, all gas ranges: • Have 4 round burner grates of equal size. • Have 4 9000 BTU/hour natural-gas rated burners (rated at 7000 or 7500 BTU/hour when used with LP gas). • Have burner controls that turn 180 degrees. • Have oven controls on backguard. • Have electronic timing controls on backguard and an electronic digital clock with 90-minute timer that counts down in seconds. • Have dial-type controls for oven. • Have separate oven, cleaning, and locked-door indicator lights. • Are inconvenient to clean under cooktop.

Key to Advantages

A–Has 2 burners rated at 12,000 BTU/hour and 2 at 9000 BTU/hour.
B–8-inch elements rated at 2600 watts; 6-inch, 1500 watts at 240 volts.
C–Burner controls turn almost 360 degrees, allowing finer adjustments than the others (but see Disadvantage b).
D–Burner-control guides most clearly marked.
E–Has electronic display, with timer that can be set to 9 hours, 55 minutes and oven temperature indicator that shows temperature as it rises, in 5-degree increments. Display also indicates broil, clean, and lock settings.
F–Tone signals when oven temperature reached.
G–Tone signals at end of timed-oven operation.
H–Door locks automatically for self-cleaning.
I–Storage drawer wider than most and easy to clean because of seamless, curved corners.
J–12-quart pot on rear elements left controls clear.
K–Panel light easier than most to change.

Key to Disadvantages

a–Cooking light must be changed by servicer.
b–Lowest heat setting too high for simmering.
c–Setting clock for timed bake or self-cleaning more complicated than most.
d–No oven indicator light.
e–Vent allows objects to fall in.
f–Manually operated oven light; special tool required to change bulb.
g–Storage drawer smaller than most.
h–Venting soils backguard more easily than most during self-cleaning and is difficult to clean.
i–Cooktop can get hotter than others.

Key to Comments

A–4 square burner grates of equal size.
B–Burner rated at 9000 BTU/hour with LP gas.
C–AT 240 volts, 8-inch elements rated at 2350 watts; 6-inch, 1325 watts.
D–2100 watts, 8-inch elements and 1250 watts, 6-inch elements were slightly slow to heat up.
E–Deep drip bowls prevent spills under cooktop but add hazard if drippings are combustible.
F–Oven selector/temperature dial at front.
G–Push-button oven control with rotary temperature setting knob.
H–Timing control is not electronic.
I–Warranty on glass parts and finishes for 30 days (**Roper and Sears**); no warranty on finish (**Hardwick**).
J–Electronic display shows when oven is self-cleaning; light shows door is locked.
K–Light shows door is locked for self-cleaning.
L–Duct that vents self-cleaning easily misaligned.
M–Self-cleaning cycle preset for 3½ hours.
N–Has two settings for broiling.
O–Oven door not removable.
P–Aluminum broiler pan and insert.
Q–Porcelain-enameled broiler pan has a chromed-steel insert.
R–Oven shelf folds in half for storage.
S–Sides of cooktop chrome-trimmed, which protects edges but is a dirt-catcher.
T–Additional 4-year warranty on heating elements and some control parts does not include labor.
U–Exterior of storage drawer painted black.
V–Special kit available for canning kettles.
W–Oven interior is light gray.

Rating scale: Better ● ◐ ○ ◑ ● Worse

⑨ Cooktop cleaning features

Electric Ranges

① Brand and model	Price	Dimensions, in.	Oven capacity	Baking	Broiling	Self-cleaning	Cooktop cleanability	Prop-up cooktop	Removable cooktop	Seamless backguard	Under-cooktop area	Porcelain drip bowls	Advantages	Disadvantages	Comments
[D] Frigidaire RSE37BA	$412	47½ x 27½ (43¼)	○	●	●	◐	◐	✓	—	✓	—	—	H,I,J	—	D,V
Gibson CEC4S6WS / [R] CEC4S6WX	520	45¾ x 27¾ (44)	○	●	●	◐	○	✓	—	—	—	—	H,I	—	D,T
Whirlpool RF375PXP / [R] RF391PXX	520	45½ x 27½ (46½)	●	●	●	○	○	✓	—	✓	✓	✓	B	i	E,K,N,O,P,V
General Electric JBP26GJ / [R] JSP26GH	445	44¾ x 27½ (45)	○	●	◐	○	○	—	—	✓	—	✓	—	—	C,K,L,O

Gas Ranges

① Brand and model	Price	Dimensions, in.	Oven capacity	Baking	Broiling	Self-cleaning	Cooktop cleanability	Prop-up cooktop	Removable cooktop	Seamless backguard	Under-cooktop area	Porcelain drip bowls	Advantages	Disadvantages	Comments
General Electric JGBP26GEJ / [R] JGP26GEN	589	47½ x 28 (45)	○	●	◐	○	◐	✓	—	—	✓	—	K	—	A,H,S,U
[D] O'Keefe & Merritt 307988 / [R] 307989	627	45¼ x 28 (45)	○	●	◐	○	◐	✓	—	—	✓	—	—	a,c,	—
[D] Tappan 303988	550	45¼ x 28 (45¼)	○	●	◐	○	◐	✓	—	—	✓	—	—	a,c,	—
Roper F8958 / [R] FGS395V	540	46¾ x 27¾ (45)	○	●	◐	◐	◐	✓	✓	—	—	—	A,C,E,F,G	b,e,f,g,h	G,I,M,N,Q,R,S,U,W
Hardwick CPG9841W579A / [R] CPT-9841-K-689 DG	501	46¼ x 28¼ (44¼)	◐	●	○	○	○	✓	—	—	—	—	D,G,K	c,d,f	F,I,J,U,W
[D] Sears Cat. No. 73781	600+	45½ x 28½ (45)	○	●	◐	◐	◐	✓	✓	—	—	—	E,F,G	e,f,g,h	B,G,I,M,N,Q,R,U,W

[R] indicates that, according to the manufacturer, model has been replaced by an essentially similar model.

[D] indicates that model has been discontinued. The information has been retained to permit comparisons.

Features of gas ranges

1 Brand and model. This table includes both tested and untested models (• indicates models tested). Manufacturers' specifications show the untested models in this table are similar in construction to those tested; they should be similar in cooktop, baking, and self-cleaning performance. Features vary, and they may affect convenience and ease of cleaning. Except as noted in the Comments, all have chrome drip bowls under cooktop burners, black-glass oven door, and storage drawer.

2 Price. Approximate retail, as quoted by manufacturer. Discounts are available.

3 Oven window. A window is a plus only if you can see inside clearly. Dark glass found in most models may cut the view.

4 Cooktop light. Unnecessary in a well-lit kitchen.

5 Clock. All have a clock and timer and can be set to bake or self-clean automatically. The clock may be an analog type (**A**) with hands, digital/mechanical (**DM**), or digital/electronic (**DE**).

6 Grates. Round (**R**) or square (**S**).

① Brand and model	② Price	③ Oven window	④ Cooktop light	⑤ Clock	⑥ Grates	Comments
Caloric • RST369	$930	✓	✓	DE	S	—
Frigidaire GPG34BN	739	✓	—	DE	S	—
• GPG38BN	829	✓	✓	DE	S	—
[D] General Electric JGBP24GEJ	619	—	—	A	S	E
[D] • JGBP26GEJ	699	✓	✓	DM	S	—
[D] • JGBP28GEJ	729	✓	✓	DE	S	A
Hardwick • CPG9841K679DG/ [R] CPJ-9841-KDG	730	✓	✓	DE	R	—
Hotpoint RGB744GEJ	579	—	—	A	S	E
• RGB746GEJ	659	✓	✓	DM	S	—
Magic Chef • 34HN-4TKXW / [R] 34JN4TKWX	824	✓	✓	DE	S	—
Montgomery Ward KTM2889 [R] 2881	699	✓	—	A	S	—
• KTM2899 / [R] 2891	749	✓	✓	DE	S	—
O'Keefe & Merritt 30-6759	599	—	✓	A	S	—
• 30-7989	749	✓	✓	DE	S	—
Roper • F8958/FGS-395V	712	✓	✓	DE	R	—
[D] Sears • 73591	796	✓	✓	DE	R	—
Tappan 30-3859	709	—	—	DE	R	—
• 30-3989	749	✓	✓	DE	S	—
30-4979	769	✓	✓	DE	S	B
30-4989	809	✓	✓	DE	S	D
Whirlpool SF365BEP	709	—	—	A	S	C
SF375BEP	839	✓	✓	A	S	—
SF376PEP	879	✓	✓	A	S	—
• SF396PEP / [R] SF395PEW	919	✓	✓	DE	S	D

[R] indicates that, according to the manufacturer, model has been replaced by an essentially similar model.
[D] indicates that model has been discontinued. The information has been retained to permit comparisons.

Key to Comments
A–Brushed-chrome cooktop.
B–Brushed-chrome cooktop; black sides optional.
C–No burner bowls; chrome burner bowls optional.
D–White glass oven door.
E–No storage drawer.

Ratings of gas ranges

As published in an **August 1990** report (model currency updated February 1991). Listed in order of estimated quality. Differences between closely ranked models were slight. Bracketed models, judged equal in quality, are listed in alphabetical order.

❶ **Brand and model.** Freestanding, 30-inch-wide, self-cleaning models, generally from the middle or top of each manufacturer's line. If you have trouble locating a model, call the company.

❷ **Price.** Estimated average price, based on prices paid and quoted during a six-month period.

❸ **Dimensions.** All cooktops are 36 inches off the floor. Height is to the top of the backguard and can be increased by adjusting the range's leveling legs. Depth includes any protrusions at the back. Figure in parentheses is depth with oven door open. Figures are rounded to higher quarter-inch.

❹ **Oven capacity.** Useful space ranges from about 1¾ to 2½ cubic feet. All ovens can hold a 20-pound turkey, but the smallest don't leave much room to spare.

❺ **Baking.** How evenly each baked four cake layers, two per shelf.

❻ **Broiling.** All broiled well. The broiling pans of the best could hold 12 burgers. The pans of those that scored a notch lower could hold 16 burgers but broiled best when we made only 9.

❼ **Self-cleaning.** We set most for a 3½-hour cycle; all left streaks of burned-on residue around the front of the oven and inside the oven door. (The **Caloric** has a three-hour cleaning cycle, not enough to burn off our tough soil.) High temperatures during self-cleaning caused hot spots on the exterior of all ranges.

❽ **Cooktop work spaces.** Based on how well the following fit on each cooktop: an 11-quart stockpot on a back burner; a 3-inch-deep, 11-inch-diameter skillet on a back burner; an 11-inch diameter skillet and a 3-quart saucepan on one side of the cooktop, with the saucepan on a back burner.

❾ **Cooktop cleanability.** How easy the cooktop was to clean.

❿ **Cooktop-cleaning features.** CU found that these design refinements make a difference. All have either a **prop-up** or **removable** cooktop; a few have both. Under the cooktop, a **deep well** and **minimum clutter** make cleaning easier. A **glass backguard** is easier to clean than a painted backguard, and it doesn't get scratched.

Specifications and Features

All: • Require 120-volt electric supply. • Have removable push-to-turn burner control dials at the front. • Have removable aluminum burners, shiny metal drip bowls, and porcelain-covered burner grates. • Have automatic spark-igniter for burners and glow-type igniter for oven/broiler. • Have oven with broiler and broiler pan (usually porcelain-coated), 2 shelves with safety stop and at least 4 shelf positions, and light. • Ovens accommodate 20-pound turkey and 14-x-16 inch baking sheet. • Can be preset to bake or self-clean. • Have door that latches manually for self-cleaning. • Have oven vents at back of cooktop; during self-cleaning and broiling, this area becomes hot. • Vents emit smoke during self-cleaning. • Get hot on door, door latch, cooktop, and cooktop control panel during self-cleaning. • Have removable black-glass oven door with window. • Have painted sides. • Have leveling feet.

Except as noted, all: • Cooktop burner controls are vertically mounted, have at least 3 marked settings, and turn 170–220 degrees. • Burners have square grates and are rated at 9000 BTU/hour (natural gas) and 7000 to 8000 BTU/hour (LP gas). • Have electronic oven controls activated by buttons; digital electronic clock with timer that can count down from 9 hours, 50 minutes; and bake/broil/self-clean (including oven-lock) information displayed on backguard. • Beep when temperature has stabilized and/or when timed cooking is done. • Have white porce-

lain cooktop and white sides. • Cooktop sides have chrome trim that protects edges but catches dirt. • Oven windows provide good visibility, and oven light turns on automatically when door is opened. • Have 1 broil setting. • Have removable storage drawer with black front. • Cooktops easily accommodate 3-quart saucepan on back burner and an 11-inch skillet on the burner directly in front. • Cooktops have some difficulty fitting an 11-quart stockpot on back burner. • Cooktops can accommodate 3-inch deep, 11-inch-diameter skillet on back burner, though pan extends under backguard's overhang. • Offer choice of self-clean durations. • Oven temperature controls can be recalibrated if they are inaccurate. • Have easy-to-change cooktop light and oven light. • Oven doors become hot during prolonged oven use. • Storage drawers become hot at top during self-clean. • Have 1-year warranty on parts and labor. • Manufacturers provide toll-free number.

None: • Of cooktop burners provide continuously variable flame.

Key to Advantages

A—Horizontally mounted cooktop controls—less likely to be turned on by small children than most (but see Disadvantage d).

B—Burner control guides very easy to see.

C—Color-coded indicators for cooktop controls behind windows; easy to see and clean.

D—Markings on cooktop controls less vulnerable to scratching than others.

E—2 front burners rated at 12,000 Btu/hour, 2 rear at 9000 Btu/hour (natural and LP gas). High-speed burners boiled water somewhat faster than others.

F—Compact burner assemblies—easy to clean around.

G—Burner controls turn 325 degrees, and flame varies more than others (but see Disadvantage b).

H—Burner grates heavier, sturdier than others (but see Disadvantages c and e).

I—Burners lift up when cooktop is propped; least clutter under cooktop among tested models.

J—Vent area was soiled very little during self-cleaning.

K—No background controls to block when 11-quart stockpot is on back left burner.

L—Top of storage drawer gets only warm to touch during self-cleaning.

M—Oven door gets only warm to touch during prolonged oven use.

N—Boiled about 6 quarts of water somewhat faster than most.

Key to Disadvantages

a–Burner controls have only 1 marked setting.
b–Lowest burner setting too high; chocolate burned in melt-and-hold test.
c–Boiled water more slowly than others.
d–Burner controls, mounted horizontally at front of range, are easily spattered with food; crevice between cooktop and control panel catches dirt, spills.
e–Removable cooktop is heavy to lift with burner grates on.
f–Cooktop props up, but access is limited, and edge of prop judged less safe than others.
g–Brushed chrome cooktop shows dirt.
h–Much hardware under cooktop; difficult to clean.
i–Self-cleaning, makes backguard above vent very dirty.
j–Vent allows objects to fall in.
k–Electronic timing controls lack Cancel switch; inconvenient to cancel automatic cooking programs.
l–Self-cleaning cycle preset for 3 hours; badly soiled oven may need more time.
m–Manually operated oven light.
n–Poor visibility through oven window.
o–Storage drawer cannot be removed.
p–Storage drawer smaller than most.

q–Instruction booklet less helpful than others.
r–Little workspace at center of cooktop.
s–11-inch skillet fits poorly on burners.
t–3-inch deep, 11-inch skillet hits backguard when placed on a back burner.
u–8-quart stockpot hits backguard when centered on a back burner.
v–Serviceperson must change cooktop light.
w–Tool required to change cooktop light.
x–Oven light difficult to change.
y–Broiler pan insert has sharp edges.
z–Oven-door handle gets hotter than others during self-cleaning.
aa–Cooktop controls and panel become hot during broiling.
bb–Oven thermostat on backguard gets hot during broiling.
cc–Oven-door handle awkward to grasp.

Key to Comments

A–2 dial-type oven controls and oven-on, cleaning, and "lock" lights on backguard.
B–2 dial-type oven controls on front panel; oven-on and cleaning lights on backguard.
C–Burner controls have 2 High settings.
D–Burners rated at 9000 BTU/hour with LP gas.
E–Burners rated at 10,000 BTU/hour with natural gas; 8000 BTU/hour with LP gas.
F–Burner controls keyed with words and symbols.
G–Round burner grates.
H–Digital mechanical clock, 60-minutes analog timer, and analog automatic oven controls.
I–Electronic timer can be set to 99 minutes.
J–Plastic electronic touchpad controls for oven and timing.
K–No audible signals.
L–Self-cleaning cycle preset for 3½ hours.
M–Has 2 broil settings.
N–Porcelain-coated broiler pan has chrome insert.
O–No chrome trim on cooktop edges.
P–Almond cooktop, sides.
Q–Almond sides.
R–No phone number for customer assistance (**Sears**), number not toll-free (**Hardwick, Magic Chef**), or number toll-free only in some states (**Caloric**).
S–No manufacturer instructions to recalibrate oven.
T–No cooktop light.
U–Warranty on glass parts and finishes for 30 days.
V–3-year parts warranty; 30 days for glass parts and light bulbs.
W–White storage drawer.

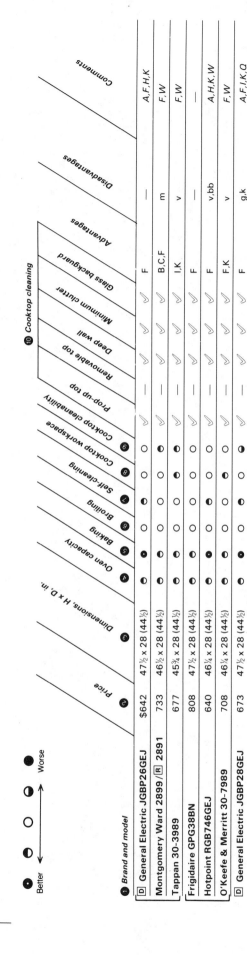

Better ● ◕ ◑ ◔ ○ Worse

① Brand and model	② Price	③ Dimensions, H x D, in.	④ Oven capacity	⑤ Baking	⑥ Broiling	⑦ Self-cleaning	⑧ Cooktop workspace	⑨ Cooktop cleanability	⑩ Cooktop cleaning — Prop-up top	Removable top	Deep wall	Minimum clutter	Advantages — Glass backguard	Disadvantages	Comments
Ⓓ General Electric JGBP26GEJ	$642	47½ x 28 (44½)	◑	●	◑	◑	○	◑	—	✓	✓	✓	F	—	A,F,H,K
Montgomery Ward 2899 / ℝ 2891	733	46½ x 28 (44½)	◑	◑	○	○	○	◑	—	✓	✓	✓	B,C,F	m	F,W
Tappan 30-3989	677	45¾ x 28 (44½)	◑	◑	○	○	○	◑	✓	✓	✓	✓	I,K	v	F,W
Frigidaire GPG38BN	808	47½ x 28 (44½)	◑	◑	○	○	○	○	✓	✓	✓	✓	F	—	—
Hotpoint RGB746GEJ	640	46¼ x 28 (44½)	◑	●	◑	◑	○	◑	—	✓	✓	✓	F	v,bb	A,H,K,W
O'Keefe & Merritt 30-7989	708	46¼ x 28 (44½)	◑	◑	○	◑	○	◑	✓	✓	✓	✓	F,K	v	F,W
Ⓓ General Electric JGBP28GEJ	673	47½ x 28 (44½)	◑	●	◑	○	◑	◑	—	✓	✓	✓	F	g,k	A,F,I,K,Q

Brand and model		Dimensions, HxWxD, in.												
Hardwick CPG9841K679DG / [R] CPJ9841-KDG	622	45¾ × 26¾ (43½)	◐	●	○	◑	◑	◑	—	✓	B,M	f,h,i,m,n,t,u,x,cc	C,F,G,M,O,R,S
Magic Chef 34HN-4TKXW / [R] 34JN4TKXW	630	45¾ × 26¾ (43½)	◐	●	○	◑	◑	◑	—	✓	B,M	f,h,i,m,n,r,t,x,y,cc	C,F,M,R,S
Roper F8958 / [R] FGS-395V	720	46¾ × 28½ (45)	○	◑	◑	◑	◑	✓	—	—	E,G,J,M	b,j,m,n,p,t,x,aa,cc	G,L,M,N,P,U
Sears Kenmore 73591 [D]	726	45½ × 28 (45½)	○	◑	○	◑	◑	✓	—	—	J,M,N	j,m,n,p,t,x,cc	D,G,J,M,N,O,R,T,U
Whirlpool SF396PEP / [R] SF-395 PEW	825	45 × 28¼ (45½)	●	●	◑	◑	—	✓	—	✓	A,B,L	a,d,k,p,s,w,x,z,cc	B,E,F,I,N,S,W
Caloric RST369	678	45¼ × 27¾ (45½)	●	◑	◑	◑	—	✓	—	✓	A,B,D,H,L,M	c,d,e,l,m,o,p,q,s,w	E,K,M,R,V,W

[R] indicates that, according to the manufacturer, model has been replaced by an essentially similar model.
[D] indicates that model has been discontinued. The information has been retained to permit comparisons.

REPAIR HISTORY

The repair index below is for gas ranges like the ones Consumer's Union tested: freestanding, self-cleaning models with one oven. It's based on nearly 7000 responses to the 1989 Annual Questionnaire.

The index indicates the percentage of gas ranges bought new between 1983 and 1989 (without a service contract) that have ever needed a repair. A difference of four points or more is meaningful. The data were adjusted to allow for the age of the range; older models are more likely to have broken down at some time. There were insufficient responses to track the repair record of several brands. GE is missing, for example, because the company only recently began selling gas ranges.

A particular brand's repair index includes many models, not just the ones tested. And the analysis is necessarily historical. Even so, the findings have been consistent over the years. Choosing a brand that's been reliable in the past will improve your chances of getting a trouble-free range.

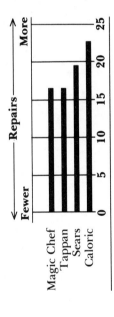

Repairs — Fewer ← → More

Magic Chef
Tappan
Sears
Caloric

0   5   10   15   20   25

Features of electric ranges

As published in a **March 1990** report.

❶ Brand and model. This table includes both tested and untested models (• indicates models tested). It should be used in conjunction with the Ratings table. Manufacturer's specifications show that the untested models in this table are similar in construction to those tested; they should be similar to cooktop, baking, broiling, and self-cleaning performance. As this table shows, features vary, and they may affect convenience and cleaning ease.

❷ Price. Approximate retail, as quoted by manufacturer. Discounts are available.

❸ Cooktop heating element. Coil **(C)** element or solid-disk element **(D).** Coils heat up and cool down faster than disks. But disks automatically lower their wattage if a pot boils dry. On a few disk ranges (see Comments), one or more elements can be set to hold a particular temperature.

❹ Drip bowls. They catch spills around coil elements, and can be cleaned at the sink or in the dishwasher. Porcelain **(P)** is easier to clean than chrome **(C)** and can be cleaned in the oven during the self-clean cycle. Chrome bowls, however, may speed up cooking.

❺ Oven window. A window is a plus only if you can see inside the oven clearly. Dark glass (most models have a black glass door) and screening to protect the glass may cut the view.

❻ Cooktop light. A nice night-light, but unnecessary in a well-lit kitchen.

❼ Clock. All models have a clock and timer and can be set to bake or self-clean automatically. The clock may be an analog **(A),** digital/mechanical **(DM),** or digital/electronic **(DE).**

Key to Comments
A–One cooktop element (two on the **Magic Chef** model) with thermostatic control.
B–Has speed-broil feature.
C–Has "power-saver" coil element, which allows heated portion to match pot size.
D–Has chrome cooktop.
E–Has black sides.
F–Model has been discontinued.

● ◑ ○ ◐ ●
Better ←——————→ Worse

❶ Brand and model	❷ Price	❸ Cooktop heating element	❹ Drip bowls	❺ Oven window	❻ Cooktop light	❼ Clock	Comments
Frigidaire							
RE34BA	$599	C	C	—	—	A	—
• RSE37BA	619	C	C	—	✓	A	—
REG36A	659	C	P	✓	—	A	—
• REG537BF	699	D	—	✓	✓	A	A
REGS38BD	770	D	—	✓	✓	DE	A
General Electric							
• JBP26GK/Ⓡ JBP26GN	579	C	P	✓	—	A	—
• JBP29GM	614	D	—	✓	—	DE	—
JB45OGK/Ⓡ JBP450GN	644	C	P	✓	—	DE	—
Gibson							
• CEC3S5WS/Ⓡ CEC355WX		C	C	—	—	A	—
Hotpoint							
RB735GJ/Ⓡ RB735GEN	469	C	P	—	—	A	—
RB737J/Ⓡ RB737GEN	514	C	P	✓	—	A	—
• RB747GJ/Ⓡ RB747GEN	594	C	P	✓	✓	DM	C
Kelvinator							
REP305C/Ⓡ REP-305G	500	C	C	—	—	A	—
• REP375G	579	C	C	✓	—	A	—
Magic Chef							
• 38HN-2CX/Ⓡ 38JN-2CX	499	C	C	—	—	A	—
• 38HN-4TXW/ Ⓡ 38JN4TXW	729	D	—	✓	✓	DE	A
Maytag							
CRE600	550	C	C	—	—	A	F
• CRE655	609	C	C	✓	—	A	—
CRE750/Ⓡ CRE755	660	C	C	✓	✓	DM	—
RCA							
• L3B325GL	$549	C	C	—	—	DE	—
Roper							
F9757/Ⓡ FES340V	559	C	C	✓	—	DE	—
• F9858/Ⓡ FES375V	629	C	C	✓	✓	DE	—
F9858X/Ⓡ FES370V	659	C	C	✓	✓	DE	D,E
Sears							
Ⓓ • 93481	536	C	C	✓	—	DE	F
Ⓓ 93581	530	C	C	✓	—	DE	F
Ⓓ 93881	660	C	C	✓	✓	DE	F
Ⓓ • 93681	624	D	D	✓	—	DE	F
Tappan							
31-3979	629	C	C	✓	✓	A	—
• 31-3969	649	C	C	✓	—	DE	—
Montgomery Ward							
• 4889	529	C	C	✓	—	DE	—
4899	599	C	C	✓	✓	DE	—
Whirlpool							
RF365BXV/Ⓡ RF365PXX	559	C	P	—	—	A	—
RF385PXV/Ⓡ F385PXX	649	C	P	✓	—	DE	—
RF367BXV/Ⓡ RE367PXX	599	D	—	—	—	A	—
• RF390PXV/Ⓡ RE391PXX	669	C	P	✓	—	DE	—
• RF387PXV/Ⓡ RE377PXX	699	D	—	✓	—	DE	—
White Westinghouse							
• KF45OG	499	C	C	—	—	A	—
KF560G	579	C	C	—	✓	A	B

Ⓡ indicates that, according to the manufacturer, model has been replaced by an essentially similar model.
Ⓓ indicates that model has been discontinued. The information has been retained to permit comparisons.

Ratings of electric ranges

As published in a **March 1990** report (model currency updated February 1991). Listed in order of estimated quality based mainly on how well each model baked, broiled, and self-cleaned; how easy the cooktop was to clean; and capacity. Differences between closely ranked models were slight. Use with Features table.

❶ Brand and model. Freestanding, 30-inch-wide, self-cleaning models, usually from the middle of each manufacturer's line.

❷ Price. Estimated average price, based on what CU paid and on a price survey during a six-month period.

❸ Cooktop heating element. Coil (**C**) or solid disk (**D**). Coils heat up and cool down faster than disks. Both types can hold a low temperature. Disks are easier to clean. But to cook efficiently, they need cookware with an extra-flat bottom.

❹ Dimensions. Cooktop is 36 inches off floor. Height is to top of backguard and can be increased with leveling legs. Depth includes any projections at back. Figure in parentheses is depth with oven door open. Figures are rounded to next quarter-inch.

❺ Oven capacity. Shelf supports and heating elements reduce useful space, which ranged from 2.1 to 2.5 cubic feet. Differences in height are small but can make a big difference.

❻ Baking. How evenly each baked four cake layers, two per shelf.

❼ Broiling. All broiled well. The best were large enough to do 16 burgers; those that scored a notch lower could do 12.

❽ Self-cleaning. After a 3½-hour cycle, all left streaks of burned-on residue around front of the oven and inside oven door. In general, models that have a dark porcelain-enamel finish were cleanest. High temperatures during self-cleaning caused hot spots on the exterior of all the ranges.

❾ Cooktop cleanability. How well the design of each range helps cleaning.

❿ Cooktop cleaning features. A **seamless backguard** means no dirt-catching seams where backguard meets cooktop. Disk models are easier to clean—spills don't go under the rangetop. The coil models that were easiest to clean have a **prop-up cooktop;** a **deep, open well** under the cooktop; and **porcelain drip bowls,** which withstand scrubbing better than chrome and can go in the oven during self-cleaning.

Legend: ◉ ◕ ○ ◔ ● Better ← → Worse

❶ Brand and model	❷ Price	❸ Cooktop element	❹ Dimensions, H × D, in.	❺ Oven capacity	❻ Baking	❼ Broiling	❽ Self-cleaning	❾ Cooktop cleanability	❿ Seamless backguard	Prop-up cooktop	Deep, open well	Porcelain drip bowls	Advantages	Disadvantages	Comments
Whirlpool RF390PXV/[R] RF391PXX	$566	C	45¼ x 27¾ (46¾)	◉	◕	◉	◕	◕	✓	✓	✓	✓	F,I,J,L	d,j,l	B,G,Q,R
Whirlpool RF387PXV/[R] RF377PXX	597	D	45¼ x 27¾ (46¾)	◉	◕	◉	◕	◕	✓	—	—	—	F,I,J,L	d,l	B,G,R
Frigidaire RSE37BA	447	C	47¾ x 27½ (44)	◉	◕	◉	◕	○	✓	✓	—	—	A,C,D,E	h	L,R,S,U
Frigidaire REGS37BF/[R] REG37BN	601	D	47¾ x 27½ (44)	◉	◕	◉	○	◕	✓	—	—	—	A,C,D,E	k	R,S,T,U,V
Montgomery Ward 4889	567	C	45½ x 27¾ (44¼)	◉	○	◉	○	○	—	✓	✓	—	H,I,J,K	b	F,Y
White Westinghouse KF450G	442	C	45¾ x 27¾ (43¾)	◕	◕	◕	◕	○	✓	✓	—	—	A,E,F	—	L,M,R,S
Tappan 31-3969	479	C	45¼ x 27¾ (44¼)	◉	○	◉	◕	○	✓	✓	✓	—	H,I,K	—	F
Kelvinator REP375G	518	C	45¼ x 27½ (44)	◕	◕	◉	◕	○	✓	—	—	—	A,E	—	P,R,S
Hotpoint RB747GJ/[R] RB747GEN	531	C	46¾ x 28 (45)	◕	◕	◕	○	◔	—	—	—	✓	C,D,F,G,J	i	H,J,M,S
Gibson CEC3S5WS/[R] CEC-3S5WX	501	C	45½ x 27½ (44)	◕	◕	◉	◕	○	—	✓	—	—	A,E	h	L,O,R,S,U,W
Roper F9858/[R] FES375	589	C	46½ x 27¾ (45½)	○	◕	◕	○	○	✓	✓	—	—	C,D,I,K	a,b,c	D,E,H,K,M,X
General Electric JBP26GK	563	C	44¾ x 27¼ (45)	◕	◕	◕	◕	○	✓	—	—	✓	F	e,i	C,M,S,Z
[D] Sears Kenmore 93481	513	C	45½ x 27½ (45¼)	○	◕	◕	○	○	✓	✓	—	—	D,I,K	a,b,c	D,E,K,M,U,X,AA
[D] Sears Kenmore 93681	579	D	45½ x 27½ (45¼)	○	◕	◕	○	◔	✓	—	—	—	D,I,K	a,b,c,k	D,E,K,M,U,X,AA
General Electric JBP29GM	608	D	46 x 28¼ (45½)	○	◕	◕	○	◔	✓	—	—	—	F,I,K	a,c,k	D,E,K,M,V
RCA L3B325GL	487	C	45½ x 27¾ (45)	○	◕	◕	○	○	✓	—	—	—	F,I,K	a,b,c	D,E,K,L,M,U
Maytag CRE655	600	C	44¼ x 27½ (43¾)	◕	◕	◕	○	○	✓	—	✓	—	B	c,e,f,g	K,S,U
Magic Chef 38HN-4TX/[R] 38JN-4TX	608	D	45¾ x 27¼ (44½)	◕	○	◔	○	◕	—	—	—	—	B,C,J,K	a,b,c,e,f,g,k	E,H,I,K,N,U,V
Magic Chef 38HN-2CX/[R] 38JN-2CX	450	C	45¾ x 27 (42¾)	◕	◕	◉	○	◕	—	—	—	—	B	a,c,e,f,g,h	A,K,L,S,U

[R] indicates that, according to the manufacturer, model has been replaced by an essentially similar model.

[D] indicates that model has been discontinued. The information has been retained to permit comparisons.

Specifications and Features

All: • Operate at 120/240 volts or 120/208 volts (but are slower with lower voltage). • Have porcelain cooktop, black-glass door, painted sides, removable storage drawer. • Have push-to-turn element controls. • Have indicator light to show cooktop is on. • Have oven with broiler, two shelves with safety stop, light. • Can fit a 20-lb. turkey or 14-x-16-inch baking sheet. • Can be preset for baking and self-cleaning. • Emitted smoke and became hot at front of cooktop during self-cleaning. • Did well in our low-heat tests of cooktop elements. • Have 1-year warranty on parts, labor.
Except as noted, all: • Have element controls on backguard clustered in a group of four. • Have controls that are blocked when 11-quart pot is on back burner. • Have flat oven shelves. • Have porcelain-enamel broiler pan and insert. • Have oven window with only fair visibility, oven light that goes on when door opens, and oven door that's removable and requires manual latching before self-cleaning. • Have one broil setting. • Offer choice of self-cleaning durations. • Have 60-minute analog timer. • Have electronic oven controls, digital electronic clock, and bake/broil/self-clean (including oven-lock) information in display. • Have anti-tip bracket. • Have dark-gray oven interior that appeared clean despite minor soiling. • Have cooktop that stayed relatively cool during cooktop- and oven-heating test. • Became hot at front of cooktop during broiling.

All disk models: • Took longer than coil models on low-heat tests. • Took longer to heat water with 8-inch element than coil models. • Reduce power to surface elements if a pan boils dry. • Require flat cookware for efficient heating.
Except as noted, all disk models: • Became soiled at cooktop vent area during self-clean. • Have two 1500-watt and two 1900- or 2000-watt elements.
Except as noted, all coil models: • Have shiny metal drip bowls. • Have removable cooktop elements, two 1500-watt and two 2600-watt.

Key to Advantages

A–Door locks automatically for self-cleaning.
B–Cooktop front edge curves up more than most to better contain spills.
C–Cooktop light.
D–11-quart pot on back burner leaves controls clear.
E–Storage drawer is wider than most and has curved, seamless corners for easy cleaning.
F–Convenient cooktop controls—2 on left side of backguard, 2 on right.
G–Power-saver coil heating element can adjust to accommodate size of cookware.
H–Stayed relatively cool at front of cooktop during broiling.
I–Signals audibly when temperature is reached and/or when self-cleaning and timed baking are done.
J–Glass backguard, easier to clean than most.
K–Electronic timer; can be set to 9 hours, 50 minutes.
L–Electronic timer; can be set to 99 minutes.

Key to Disadvantages

a–Little clearance behind oven handle; you could burn your hand if you grasped during self-cleaning.
b–Manually operated oven light.
c–Oven light hard to change and/or requires tool.
d–Aluminum broiler pan and insert; hard to keep clean.
e–8-quart pot on back burner blocks controls.
f–Storage drawer smaller than most.
g–Has optional broil shield which gets very hot during boiling.
h–Elements are lower in wattage than most (1250 and 2100 watts) and were slow at heating.
i–Elements are lower in wattage than most (1325 and 2350 watts) and were relatively slow at heating.
j–Elements have the same wattage as most yet were relatively slow at heating.
k–Cooktop became hotter than most during cooktop- and oven-heating test.
l–Cooktop became much hotter than most during cooktop- and oven-heating test.

Key to comments

A–Cooktop lifts, but does not prop up.
B–Oven door not removable.
C–Duct that vents self-cleaning fumes can become misaligned.
D–Self-cleaning cycle preset for 3½ hours.
E–Has two broil settings.
F–Has six broil settings.
G–Custom-broil feature can be set on high or from 150° to 325°F.
H–Chrome-trimmed cooktop sides protect edges but catch dirt.
I–Oven vent at backguard is painted black so soil is less visible.
J–Power-saver element lifts up for cleaning, but it cannot be removed.
K–Oven interior is light gray.
L–No oven window.
M–Porcelain-enamel broiler pan has chrome steel insert.
N–On our sample, the two thermostatically controlled disks began to work erratically at the end of our tests and had to be repaired.
O–Lacks anti-tip bracket.
P–On our sample, window shattered during self-cleaning.
Q–Deep drip bowls prevent spills under cooktop, but can be hazardous with combustible drippings, such as grease.
R–One of two oven shelves is offset, providing more room for covered casseroles.
S–Rotary oven dials and analog clock (**Hotpoint** has digital mechanical clock). Oven indicator light on backguard cycles.
T–One large element is 1910 watts: largest one is 2670 watts.
U–No phone for customer assistance or number is not toll-free.
V–5-year warranty on disk replacement.
W–5-year warranty on surface and oven elements, switches, and thermostats.
X–Warranty on glass parts and finishes for 30 days.
Y–On our sample, one small element rated at 1500 watts measured only 1220.
Z–Current designation of model is **JBP26GN.**
AA–Model has been discontinued.

GLOSSARY

Air duct. A formed conduit that carries warm or cold air to rooms from the the furnace or air-conditioner and back again.

Aisle space. The space through which traffic flows in the kitchen. Traffic should be directed away from the path of the cook.

Ampere. Also referred to as *amp,* the rate of flow of electricity through electric wires.

Ballast. Required in all fluorescent fixtures, it is an electrical component that limits the flow of electricity into a bulb.

Baseboard. A board along the floor against the walls and partitions; among other functions, it hides gaps.

Batt. Insulation in the form of a blanket, as opposed to loose filling.

Beam. One of the main horizontal wood or steel members of a house.

Bearing wall. A wall that supports a floor or roof of a house.

Butt joint. The joining point of two straight-cut pieces of wood or molding.

Casement. A window sash that opens on hinges at the vertical edge.

Casing. Door and window framing.

Chair rail. Wood molding on a wall around a room at the level of a chair back.

Chamfered edge. Molding with pared-off corners.

Chase. A groove made in a masonry wall or through a floor to accommodate pipes or ducts.

Circuit breaker. A safety device that opens (breaks) an electric circuit automatically when it becomes overloaded.

Clearance. The amount of space needed for the proper and/or safe use of various installations—for opening appliance and cabinet doors and drawers, for example.

Corbel. A horizontal projection from a wall, forming a ledge or supporting a structure above it.

Corner bead. A strip of wood or metal for protecting the external corners of plaster walls.

Cornice. A horizontal projection at the top of a wall or under the overhanging part of the roof.

Cove lighting. Concealed light sources, placed behind a cornice or other horizontal recess, that direct the light on a reflecting ceiling.

Crawl space. A shallow, unfinished space beneath the first floor of a house that has no basement.

Used for visual inspection and access to pipes and ducts. Also refers to a shallow space in the attic, immediately under the roof.

Delamination. The separation of layers of plies through the failure of adhesive bond.

Double glazing. An insulating windowpane formed of two thicknesses of glass with a sealed air space between them.

Double-hung windows. Windows with an upper and lower sash, each supported by cords and weights.

Drywall. A wall surface made of plasterboard or of a material other than plaster.

Fascia. A flat vertical face of a cornice; the filler from wall cabinets to the ceiling, for example.

Fill-type insulation. Loose insulating material that is applied by hand or mechanically blown into wall spaces.

Flashing. Noncorrosive metal used around angles or junctions in roofs and exterior walls to prevent leaks.

Floor joists. Framing pieces that rest on outer foundation walls or interior beams or girders, to support the floor.

Footing. The concrete base on which a foundation sits.

Foundation. The lower parts of walls on which the house is built. Foundation walls of masonry or concrete are mainly below ground level.

Framing. The rough lumber of a house: joists, studs, rafters, and beams.

Furring. Applying thin wood or metal to a wall to level the surface for lathing, boarding, or plastering; or to create an insulating air space and to damp-proof the wall.

Fuse. A short plug in an electric panel box that opens (breaks) an electrical circuit when it becomes overloaded.

Girder. A main member in a framed floor supporting the joists that carry the flooring boards. It carries the weight of a floor or partition.

Glazing. Fitting glass into windows or doors.

Grain. The direction, size, arrangement, and appearance of wood or veneer fibers.

Green lumber. Lumber that has been inadequately dried and that tends to warp or "bleed" resin.

Hardwood. The close-grained wood from broad-leaved trees such as oak or maple.

Headers. Double wood pieces supporting joists in a floor or double wood members placed on edge over windows and doors to transfer the roof and floor weight above the openings to the studs at the side.

Heartwood. The nonactive center of a tree; generally darker in color than the outer portion (sapwood).

Jalousies. Windows with movable, horizontal glass slats angled to admit ventilation and keep out rain; also, outside shutters of wood constructed in this way.

Jamb. An upright surface that lines an opening for a door or window.

Joist. A small rectangular sectional member arranged parallel from wall to wall in a house, or resting on beams or girders. Joists support a floor or the laths or furring strips of a ceiling.

Kiln-dried. Artificially dried lumber, a method that produces lumber superior to the more commonly air-dried product.

Lath. One of a number of thin, narrow strips of wood or metal nailed to rafters, ceiling joists, wall studs, etc., to make a groundwork or key for slates, tiles, or plastering.

Lintel. The top piece over a door or window that supports walls above the opening.

Load-bearing wall. A wall capable of supporting weight; removing a load-bearing wall without proper support will destabilize the structure it is supporting.

Miter joint. A joint formed by fitting together two panels or pieces of wood that have been cut at a 45-degree angle.

Moisture barrier. Treated paper or metal that retards or bars moisture from passing into walls or floors.

Molding. A strip of decorative material having a plane or curved narrow surface prepared for ornamental application. These strips are often used to hide gaps at wall junctures.

Mullion. Slender framing that divides the panes of windows, which are often called "lights" or "lites."

Plates. Pieces of wood placed on wall surfaces as fastening devices. The bottom member of the wall is the sole plate, and the top member is the rafter plate.

Plumb. Exactly vertical. Most walls in older homes and apartments are not plumb.

Pressed wood products. A group of materials used in construction that are made from wood veneers, particles, or fibers bonded with an adhesive under heat and pressure.

R-value. A measurement of thermal resistance; ability to retard heat transmission. Calculation method to determine insulating capabilities.

Rabbet. A groove cut in a board into which another board will fit.

Routing. Carving into wood. Some cabinet doors have designs or patterns routed into them, for example. The technique can also be used to create interesting countertop designs.

Sash. The movable part of a window: the frame in which panes of glass are set in a window or door.

Shim. A thin, tapered piece of wood used for leveling purposes.

Sill plate. The lowest member of the house framing resting on top of the foundation wall. Also called the mud sill.

Slab. A concrete floor placed directly on earth or on a gravel base; usually about 4 inches thick.

Sleeper. A strip of wood laid over a concrete floor to which the finished wood floor is nailed or glued.

Soffit. The visible underside of house parts such as staircases, cornices, beams, roof overhangs, and eaves. In a kitchen, soffits extending over wall cabinets are often used for lighting fixtures.

Softwood. Wood that is easily worked or comes from a cone-bearing (evergreen) tree.

Soil stack. Vertical plumbing pipe for waste water.

Studs. In wall framing, the vertical members to which horizontal pieces are nailed. Studs are spaced either 16 inches or 24 inches apart.

Subfloor. Usually, plywood sheets that are nailed directly to the floor joists and that receive the finish flooring.

Tambour door. A door, made of narrow slats, that opens by rolling up rather than opening out. It has no hinges.

Toenail. Driving nails at an angle into corners or other joints.

Tongue-and-groove. A carpentry joint in which the jutting, cutaway edge of one board fits into the grooved end of a similar board.

Trap. A bend in a water pipe to hold water so gases will not escape from the plumbing system into the house.

Veneer. A thin sheet of wood, called a ply when assembled into a panel.

Vent pipe. A pipe that allows gas to escape from plumbing systems.

Ventilation rate. The rate at which outside air enters and leaves a house. Can be expressed as the number of changes of outside air per unit of time (ach: air changes per hour) or as the rate at which a volume of outside air enters per unit of time (cfm: cubic feet per minute).

Volt. A unit that measures electrical pressure. Common voltages used in the kitchen are 120 and 240.

Volume ceiling. A ceiling that is higher than the standard 8 feet. It can be angled or arched or simply horizontal.

Wainscoting. The lower 3 or 4 feet of an interior wall distinguished from the rest of the wall when lined with paneling, tile, or other material.

Wall sheathing. Sheets of plywood, gypsum board, or other material nailed to the outside face of studs as a base for exterior siding.

Wattage. The measure of the rate at which electricity works. To determine watts, multiply volts by amperes.

Weather stripping. Metal, wood, plastic, or other strips installed around door and window openings to prevent air infiltration.

Weep hole. A small hole in a wall that permits water to drain off.

INDEX